Lamentation as History

W9-BOO-076

Lamentation as History

NARRATIVES BY KOREANS IN JAPAN,
1965–2000

MELISSA L. WENDER

Stanford University Press
Stanford, California
2005

Stanford University Press
Stanford, California

© 2005 by the Board of Trustees of the
Leland Stanford Junior University.

All rights reserved.

No part of this book may be reproduced or transmitted
in any form or by any means, electronic or mechanical,
including photocopying and recording, or in any information storage or retrieval system without the prior
written permission of Stanford University Press.

Printed in the United States of America on acid-free,
archival-quality paper

Library of Congress Cataloging-in-Publication Data

Wender, Melissa L.
Lamentation as history : narratives by Koreans in
    Japan, 1965–2000 / Melissa L. Wender.
        p.   cm.
    Includes bibliographical references and index.
    ISBN 0-8047-5040-8 (cloth : alk paper)—
        ISBN 0-8047-5041-6 (pbk : alk. paper)
        1. Japanese literature — Korean authors —
    History and criticism.   2. Japanese literature —
    20th century — History and criticism.   3. Koreans —
    Japan.   4. Japan — Ethnic relations.   I. Title

PL725.2.K67W46 2005
895.6'098957'09045 — dc22   2005014913

Original Printing 2005

Last figure below indicates year of this printing:
14   13   12   11   10   09   08   07   06   05

Typeset by BookMatters in 10/14 Sabon

To the memory of my mother, Dorothea Schmidt Wender

Contents

A Note on Names

Unless those being referred to are writing in English, Korean and Japanese names appear in their standard order in those languages — that is, last name first. When I know someone's preferred English spelling, I use it, but I provide a phonetic reading in parentheses. For well-known people and places, I use the common spelling and order. Many of the Resident Korean authors and activists I write about use several names. I have decided to refer to them using the McCune-Reischauer phonetic spelling of their names unless (as in the case of Ri Kaisei and Kin Kakuei) they are known to prefer a Japanese reading of the characters of their names.

Acknowledgments

The support of a number of organizations helped make this book possible. I want to thank the Fulbright Commission and the Japan-U.S. Education Commission for awarding me a dissertation research grant. Iwata Mizuho in particular was kind beyond the call of duty. At the University of Chicago, the Center for Japanese Studies and the Regional Worlds Program (supported by the Ford Foundation) provided me with much-needed funds, and I am grateful for their support. Bates College has generously supported me in follow-up research, and the Council on East Asian Studies at Yale University provided me with a postdoctoral fellowship that allowed me the time to rethink the ideas I had originally developed in the dissertation on which this book is based.

There are also a great many people without whom I never could have gotten this far. In the course of conducting research in Japan, I received assistance, advice, shelter, and nourishment from a seemingly countless number of people. I want to thank everyone who provided these services to me. Particular thanks go to all the members of the Zainichi no jūgun ianfu o sasaeru kai and Uri yoson nettowaaku, particularly Kobayashi Eiko, Kim Yŏng-hŭi, Yang Chin-Ja, Chu Su-ja, Pak Hwa-mi, Pak Chae-chŏl, and Kinomura Terumi; to Chŏng Yang-yi, Nakane Shōichi, Kim Kugo, and Bae Chung Do of Fureaikan; to Ha Hyeon-il and the staff at Minkenkyō; to Saitō Nobuyuki and the staff at Research/Action Institute for Koreans in Japan; everyone at the Osaka KMJ (Korean Minority in Japan) Center; all the members of the Hangyore kenkyūkai; and all the members of my Korean dance class. I'm indebted the following people as well: Kim Duk Chul, Kyō Nobuko, Kawakami Chiori, and Pak Poe. I'm also grateful to Seok Soon-hi, Kang Je-suk, Miyachi Tadahiko, Koyanagi Akiko, and Kim Kyong-yun for great conversation. Yū Miri was kind enough to agree to meet with me. Ri Kaisei took more time than he needed have to answer my questions. Nakata Tōichi was forthcoming and encouraging over e-mail and in person. Days spent with Chong Ch'u-wŏl and Kim Ch'ang-saeng were thought-provoking and immensely enjoyable; I hope they'll both be lifelong friends. Song Youn-ok's friendship and always witty conversation were invaluable; her provision of a bed in Osaka, a godsend. Her sister and nieces were also unnecessarily generous. Suh Kyung-sik and Funahashi Yūko were always giving, intellectually and otherwise. The members of the "Meri-ken," Kim Suna, Furukawa Atsuko, Kuribayashi Reiko, and Morishita Ikuhiko, both indulged and challenged me. I'll never forget the many hours spent talking with Furukawa-san and Nishi Ken-san and Kim Suna and Kim Hyunchul. I owe more gratitude than I can express to the members of the Kim-Ri family: Ri Mun-ja's strong will has guided me throughout the writing of this book, and Kim Suna has become such a part of my life that I'm not sure how to thank her. Alexis Dudden was a research buddy extraordinaire. My dear friends Inoue Yuka and Endō Shō provided me with much-needed nourishment, both bodily and psychological. They know already, I hope, how grateful I am. Once more: Thanks! Finally, I want to extend my gratitude to Mihashi Osamu, whose intellectual curiosity, humor, generosity, and sense of perspective will, I am sure, continue to inspire me for the rest of my career.

Many in the United States have helped me as well. Many people have listened to, read, and helped me revise portions of the pages that follow. Everyone who attended presentations of the many versions of this work, thank you. Kudos to Sarah Frederick and Amanda Seaman for cheerfully reading drafts (and to Chris and Sean for looking over their shoulders). I send Yoshiko Nagaoka and her family a heartfelt "thank you" for all they have given me. Thanks to Howard Ro for his great confidence in me. Pamela Johnson worked through ideas with me with great spirit. Kathy Rupp has been the most dedicated of friends, never failing to engage in the discussion of anything, and never giving up on me. Carol Haney, Sam Farwell, and Abbe Friedman have let me join their family; I couldn't have written this book without them.

I've learned an immense amount from Harry Harootunian, and I'm grateful to him for all he has given me. Much gratitude goes to Tetsuo Najita for his incisive but good-natured criticisms and his consistent support. Kyeong-Hee Choi has served as a behind-the-scenes coach; I am grateful for all the inspiration she provides. I cannot thank Bill Sibley enough acumen for his careful attention to all that I've written. All he's taught me makes me a better reader of literature than I might be otherwise. Finally, Norma Field has been a wonderful teacher and friend. She never ceases pushing me to ask the most challenging questions in scholarship and in life. Her encouraging voice is with me all the time. Whatever I can say surely isn't enough.

My family deserves more gratitude than I can give. Thanks to Leslie and Jocelyn for putting up with my crabbiness and self-righteousness and supplying all the emotional support I've needed, and to my father and stepmother Frances, who have encouraged my hunger to learn and who have unfailingly answered queries about matters psychiatric. My husband John has supported me from near and far through the challenges of making what was a dissertation into a book. His political feistiness, his sense of the absurd, and his faith in me have made it possible for me to keep my true passions in sight.

Finally, I thank my mother, who taught me the wonder of humanity with great humor and a healthy dose of skepticism.

Lamentation as History

Introduction

On a September evening in 1995, in a dimmed auditorium in Tokyo, I sat listening to a benefit concert sponsored by an organization supporting Song Shin-do, the sole Korean former comfort woman living in Japan to have filed claims against the Japanese government. Midway through the performance, the band receded into the background, as first Song and then a former comfort woman from Korea, Yi Yŏng-su, rose to dance and sing to a rendition of the Korean folk song "Arirang." Soon Yi was on stage alone. Before long, her singing gave way to storytelling. At one point in her narration of her experience of having been forced to sexually service members of the Japanese military, she suddenly wailed "Mother!" in Japanese. The tension in the auditorium was palpable.

Earlier that same day, I had attended a court appearance by Song Shin-do in her suit against the Japanese state. Next I followed along with a group of people, mostly women, to a small room where her lawyers gave a debriefing. The court proceedings were predictably stiff, filled as they were with legal jargon. The explanatory session, in contrast, was lively, and I found myself in immediate agreement with the objective of the case as presented by Song's lawyers: to force the government to acknowledge the right of individuals to make claims against the state for crimes perpetrated against them. The concert was the culminating event of a day many had spent carefully planning. When I left the concert hall, I went to a coffee shop with a number of the planners, and as I listened to them, they talked about any number of things, including the remarkable experience of Yi's storytelling. When I finally went home, I continued to ponder how the darkness, the music, and the audience of supporters — many of them Zainichi Koreans, people of Korean descent residing in Japan — had enabled Yi to communicate the depth of her pain in a manner not possible in either of the other forums.[1] I lamented the limited efficacy of legal and political struggles for compensation and apology in helping these victims to overcome their agony. At the same time, I marveled at what this occasion might have made possible for Yi, and indeed for everyone in the auditorium that night.

THE ISSUES

This is a book about the emergence of, and transformations in, discourses of ethnic identity in the literature of Koreans in Japan from the mid-1960s through 2000. I begin with this anecdote rather than with a more standard review of what has been written on the subject because the issues it raises help me to explain why I take the complicated and somewhat unusual approach of weaving together readings of literature and grassroots legal movements in my analysis. I do so in an effort to understand ethnic identity as something experienced in a manner that is deeply internal, psychological, and individual and radically public, political, and communitarian. I begin by highlighting three points revealed in the above story, each of which relates to the intertwined nature of discourses of politics and fiction. Next I step back to say a bit more about who Zainichi Koreans are and how they fit with academic discourses about ethnic diversity in Japan and elsewhere. I expand upon the three points, and I conclude with a brief outline of the chapters to follow.

The first issue that the above story elucidates for us is that Zainichi Koreans' legal activism, although often focused on a particular case, has invariably held goals extending beyond the specific issue at hand, and that even as far as the given matter is concerned, has had important ramifications that reach beyond the courts themselves. Lawsuits like this one aimed to obtain both monetary compensation and apology for individual comfort women, as mentioned above. At the same time, their lawyers also held the explicit objective of convincing the state to recognize the right of individuals to make claims against it. In addition, this anecdote points to the fact that the legal battles have significant impact regardless of their outcome. For one thing, they and the broader movements surrounding them have attracted media attention and thus have had the ability to expand mainstream awareness of Zainichi concerns. In addition, and crucial for my project, the organizing for these causes has provided a vehicle for individual members of the Korean community to meet one another and sympathetic Japanese (such as those who ferried me along to the trial, concert, and coffee) and in so doing, to transform their sense of who they are. In others, legal movements transform both groups and the people who constitute them.

The next issue this episode highlights is the importance, for both the speaker and the audience, of the telling of life stories. One of my main concerns in this book is to show the pivotal place of the narration of personal experience in both the literary works and legal struggles of Resident Koreans. The lives of those people, real or fictional, often have been taken to stand in for the whole, as is so often the case for representatives of minority groups. The events of their lives, particularly those events somehow shaped by their stance toward their ethnicity, then sparked vibrant discussion over the meanings of being Korean in Japan. As such, I feel that a consideration of Zainichi Korean identity over the past thirty-odd years needs to take into account the specific stories that have come into the public realm and been tossed about together in it. To help me understand the possible significance of this occurrence, I draw upon a growing body of work on narrative, storytelling, and the world of law in the United States. I also take into consideration the specific conditions — economic, cultural, and political — that may have made a focus on identity so popular in late twentieth-century Japan.

Finally, this anecdote draws our attention to the place of sexuality and gender in Resident Korean politics and literature. The comfort woman movement, which began in the 1990s, was the first political struggle addressing sexual and gender discrimination and the first to attract women to activism in droves. In contrast, women began writing as early as the

1970s, and gender and sexuality have always been central to both men and women's literary imaginations of ethnicity. If we read this fiction as decidedly based in reality, or as a peephole into social life, as most readers have, it surely suggests to us that Zainichi women have been dually oppressed — as Koreans and as women. My goal, however, is to get beyond this point. I therefore examine the repeated metaphorical uses of gender and sexuality: pure woman as symbolic of beautiful nation, raped woman as metaphor of oppressed nation, reproduction of children as preservation of culture, heterosexual union with a Japanese as assimilation into Japanese culture, and so on. I then want to ask if ethnicity is always gendered (and sexualized) for Resident Koreans only in the literary imagination. Or, perhaps, do such ideas affect the way that Zainichi people of different genders and sexualities relate to the majority Japanese culture? Are they more or less inclined to want to belong, to become active citizens (in the broadest sense of the term) in that society?

WHO ARE RESIDENT KOREANS?

Zainichi Koreans are not only Japan's only significant immigrant minority but the only substantial population that is a direct legacy of Japan's overseas empire: Japan colonized Korea between 1910 and 1945. Their numbers are uncertain. Official estimates hover around 650,000, but this figure includes only people who are citizens of South Korea or whose foreign registration cards designate their nationality as "Korean," a status comparable to North Korean citizenship.[2] The actual number, however, may be closer to a million. The discrepancy derives from the fact that the government does not keep statistics on the ethnic background of its citizens, and large numbers of people who are either wholly or partly ethnically Korean have obtained Japanese citizenship through naturalization, marriage, or having one parent who is a citizen.[3]

Even at one million, however, Koreans would constitute less than 1 percent of Japan's entire population. If this is a statistically insignificant figure, the community is nonetheless of considerable symbolic importance. It is still one of Japan's largest ethnic minorities (second only to people of Okinawan ancestry, whom some consider ethnically distinct) and, as mentioned, its only major immigrant population. In addition, although there has been a recent influx from South Korea, the majority of this one million are the descendants of people who came to Japan when Korea was colonized by Japan, and thus Resident Koreans serve as a signal reminder of Japan's militarist past.

One of the most fraught matters for Resident Koreans — unlike Okinawans or Ainu, the ethnic group native to Japan's northernmost island, Hokkaido — is that of citizenship.[4] Under colonial rule, Koreans were citizens of the Japanese empire — second-class citizens (legally and otherwise), but citizens nonetheless. Although the majority of Resident Koreans are descendants of these people, as the above statistics testify, most are not legally Japanese, for Japan grants citizenship based not on place of birth (jus solis) but on parentage (jus sanguinis), and no special dispensation has been given to this community.[5] The laws governing their status, therefore, are less a legacy of colonialism than a sign of the Japanese state's effort to forget this blemish on its past.

At the end of the war, there were roughly two million Koreans in Japan, many of whom had been drafted as laborers to work in mines, munitions factories, and so on; others had been pushed off the land they had farmed and had migrated in search of employment.[6] The vast majority of these Koreans returned to the Korean peninsula as soon as it became possible; roughly 600,000 stayed.[7] Between 1945 and 1952, under the U.S. Occupation of Japan, Koreans' legal status was ambiguous: under the Alien Registration Ordinance passed in 1947 they were designated as "Korean" and were supposed to register as aliens and to carry identification papers, yet they were still considered legally Japanese.[8] It was not until 1952, when the United States and Japan signed the San Francisco Peace Treaty and when this ordinance became an official law, that they were unequivocally stripped of their Japanese citizenship.[9]

In fact, although Koreans were allowed to remain in Japan, they had no right to live in Japan legally until 1965, when Japan and South Korea entered into formal diplomatic relations. Even at this point, however, because South Korean citizenship was a prerequisite for the new category of "permanent resident" and many felt either sympathy with North Korea or animosity toward South Korea and thus refused to apply for South Korean citizenship, the right to live in Japan was secured for only a portion of the population.

In addition, these terms applied only to colonial-era immigrants and their offspring, leaving the legal status of subsequent generations to be decided twenty-five years later, that is to say, by 1991. The problem of the status of non–South Korean citizens was finally resolved in 1982. In 1979, Japan ratified the International Human Rights Convention, and in 1981, the Convention on Refugees. In 1982, in order to bring its domestic laws into accordance with these conventions, it passed a new Immigration Control and Refugee Recognition Act, which allowed stateless Koreans, such as those with the "Korea" designation, to obtain "general permanent resident" status, and in so doing gave them access to a range of state benefits, including pensions and welfare benefits for children.[10] In 1991, Japan and South Korea passed an addendum to the 1965 treaty agreeing that the right to permanent residence should be extended to those of subsequent generations. Then, in the same year, Japan enacted a new law granting all Resident Koreans — who, as we have seen, had previously been classified under different categories — the new united status of "special permanent residence."[11]

This series of laws reveals something of the postwar Japanese state's attitude toward the presence of people of Korean heritage. Persistent legal exclusion shaped the way that Koreans in Japan defined themselves and the kinds of political rights that they demanded. Although Resident Koreans fought for rights to welfare benefits, rights to live in public housing, and against certain requirements of the Alien Registration Law (in particular its fingerprinting requirement, as we will see in Chapter 4), they did not demand Japanese citizenship itself.[12] In the late 1990s, however, as the process became less of an ordeal, increasing numbers of people began to apply for naturalization. At the same time, however, among the most vibrant struggles were those by noncitizens asserting that they should be allowed to hold government jobs at the management level and to stand for and vote in local elections.[13] In part as a result of this legal history, Resident Koreans have been reluctant to take on Japanese citizenship. One can only speculate whether things might have been different if Japan had offered former colonial subjects citizenship in 1952.

There are of course other reasons for Koreans' perception of naturalization as a form of betrayal. As in Japan, people in Korea have placed a high value on blood relations and have commonly equated citizenship with ethnicity and race. In addition, in contrast to Germany, for example (this is a common comparison), Japan has been negligent about teaching the postwar generation about its militarist past, including its colonial rule of Korea. Finally, there is the matter of the division of the Korean peninsula, which not only left this diasporic population split in two but encouraged an intensified sense of longing for a utopian wholeness that could be, if only the country were one again.

Several organizations emerged in the early post-1945 era, but for most of its history, the two dominant groups of the Resident Korean Community have been the Zainihon Chōsenjin Sōrengōkai (Chaeil Chosŏnin Ch'ong-ryŏnhaphoe in Korean; General Association of Korean Residents in Japan), usually known as simply Sōren (Ch'ongryŏn), and the Zainihon Daikan-minkoku Mindan (Chaeilbon Taehanminguk Mindan; Korean Residents Union in Japan), abbreviated Mindan.[14] The former, begun in 1955, successor to several other left-leaning groups founded as early as 1945, sees itself as an "overseas" organization of North Korea; Mindan, in existence since 1946, is composed of South Korean citizens (although membership is not mandatory).[15] Sōren was the more influential by far. Between 1959 and 1967, it helped more than 80,000 Koreans "repatriate" to North Korea.[16] It also educated and employed a significant portion of Resident Koreans: it has its own schools from kindergarten through university, as well as its own publishing house, newspapers, and banks.[17]

Although these organizations played a pivotal role for Zainichi Koreans in the first several decades after the war, Sōren's membership was beginning to decline at the date I begin my study, and Ri Kaisei, the author I examine in the next chapter, was one of those whom the association lost. The attrition rate seems to have increased as information about the true state of affairs in North Korea began to trickle into Japan and out into the world at large. In addition, many who had long been dismayed by South Korea's string of dictatorships began to feel hope in the 1980s as first the student movement, and then a broader democracy movement, burgeoned. These changes, together with the improved living conditions resulting from an improved economy, led many Resident Korean and Japanese students to develop interest in Korean culture and to visit South Korea for travel and study. By the end point of my enquiry, with news of starvation and atrocities in North Korea, Sōren's schools, although trying to adapt to the times by changing their curriculum, were losing students; its banks were failing, and it was losing members in droves. Indeed, as we shall see, group affiliation in general was on the decline, and with it, an identity shaped by the ideologies of these state-linked organizations.

CHALLENGING THE MYTH OF JAPANESE HOMOGENEITY

By the end of the twentieth century, when I sat in the Tokyo auditorium, what it meant to be Korean in Japan was radically different from what it had meant in 1965, the starting point of my enquiry. This was true not only because of the changes in legal status that I have just outlined. Despite the recession following the economic soar of the 1980s, Japan in the 1990s was still one of the world's most affluent countries, and its problems were those afflicting such nations. Among those included a falling birthrate, an aging population, and a well-educated populace for the most part unwilling to engage in manual labor. This confluence of circumstances led the authorities to overlook an influx of illegal immigrant laborers from Asia (including Korea) and the Middle East, and to make it legal for Nikkeijin (people of Japanese descent) to work in Japan, resulting in the arrival of additional workers from Latin American countries, notably Brazil and Peru. United Nations data suggest that in order to keep the working age population stable through 2050, Japan would need to add approximately 33 million immigrants.[18] As Stephen Murphy-Shigematsu points out, this would make roughly 30 percent of the population foreign-born, and would require the Japanese government (and society) to radically alter policies and attitudes toward immigration and immigrants.[19]

Given such conditions, it is unsurprising that the attitude toward Resident Koreans, sometimes specifically identified as "oldcomers," had shifted. Multiculturalism and diversity, even in the comparatively linguistically, culturally, and ethnically homogeneous nation of Japan, became buzzwords. Academics both inside and outside Japan authored tomes about Okinawans, Ainu, a former outcaste class often referred to in English as Burakumin ("people of the villages"), Japanese-Brazilian return immigrants, and of course, Zainichi Koreans.[20] Many of these works point out that Japan is more diverse than has typically been acknowledged, and that the ideology of homogeneity purveyed by Japan's state and culture has been oppressive to both its minorities and the Japanese themselves. They also made comparisons with, and drew on models based on the experience of, groups in similar positions outside of Japan.

ZAINICHI KOREANS AS IMMIGRANT ETHNIC, RACIAL MINORITY, AND/OR POSTCOLONIAL POPULATION

That they would do so is unsurprising. The fate of Resident Koreans is important not only for those wishing to understand Japan, but also for those concerned with immigrants, minorities, or so-called postcolonial populations everywhere. Unlike the United States, or even France, Japan is not the home to many immigrants and has not developed a narrative of how one might become Japanese in the way one becomes American or French. Yet the parallels are numerous, and this difference might productively serve to show how mainstream ideology can affect the experience of immigrants.

In a postdoctoral fellowship interview I participated in shortly after I had drafted the first version of this book, a scholar of American literature noted that she thought the creative work of Zainichi Koreans sounded as if it had followed a path analogous to that of Italian, Jewish, and other European immigrants to the United States. She observed that they had engaged in a comparable twisting of literary language and form, in comparable political and cultural resistance to mainstream society, but had ultimately ended up trying to maintain distinctiveness while staking a claim for a place within the national culture. I did not do a good job of responding to her insights, and her comments have stayed with me since. There are certain affinities that I would be foolish to ignore. Like European immigrants to the United States, Korean immigrants can "pass" in Japan. In addition, Resident Koreans have similarly tried to strike a balance between affirming distinct politics, culture, and rituals, and assimilating into the Japanese world around them.

Yet much is obscured by highlighting these affinities. As mentioned above, the society to which Koreans came was nothing like the United States. Not only has there been no immigrant, melting pot, or salad bowl myth, but, as mentioned, citizenship has been based on blood rather than birthplace, naturalization laws have been famously discriminatory, and Koreans immigrated to Japan as subjects of its empire — an immigration voluntary only in the strictest understanding of that term. The place Koreans came from, too, was signally homogeneous and held nearly identical views of blood and belonging.

Once again, this is not to say that Zainichi Koreans do not, in their lives and their literature, follow a trajectory through conflict to assimilation as has been argued is the case for the experience of European immigrants to the United States, but rather to suggest that this mode of analysis itself is problematic.[21] As Michael Omi and Howard Winant point out in the book that has now become a must-read for all students of race and ethnicity in the United States, *Racial Formation in the United States*, the so-called ethnicity paradigm has a number of significant flaws. One of these is that a form of the paradigm that they call the "bootstraps model" posits that groups do better or less well (that is, integrate/assimilate or do not) according to the "norms" and "circumstances" of the group: "If Chicanos don't do well in school, this cannot even hypothetically, be due to low-quality education; it has instead to do with Chicano values."[22] There is no room for considering not only the unequal distribution of resources, but also their potential cause: discrimination. A second criticism they make is of the fact that such models assume that all minority groups — be they classified what we normally think of as racial (for example, black Americans) or ethnic (for example, Irish) — are seen as equivalent. They acknowledge that the "ethnicity paradigm" has often described blacks' experience as being distinct from other ethnic groups, but "there is something awkward, something one-dimensional, about ethnicity theory's version of Black exceptionalism."[23] Not only is there no recognition of the ethnic diversity among blacks, but, as they go on to argue, other nonwhite immigrants to the United States have been racialized in much the same way that blacks are; hence we speak of Asian Americans, Latin Americans, and Native Americans, brushing aside the significant diversity within these groups.[24]

In the case of Japan, although recent immigrants from Arab countries are racialized, those from Korea are distinguished from those from China just as in the United States, Irish immigrants were distinguished from

English immigrants. What I want to take from Omi and Winant is not so much their specific observation about race, however, because it does not aid us in analyzing the case of Resident Koreans. What does help me is their observation that the dynamic of integration (or nonintegration) of any minority group depends on a myriad of factors including, but not limited to, the host society's attitudes toward that group, the group's internal history, structural factors such as the economy, and finally the relationship between the given group and other such groups within and outside of the country.

This brings me to one of the main points that I want to make here: Zainichi Koreans themselves have at times compared themselves to different oppressed groups around the globe, as we shall see. Several times during my research, people (including the writer Ri Kaisei, whom I discuss in the next chapter) asked me about my own ethnic background, and made "aha!" comments when I mentioned that I am part ethnically Jewish. They then would recount some experience they had reading Jewish literature or history. The critic Suh Kyung-sik, who kindly befriended me during my time in Japan, has written about the Italian Jewish holocaust survivor Primo Levi and was interested in the fact that one of my sisters had studied Italian and was a fan of Levi's writing. He also has a sustained concern for the plight of Palestinians. Kim Ch'ang-saeng, whom I discuss in Chapter 4, talked to me about reading African American writers. As I mention in Chapter 3, the Resident Korean Christian Church, largely through the fostering of Yi In-ha, a Korean-born minister, became involved with the African American church and drew on ideas from the U.S. civil rights movement. Although Christianity never took root in Japan, in Korea, the situation was radically different, and through figures like Yi In-ha, progressive Christian ideas and the support available through church networks trickled into the Zainichi community.

Given the fact that so many Resident Koreans liken their own experience to that of minorities elsewhere (not to mention in Japan), it would be imprudent for me to brush aside such comparisons. In fact, I am intrigued by the way that the people I met and the people I write about do so, and I feel that this part of the story needs to be included. Zainichi Koreans' sense of self has been influenced by what they read and watch and hear, which in late twentieth-century Japan, is so vast in scope it is impossible to track.

When I began the research for this project in the early 1990s, ideas about postcolonialism were in vogue in the American academy. These ideas had originated in the expansion of English literature to include Commonwealth literature — that is to say, writings in English by people who were residents of places formerly parts of the British empire. Before long, scholars expanded their scope to examine the literature of populations everywhere who were affected by the legacies of colonialism — both colonizers and colonized. In the mid-1990s, when I went to Japan, however, the term had not yet caught on despite its potential applicability. By late in the decade, it was everywhere, and we find in print scholars of Zainichi literature like Ri Takanori advocating the use of the term for Resident Koreans.[25] In 2002, at the Association for Asian Studies, respondent Lisa Yoneyama asked me and my copanelists why we had not taken up the body of work on the subject or used this term to help us describe Resident Korean culture. On occasion, I do use this term, and I do draw on postcolonial criticism. In fact, I think those who study postcolonialism will have much to gain from learning about Koreans in Japan.

Postcolonialist critics frequently have portrayed the world as divided into two distinct camps: the white, Christian, Euro-American, quick-to-modernize colonizers, and everyone else. This scheme may work fine for understanding the modernizing process of much of the world, but Japan does not fit into it so well. Japan, although it too is a colonial power, has sometimes been lumped together with those oppressed by imperialist modernity. As Iwabuchi Kōichi points out, in his book *Culture and Imperialism* Edward Said refers to Japan "predominantly as a non-Western, quasi–Third World nation which has been a victim of Western (American) cultural domination."[26] Surely this is because the Japanese, like the Koreans (and others) they oppressed, are nonwhite and traditionally non-Christian, and they came to modernity and capitalism later than other imperialist states. It was only after the threat of being colonized by the United States that Japan embarked on its own imperial ventures. The relationship between Japan and Korea, in other words, has long been triangulated by the "west" generally and the United States specifically. We must be careful, then, not to overlook the equally important influence on Zainichi Koreans of that country more usually thought of as imperialist, both culturally and politically: the United States. It does not loom as large or as negatively as Japan itself, but as for other residents of the islands, it is a towering presence. At the same time, we must not lump the experience of Koreans, Zainichi or otherwise, together with Japanese. Japan was an imperialist state, and the legacies of that fact persist to this day. For these reasons, postcolonial theories alone will not suffice to explain the diverse ways in which Koreans and Japan have defined themselves both politically and culturally.

What is invaluable for me in postcolonial criticism is that it attempts to locate individual human agency, and that it does so, in many cases, by examining literary and other texts produced by oppressed peoples. Following Edward Said's *Orientalism* and Benedict Anderson's *Imagined Communities*, most scholars have acknowledged the importance of discourse in the nation's, and the empire's, ability to rule. As a consequence, scholars writing about ethnic and/or postcolonial minorities have championed the place that narratives — and particularly fictional narratives of alternative identities — have both in making possible and in challenging the dominant political forms of the modern era, nation-state, and empire. This book focuses on literary works that do just that: propose and produce identities that counter the hegemonic ideology of the Japanese nation.

On the other hand, intense focus on literary works can sometimes make it appear that these texts alone monopolize national discourse, or worse, that discourse alone controls the functioning of the political world, even when the critic believes no such thing. Although I believe firmly in the power of literature (and discourse more generally), I want to situate my analysis of it in relationship to what I see as a distinct, extradiscursive reality to which language, and even literature, can help give us access. In this book, I therefore strive to show that Resident Koreans' literary works forced a redefinition of the place of this minority within the Japanese nation, but not on their own. I want to show instead that this literature is important because it has worked in a symbiotic relationship with political discourse and action, often through the legal system, to effect a change in this community's legal status as defined by the postwar Japanese state.

POLITICS AND LITERATURE, LAW AND LIFE STORIES

I now finally return to the issues I raised in the beginning of the chapter. The first two of these — the broad meanings of legal activism for members of the community and the importance of individual life narratives — meld together here into a single concrete point. The stories of individual people stand out everywhere: in literary works, trial transcripts, the newsletters of grassroots struggles, and books about all of these. Those stories, and the multitude of abstract ideas associated with them, including legal reasoning, come together to paint an intricate but remarkable coherent mural of the diverse ways that Resident Koreans formed identities in the decades I examine. I first learned of Resident Koreans through the newspaper and was outraged by the political oppression I read about, often in the form of stories about individuals. However, as I invariably do when I want to learn about a foreign place or a different time, I went to literature. And as is so often the case, it helped me understand how the individuals whose experiences diverged so much from my own had made sense of their own world. Although studying literature is what I do for a living, I still read for more basic reasons — for pleasure, in search of knowledge, to help me unravel the quagmire of life. I want to keep in mind that these are among the reasons ordinary folk pick up volumes of fiction and poetry. I strive for an analysis that does not forget this sort of passionate engagement with literature.

If I myself had first read Zainichi fiction to learn, as I began to do research, I discovered that contemporary readers, both Japanese and Resident Korean, had done so as well. As a consequence, in the time period I examine, there is a striking amount of mutual influence between the literary and the political, particularly in the form of legal struggles for civil rights. Literature played a key role, I argue, in enabling these people to recognize their own agency. Fiction allowed Koreans to see their lives as having meaning, even beauty; it gave Japanese insight into how it felt to contend with prejudice. Legal struggles fed off such literature: lawyers not only called fiction writers as expert witnesses but learned to use the narrative structure of fiction, telling life stories with emotional conviction in order to persuade the judge of the claims of litigants. Literature fed off legal battles in turn: writers turned legal material into literary themes and manipulated pithy phrases used by legal activists. By toying, twisting, and misusing words and linguistic forms, they undermined the seeming immutability of the laws and practices that refused to recognize Koreans' right to live in Japan. If literary texts refer to and make points about economic, social, and political belonging, the political documents not only refer to specific authors but use strategies found in their narratives — particularly that of telling the individual life story — to argue their case. The mutual influence between these realms is stunning.

Although it is surely possible to find ways that literature and politics feed off one another in any place and at any time, in this instance, the two are particularly closely intertwined. I return here for a moment to the central assumption of the postcolonial theorists. In my own words, it is thus: imperialist states used discourse to bolster material methods of control, and the legacies of discursive control are still alive today despite the dismantling of colonial governments. As a consequence of the complicated intertwining of material and discursive control, for postcolonial peoples to become truly liberated, they must engage in activism of the body and of language. It is natural, then, that for Resident Koreans, who as a postcolonial (immigrant minority) people have been oppressed by both state policies *and* the national culture, would find literature and grassroots activism to be of a piece.

When I examine the literature of the Resident Korean community in the pages that follow, I do so with great concern with how certain individuals came to see themselves as having historical agency. It is as important to understand why and how people acted politically as it is to know that they did so. Therefore as I trace the legal activism of the community, I analyze the rich texts which opened people's eyes to, in Herbert Marcuse's words, the "imperative: 'things must change.'"[27] More specifically, I try to unearth the concrete ways in which literature enables people to see that what seem like fixed structures — for example, institutions — are in fact mutable. I take to heart the insight of Raymond Williams that "art is never itself in the past tense" because it takes on new meanings every time people read it, and because it affirms and reaffirms the primacy of personal life, in which change is of the element.[28] In addition — and this point overlaps with Marcuse's ideas — there is potential in the fact that literature often concerns itself with "experiences to which the fixed forms do not speak at all."[29] This is true because the aesthetic "is in large part a protest against the forcing of all experience into instrumentality ('utility'), and of all things into commodities."[30]

I see just such a dynamic at work in the history I examine. As I mentioned when explaining the anecdote with which I began this chapter, individual life stories are a preeminent feature of Zainichi literature and, perhaps more surprisingly, grassroots politics. Williams's assertion helps me to suggest how literary works may have roused people to activism. Delving into the growing body of texts exploring the place of narrative within the law then furnishes us with reasoning for why legal activists may have decided to bring literary strategies into the political arena.[31] A number of scholars, for example, observe that the telling of human stories has been used effectively by minority populations in particular, but that more generally it has been useful for "countermajoritarian argument . . . [as] a way of saying, you cannot understand until you have listened to our story."[32] In the chapters to follow, I will show how Zainichi activists used such a strategy, perhaps having learned from this style of argumentation as used by minorities in the United States, but certainly also having taken note of the communicative power of the fiction and autobiography of fellow Resident Koreans.

GENDER AND SEXUALITY

There are of course multiple discrepancies between the narratives of fiction and those of politics. This fact is most evident when we examine the place of gender and sexuality in each. As I mentioned above, until recently, women and their concerns seldom appeared in political activism, histories of the community, or discussions of ethnic identity. In contrast, women have always played a central role in literature. Their representation is often interwoven with that of sexuality, in the form of reproduction, prostitution, masochism, rape, masturbation, and incest. In my analysis of specific works, therefore, not women broadly speaking, but women's sexuality, a sexuality devoid of pleasure and often warped by violence, comes to the fore.

Both men and women use instances of sexuality metaphorically. For example, they may use rape to stand in for the oppression of the Korean people, or childbearing to refer to the reproduction of Korean culture. At the same time, writers of both genders have tended to base their fiction on real-life experience; however, men write as witnesses to their mother's experiences, whereas women write of their own. In political realms, where men's voices long predominated, we find a similar trend. To the extent that sexuality as served as metaphor rather than representation of the real, it has had the effect of making Zainichi women's particular oppression as women invisible. Even today some male politicians continue to deploy the discourse of women's victimization as a sign of the general oppression of Koreans under colonial rule. However, they do so in a changed context. As a result, both the shifts in global discourses of sexual crimes and the disclosure of historic, state-sponsored brutality against women activists have found tools for understanding and naming this violence and seeking legal amends.

In doing so, however, women are not engaging in Zainichi activism in the same way that men did. The abstract Zainichi Korean — both in discussions of identity and in concrete legal struggles — generally has been ungendered. What this most often really means — as has been pointed out by feminists in the United States beginning in the 1970s of African Americans and other minorities — is that it is male. In the case of the fictional narratives I examine, however, this is not the case; the protagonist is always a man or a woman, usually matching the gender of the author. On the most literal level, the characters relate to Japanese or Zainichi culture in ways determined by their gender; metaphorically and thematically, too, as mentioned above, works can be divided on gender lines.

This is not at all surprising, for women surely are subject to different legal, economic, and cultural treatment within both Japanese and (Resident) Korean societies. Men and women have different stakes in participating in or excluding themselves from both. Men stand to gain from becoming part of Japan's powerhouse economy, for example; women do not to the same degree. Women have less to lose by giving up all associated with Korea, for women's position in Korean culture is usually thought to be even more subordinate than in Japanese. It behooves us to keep this fact in mind as we ponder the ways that Resident Koreans choose to join or reject affiliation with various groups.

THE CHAPTERS

My account is roughly chronological. In the next chapter, I analyze the literature of Ri Kaisei, who in 1971 was the first non-Japanese writer to win the prominent Akutagawa prize. I juxtapose his fiction with debates surrounding a crime by a man named Kim Hŭi-ro in 1968, which was made a spectacle of and catapulted Zainichi Koreans into the mainstream Japanese media. Both Ri's work and Kim's defense, in which Ri and other intellectuals participated, are obsessed with the question of the way people's perception is shaped by language. Each proposes that the Japanese language denies Koreans dignity because of the nuances associated with the words used to describe them. Ri thus infuses his fiction with the Creole of first-generation immigrants and traditional Korean oral literary forms. Members of Kim's defense cite Frantz Fanon to make the argument that Koreans will only be able to become subjects and not objects of history when they use Korean names and learn Korean language and history. In order for this to be possible, they argue, both Resident Koreans and Japan must change. Of particular interest to me is the extent to which the model of subjectivity they propose is gendered.

In the third chapter, I consider a pair of stories by Kin Kakuei, a contemporary of Ri's, and a battle against employment discrimination often called the first citizens' movement by Koreans in Japan. Both Kin's fiction and this struggle confront the stark reality faced by this community: they are neither purely Korean nor purely Japanese and are condemned to face discrimination from both sides. Each asserts the importance of becoming full-fledged members of Japanese society but at the same time attempts to challenge its developmentalist system of values.

Two women based in Osaka, Chong Ch'u-wŏl and Kim Ch'ang-saeng, who have published from the 1970s through the present, are the subject of the fourth chapter. Their work explicitly and implicitly comments on the best-known Resident Korean grassroots movement, which in 1986 succeeded in winning the repeal of a fingerprinting requirement stipulated in the Alien Registration Law. Many Koreans saw the fingerprinting system as a symbol of the state's view of Koreans as potential criminals who needed monitoring, not as equal participants in a democratic society. Although the movement attracted international attention, its core philosophy was one of local action, and employees of the local government offices where fingerprints were taken joined the fight. These women's texts likewise focus on the local, specifically on women in Ikaino, the Korean neighborhood in Osaka. Both the antifingerprinting movement and their work honor individual experience and propose ways to identify in Japan but not with Japan the nation.

In the fifth chapter, I turn to the fiction of Yi Yang-ji. I analyze her texts in relation not to a social movement but to two general trends: first, that within Japanese mainstream literature toward a focus on interiority; second, that within the Resident Korean community toward a self-definition based on culture rather than politics. In particular, I concentrate on Yi's literary appropriation of Korean shamanism and her portrayal of characters who challenge prevalent ideologies of women's sexuality by engaging in sex for money, receiving financial support from married lovers, and rejecting motherhood. I do note also the frequency in her work of references to the way people are shaped by the way that educational systems teach them about history, a poignant fact given the prominence during the 1980s of Ienaga Saburō's lawsuits trying to persuade the state to accept his history textbooks, which frankly recounted Japanese aggression in Asia.

In the final chapter, I contemplate the preoccupation with trauma in 1990s Japan. I examine the fiction of Yū Miri and debates surrounding the inclusion of the history of comfort women in middle school textbooks. I propose that Yū's reluctance to engage in debates about the comfort women and her refusal to claim either Resident Koreanness or feminism as a primary identification are central to understanding her texts. Reading her with these facts in mind discourages us from assuming that her fiction, which often treats dysfunctional families and child sexual trauma, is necessarily a commentary on the discrimination faced by the Resident Korean family or on women's oppression as a result of their gender. We then see that her work instead proposes that much of the real violence and oppression in Japanese society are rather the result of decades of striving for economic growth.

The chronological history I present does, as I mentioned, track changes in Resident Korean self-definition that parallel the model of ethnic immigrants. I wish to remind the reader once again to pay heed also to what differs from such cases elsewhere: the specificities of the economic, political, and social histories of Japan and Korea, which have so deeply conditioned the manner in which Zainichi Koreans have been able to conceive of themselves as individuals, of their minority community, and of the relationship of each to the many broader communities in which they live.

2

Mother Korea

The 1960s was a tumultuous decade for Japanese and for Koreans living in Japan, just as it was for people elsewhere across the globe. In 1960, the populace staged massive protests against the renegotiation of AMPO, the U.S.-Japan Mutual Security Treaty. By 1968, the broad-based and often violent student movement that had grown out of the 1960 activism reached its peak with a temporary shutdown of Tokyo University. By 1970, however, when the treaty came up for renewal a second time, the fervor had receded. Some students joined farmers in fighting the government's repossession of their land to build Narita International Airport.[1] The year 1970 is often considered a turning point in Japanese grassroots politics. After it, we see a shift from broadly defined struggles based on abstract principles such as those espoused by the New Left Marxists, who had been central in the 1960 and 1968 movements to ordinary citizens organizing around single issues.[2] Perhaps the best-known example of this new politics was the mobilization of residents of Minamata against industrial lead pollution, which has often been hailed as the first "citizens' movement."

These events were meaningful for all residents of Japan, including people of Korean descent. By this time, Japan-born Koreans outnumbered their immigrant parents. Born, raised, and educated in Japan, most spoke

Japanese better than Korean, which many didn't know at all. Although some followed their parents in engaging in Korea-based politics, some had joined their peers in the 1960 demonstrations against the U.S.-Japan Security Treaty. Yet through their participation, they had become aware that even winning that particular battle would not help them overcome the discrimination they faced as resident aliens. They thus directed their efforts to a single issue and protested the signing of a treaty initiating formal relations between Japan and South Korea, a treaty they thought inadequately addressed the legacies of colonial rule, including the legal status of Koreans in Japan.[3]

Their efforts were in vain. The treaty, signed in 1965, shaped their lives in ways that they could not have anticipated. As mentioned in the Introduction, this agreement compelled Koreans to take on South Korean citizenship if they wished to obtain permanent resident status. As a consequence, by 1970, the number of Resident Koreans with South Korean citizenship for the first time overtook those who were aligned with the North.[4] Because it had forced people to choose an affiliation, the treaty deepened the division of Koreans in Japan into North and South–affiliated camps.

Yet as a result of escalating authoritarianism under Pak Chŏng-hŭi in the South and increasing emphasis on Kim Il-sung worship in the North, the organizations linked with those governments and long the mouthpieces for Koreans in Japan, Mindan and Sōren, lost much of their appeal. Zainichi Koreans therefore began to seek other ways in which to air their concerns. One of the main methods they found was single-issue activism, although this time they directed their efforts domestically. Specifically, they targeted laws they saw as discriminatory.

Politics was not the only forum in which the issues of Resident Koreans began to emerge into public view. In fact, the late 1960s and early 1970s saw what one Japanese critic identified as a Korea "boom."[5] Young Resident Koreans began publishing in mainstream journals, even winning prizes for their largely autobiographical fiction. Of course, without interested Japanese, the legal struggles of Koreans would not have succeeded, and the writing of Koreans would never have been honored. Japan as a whole was aware of goings-on elsewhere in the world, and particularly in the United States. As such, they knew not only about struggles

for civil rights but the newly popularized concepts of individual and ethnic identity, an awareness that seems to have made them receptive to both
the politics and the fiction of Zainichi Koreans.[6]

In 1966, a young Japan-born Korean named Kin Kakuei (Kim Hak-
yŏng) won a literary prize sponsored by the magazine *Bungei* [The Arts].
In 1969, Ri Kaisei (Yi Hŏe-sŏng) won the *Gunzō* new writers' prize, and
in 1971, the most coveted prize of all, the Akutagawa. His acclaim in the
Japanese literary mainstream attracted attention to other Zainichi writers, and provoked a number of debates about the meaning of Koreans'
writing in Japanese and about how they might resist assimilation.

Because, as mentioned above, the majority of the community was of
the second generation, attended Japanese schools, and spoke mostly
Japanese, Koreans could easily pass as Japanese — and often did. Because
discrimination persisted, in order to get housing or jobs, most Koreans
used a Japanese name as well as a Korean one. To top it all off, a good
third of Koreans were marrying Japanese.

In this chapter, I focus on two people who drew the attention of the
Japanese populace to these issues and who entreated them to see these as
problems as their own and not just Resident Koreans'. The first is Ri
Kaisei, winner of the Akutagawa prize, and the second is Kim Hŭi-ro.
Kim's fame preceded Ri's and certainly was more extensive, for what Kim
is known for is a spectacular crime. In February 1968, Kim shot and
killed two members of the Japanese mafia to whom he owed money. He
started to call the police station to confess, planning to turn himself in.
But then he changed his mind. This is where the real spectacle began.
After driving to a remote mountain inn where he took the owners and all
the guests hostage, he spent the next day contacting the mass media. He
made a specific demand: that he receive a broadcasted apology from a
member of the police department who had formerly assaulted him with
racist insults. Before long, he went on camera himself. Standing with a
rifle in one hand, he claimed that it was this racism that had led him to
commit these crimes and lamented the terrible discrimination he had
faced as a Korean. He also indicated he planned to commit suicide in
order to take responsibility for his deeds.[7] In the end, however, Kim was
arrested by a police officer disguised as a reporter. He had held his hos-
tages for eighty-eight hours.

Japanese and Zainichi intellectuals were spurred to action as soon as they heard what had happened. Dissatisfied with the spectacle of the media coverage (Kim on camera touting a rifle and so on), a group of college professors, writers, and lawyers drafted a statement that they sent to the media. They then set out to see this man and hear his story for themselves. They spent a whole night trying to convince him not to commit suicide and to let them help him use his trial — rather than his death — as a way to inform the Japanese public about the discrimination faced by Resident Koreans. Surprisingly enough, they succeeded.

As a consequence, the transcripts of Kim's defense read like a textbook on the history of the conditions of Resident Koreans.[8] Yet if at moments it approaches an academic historiographic style, those who crafted it knew the persuasive power of personal narrative. That is to say, people tell Kim's or their own life story using narrative rather than argumentative strategies, relying on identification or emotional response rather than logic. This approach worked, at least to a degree. Although Kim was convicted of his crimes in 1973 and remained in prison until 1999, the trial was nonetheless successful in alerting the Japanese public to problems faced by Koreans in Japan. In my discussion of the trial, it will become clear that the notion of identity, and identity as something that people construct through the telling of individual histories, was crucial to these intellectuals' understanding of the way that Resident Koreans could overcome their oppression.

As I discuss in the Introduction, I will examine such political and legal efforts to define Koreanness alongside fiction. Here, that will mean looking at the Kim trial and Ri Kaisei's fiction, particularly his Akutagawa prize–winning story. My intent in making pairings such as this one is not only to highlight the temporal contemporaneity of a literary work and historical events but also to show how they might be intertwined. Although direct links — for example, the fact that Ri Kaisei provided testimony at Kim's trial — are clearly significant, some of the less direct connections are just as much so. Throughout the book, I will mine both fiction and traces of history in an effort to reveal how authors and activists drew on common ideas and worked toward common ends.

Ri Kaisei and Kim Hŭi-ro's defense team, for example, seem to share an objective: they want to reshape common perceptions of what it meant to be Korean in Japan. Until this point, many had a view of Koreans as downtrodden, living amidst poverty, violence, and discrimination. It was their goal to help the public to see Koreans in a more positive light. Each believed that knowledge was the key to transforming the meanings of Korean ethnicity. Ri's literature was about self-aware Resident Koreans who were proud of their history, while the intellectuals who testified in Kim's trial contrasted Kim, who didn't know the Korean language or culture or anything of the homeland, with successful and well-adjusted Zainichi Koreans who did. Mainstream and literary journalists picked up on these hints and glommed onto the idea that ethnic identity involved a "recovery" of something lost. At the same time, they furthered the notion that a strong sense of ethnic identity provided a sense of purpose and well-being.

Literary critics thus favored Ri over his contemporary, Kin Kakuei, who had a far less sanguine view of the possibilities of ethnicity. His stories also focused on young Koreans living in Japan, but in contrast to the young men in Ri's work, who derive a sense of pride from their history and purpose from political activism, his largely disaffected protagonists find little solace in anything. In the same vein, although the press paid a great deal of attention to an employment discrimination case, *Pak v. Hitachi*, many Zainichi Koreans vilified it. The idea that one could still maintain a Korean identity while speaking Japanese, participating in the Japanese economy, and either being apolitical or focusing one's political efforts on changing Japan, was perhaps threatening at the time. It came to shape the later course of Zainichi Korean politics and literature, however, and so I devote the next chapter to the impact of Kin Kakuei and the *Pak v. Hitachi* trial.

In this chapter, I hold my attention to Ri Kaisei, Kim Hŭi-ro, and discussions of both. Doing so reveals that at the time, ethnic identity appears to have been felt to have almost mystical powers of human healing, recalling for me immediately words by Cornel West: "believe me, identity cuts at that deep existential level where religion resides."[9] In the Kim trial, as in Ri Kaisei's prize-winning story, which I will analyze later, among the most important markers of Korean identity, not only in Japan, but in Korea itself, is one's name.

Not long after Kim Hŭi-ro was convicted, the Zainichi poet Kim Shi-jŏng wrote an essay about his experience of the trial in which he observed that including the name "Kwon Hŭi-ro," the name appearing on Kim's South Korean family registration (and a name that Kim himself was unaware of), Kim had a total of eight names.[10] It was not uncommon then, nor is it now, for Resident Koreans to use both Korean and Japanese names. Eight names, however, was something of an extreme. Kim was unstable, his defense team argued, because he lacked a solid sense of self, at least in part because he had so many names.

Such a proliferation of names might cause anyone confusion, but it had particularly detrimental effects on someone of Korean ancestry. A young scholar of Korean history called attention to the fact that in Korean society, changing one's name is such a rarity (and presumably a shameful thing, because it is an insult to one's ancestors) that when people make promises, he said, they use the phrase, "if I break this promise, I'll change my name" to indicate how sincere they are. As such, the Japanese colonial law forcing Koreans to change their names had been particularly cruel.[11] He did acknowledge that many Resident Koreans did use Japanese names, but stressed that they did so to avoid discrimination.

Kim's case was different, however. He had two different Korean last names, and this historian knew of no other such person in all of Korea's modern history.[12] The reason Kim had two surnames was that he had taken his stepfather's. The scholar emphasized that this was highly unusual, and he indicated that Kim's family situation must have indeed been quite "complicated." Kim's mother, he surmised, did not want others to know that this was not her current husband's child.[13] In the end, the defense argued that Japanese colonialism and its legacies were responsible for Kim's lack of a coherent identity and thus for making him into the criminal he had become. Not only did he use a Japanese name (no doubt first created under colonialism) to avoid discrimination, but his mother had ended up relinquishing her own culture and ignoring the presumably healthy taboo on changing her son's name.

Members of the defense team similarly contended that knowing the language of one's ancestors — in Kim Hŭi-ro's case, Korean — was essential to a "rightful, unified" identity. This point relates to the main thrust of their defense: that Kim should be deemed innocent because he had been pushed into this crime by the discrimination he had faced for his lifetime in Japan, and more immediately by the slurs of a police officer. In their opening statement, they argued that the fact that the only language Kim knew was Japanese meant that the only access he had to the concept "Korean" was through the word "Chōsenjin." They pointed out that the word had numerous negative connotations across its history, such as "someone who is not Japanese, a former colonial subject, one deserving of contempt, someone pitiful, someone reeking of garlic, a ragpicker, a dirty guy, someone who is rough, someone suited for manual labor, a bad guy, someone who is not one of 'us,' that is to say, 'them,' and so on."[14] The fact that Kim only had access to Japanese was even more serious, they proffered, because children usually attain their ethnic consciousness just as they enter their teens — and for Kim, this was in the early Shōwa era, when Korea was still a colony and thus not only at time when was discrimination particularly severe, but when the use of the Korean language was still officially prohibited.[15]

The most intricate argument about language came from Suzuki Michihiko, a professor of French literature.[16] In order to explain how he became concerned with Resident Koreans' plight, Suzuki told of his experiences as a student in France. He had gone there in 1954, the year that the Algerian War began, and was appalled to find that most of the French people he met were ignorant about Algeria and not supportive of its independence. He concluded that when one nation/people rules another, it is often blinded to the oppression faced by the people it is ruling.[17]

He continued to hold this notion when he returned to Japan and became more attentive to issues affecting Zainichi Koreans. For example, in 1963, when the debate over the normalization of relations with South Korea began, he found himself enraged by the standard position of the Left: that the real problem was American imperialism, and that Japanese, who were, like the Korean people, victims of this American imperialism, needed to join with the Koreans in a battle against it.[18] In 1966, he also sponsored a symposium on the so-called Komatsugawa Incident (1958), in which a Korean student named Yi Chin-u had confessed to killing a Japanese female classmate. At that time, Yi had contacted a newspaper himself, and the event attracted a great deal of media attention. In addition, Yi began exchanging correspondence with a Zainichi woman named Pak Su-nam. When he read those letters, Suzuki said,

What stuck in my head was that this boy Yi could only speak Japanese, and that when dealing with the outside world, that is to say in the society around him, he used the Japanese name Kaneko Yasutaka, and presented himself as Japanese. In other words, he was performing. . . . Of course inside he knew that he was Korean. He had kept telling himself he was Korean, but the language in which he was telling himself this was Japanese.[19]

When it came to the Kim Hŭi-ro trial, he was convinced that language had played a large role.[20] Suzuki's attention to this question of language and its significance in colonial and postcolonial situations was not entirely one of chance: he was the translator of Frantz Fanon.[21] After asking about the Komatsugawa Incident, the defense lawyer proceeded to ask him to outline Fanon's basic argument. He stressed the following points: languages contain value systems; in French, the word *blanc* ("white") does not indicate simply color, but also white people — that is to say, those of French origin. In addition, its connotations are positive ones, such as purity. As a consequence, blacks who speak French have only *noir* ("black") or *négre* ("negro"), which had negative connotations, to refer to themselves. Fanon's contention, Suzuki pointed out, was that only being able to refer to themselves in this language, through this value system which saw them in a negative light, caused them a sort of "perversion" of their being.[22]

Resident Koreans, he continued, because they speak only Japanese, and because of the negative connotations attached to the notion of Chōsenjin, are in a position not unlike formerly colonized Africans who can only speak French.[23] It is apparent that the logic of the defense, as outlined in its opening statement mentioned above, had relied heavily on the views of Frantz Fanon. Perhaps such views painted a view of Kim Hŭi-ro that placed the blame for his actions not so much on him but on the society that colonized his ancestral land. The legacies of Japan's colonization included the presence of Koreans in Japan, a group of people unable to speak their native language and discriminated against when they asserted their presence by using Korean names.

However simplistic this argument may seem now, it was seen as credible at the time. Nonetheless, it left one question unanswered. If such legacies of colonialism were so harmful, then why did not all Resident

Koreans take actions like Kim Hŭi-ro's? Many commenting on the trial, including members of the committee supporting the defense team, saw this as the central question. One such member, Mihashi Osamu, later professor of human relations and president of Wako University, remarked in March 1971, partway into the trial, "We are setting an individual's actions against a social backdrop in order to determine the meanings of those actions. Strictly speaking, however, all we are doing is noting a series of chance events. . . . Our purpose is to objectify, clarify, and expose the degree to which this chance is determined by a class society."[24]

Zainichi Chōsenjin who testified at the trial, most of whom were prominent intellectuals, likewise saw the element of chance as fundamental: nearly all claimed that they could easily see themselves in Kim's position. The poet Kim Shi-jŏng claimed that it was only because he had grown up in Ikaino, Osaka's Koreatown, and thus had a strong sense of his Koreanness, that he had been spared such a fate.[25] Ri Kaisei also testified at the Kim Hŭi-ro trial in December of 1971, just a few months before he won the Akutagawa prize.[26] In this testimony, Ri observed,

> Just a moment ago, I stood here and took the oath, and for an instant, I felt that I could have been taking the stand as a defendant, not as a witness. That is, looking back at the path that I have taken, I see that there were times when I just barely avoided becoming a criminal, and this makes me think that again and again, [as Koreans] we have been thrown into circumstances that made that option seem tempting. I was able to avoid that fate myself, but, sad to say, many people aren't so lucky.[27]

These striking confessions dramatize the element of chance. Indeed, there may be no *reason* for the success of people like Ri. The specific circumstances that made up Ri Kaisei or Kim Shi-jŏng's life were simply different from those of Kim Hŭi-ro's, despite all the concurrences.

The strong determinist bent of Kim's defense should by now be apparent; they attempted to show him as a passive victim of his economic class and of the real discrimination he faced. In part, of course, this is the psychological determinism taken from Fanon. At times it seems also in part Marxist; there is great attention paid to Koreans' poverty. Yet members of the defense team attempt to salvage agency for Koreans in Japan, *not* a simplistic, unmediated agency derived from recognition of their class position, but rather from an enlightened understanding of a link between their nationality (ethnicity/race) and their economic oppression. Zainichi intellectuals who testified suggested ways that Kim Hŭi-ro could become the master of his own life, by becoming Korean, albeit at a late date. It is implied, additionally, that other Resident Koreans could learn a lesson here. If they came to see how many facets of their degradation, including the economic, resulted from the state and industry's manipulation of pre-existing practices of discrimination (legacies of colonialism); that is, they would rise up and fight against these powers. Yet none of this is stated openly. Instead, the directives deal mostly with overcoming the psychological component of oppression, by attaining a new, positive identity for themselves.

Perhaps the most poignant example of this advice came from Kim Shi-jŏng, who entreated Kim to "go to" or find "Korea," not so much through superficial measures like putting on Korean clothes sent to him from South Korea or marrying a Korean woman (both of which Kim had done since his crime), but in some more meaningful sense.[28] Although he would not assume that his way would be right for Kim Hŭi-ro, his own way of doing this, he added, was to learn Korean but to continue to write poetry in Japanese, for "I can only find my own Korea by going through Japan."[29] He further stressed that learning the Korean language (which Kim Hŭi-ro was also doing) would not make him "completely Korean." Instead, he urged Kim to try to understand himself better by looking more deeply into himself and his memories of his parents; he also entreated him to avoid the tendency to blame everything on Japan and to acknowledge that his passivity had exacerbated his oppression. He then added, "I am not saying this just to Kim Hŭi-ro, but to myself as well."[30]

When I first began to peruse the musty pages of the compiled trial transcripts passed on to me by my advisor in Japan, Mihashi Osamu, who, as mentioned above, was one of the Japanese intellectuals engaged in strategizing Kim's defense, I was intrigued to find Kim Shi-jŏng's testimony. The fact of a poet taking the stand reinforced my perception that literary and political pursuits were intertwined in this era, and the words he imparted, in a legal forum, were about the power Zainichi Koreans could gain over their own circumstances by making the Japanese language their own. He had himself been passive, but through writing literature in

Japanese, he recounted, he had ultimately found the way to his own Korea.

Kim Shi-jŏng, much less involved in politics than Ri Kaisei, is probably the first Zainichi writer to have asserted the importance of writing in Japanese, and has been one of the most fervent advocates of doing so. In the late 1950s, Sōren, the North Korea–affiliated group, had criticized him for this view, leading him to quit the organization.[31] But he was ahead of the game. It was not until more than ten years later that mainstream Japanese intellectual circles began to see the significance of Koreans' writing in Japanese. A notable example of their interest is a discussion between Ri Kaisei, Ōe Kenzaburō, and the first-generation writer Kim Sŏk-bŏm published in the journal *Bungaku* [Literature] as "Nihongo de kaku koto ni tsuite" [On Writing in Japanese] in November 1970.[32]

Ōe and Ri both stress the phenomenon of unwitting assimilation among Resident Koreans, assimilation that was both linguistic and behavioral. In 1972, close to half of the marriages of Resident Koreans in Japan were to Japanese.[33] This statistic signals, of course, the loss of pure Korean blood. In addition, more important for ethnic identity than genetic purity was behavior. Mixed marriages meant that families would gradually lose cultural markers of Koreanness, such as eating certain foods, wearing Korean dress, celebrating traditional holidays, and performing ancestor worship.

This was making everyone nervous. Pak Shil, however, has made an interesting observation about what was really happening. Looking only at the number of *marriages* of Resident Koreans to Japanese (versus those to other Resident Koreans), he argues, distorts the perception of the number of Resident Koreans marrying Japanese. In 1970, for example, 2,922 out of 6,845 marriages were to Japanese, 3,923 between Resident Koreans. When we count in couples, then, it seems that almost as many Koreans were marrying Japanese as other Koreans. But in fact, each Korean couple is not one individual person but two. Thus, if we use as our unit not couples, but individuals, we see that 1,466 Resident Koreans married Japanese, and 7,846 Resident Koreans married each other. So actually only 27.25 percent of the total number of Resident Koreans marrying that year were taking Japanese spouses. If we continue to look at the number of *individuals* marrying Japanese, we learn that not until 1984 did the number of Resident Koreans marrying Japanese pass the 50 percent mark.[34] Nonetheless, the fact that statistics were being reported in such a manner indicates that there was clearly anxiety (on the part of all involved) that Resident Koreans were capable of becoming Japanese and were choosing to do so.

The debate on writing in Japanese is a manifestation of precisely such a fear.[35] Ri Kaisei's key point in the exchange with Ōe and Kim Sŏk-bŏm was that he believed that Zainichi writers — if they chose to write in Japanese — should resist linguistic assimilation by making certain that their language has a "Korean flavor."[36] Kim also stresses that their language should be in some way unique, if they are to avoid becoming Japanized in the process of writing in Japanese.[37] All seem to have agreed that they should resist the Japanese language, at least in part because it was "the language of extremely invasive rulers in Asia, not only in the political sense, but morally as well."[38]

Although all three concurred to a certain extent, Ri took pains to distinguish his own efforts from that of his predecessors, including Kim Sŏk-bŏm. For him, he said, it was not enough to preserve some old vision of Koreanness, for within it were things that he would wish to reformulate.

> It's not so much that I wish to . . . tear ethnic subjectivity and literary creativity apart. Rather I think we need to use that creativity for broader exploration. For example, as Resident Koreans we live on Japanese soil and in the Japanese climate. If we accept what's here, surely there is plenty that we can learn. If we let ourselves learn from the Japanese people and from the advanced elements that Japanese have brought to the world from their culture, won't we become more advanced too? . . . Don't we need to work in harmony with the international while keeping a Korean "flavor" at the core? If we don't, I fear that we'll just see the old as old, and let it drift away as if it were sediment at the bottom of a stream.[39]

This passage makes perfectly clear that Ri believed firmly that Koreanness could be created. His is also a vision of a critique of the oppression of Japanese society, state, and culture from within its own frame. In 1972, Ri also wrote several essays on the subject of writing in Japanese. In them, he refined his point somewhat, quoting Miki Takashi's argument that language changes with each speaker; in other words, that users change language.[40] He adopts a number of new terms as well, such as *shutaisei* ("subjectivity"), a word central to early postwar discussions of Japan's war experience. Because this term refers in particular to the individual in history and its relationship to the modern state, we see that Ri is attempting to forge a role for Resident Koreans in determining their own fate. More familiar to us as contemporary readers is another keyword he picks up: identity (for which he uses the English together with Japanese characters coined to mean identity, indicating self-sameness, referring to the psychological usage of the term). In his piece, he argues these things writing cannot be "good."[41] Thus, although Ri is best known for advising Zainichi readers to find themselves by forming links with the homeland, we see that he simultaneously struggled to define ethnicity not as innate but as something that people themselves have a place in fashioning.

Of course, Ri was not working in a vacuum. His ideas about the use of Japanese are not unlike those discussed in the Kim Hŭi-ro trial. Both Kim Shi-jŏng (in his testimony) and Ri Kaisei (in this discussion) find their way out of the oppression inflicted by Japanese language and society through an exploration of not spoken but written language. And this is not just any written language, but literature. But where would that leave ordinary second-generation Resident Koreans? Are their only choices to speak only Korean (which nearly everyone had determined was impossible), or to write a resistant, Koreanized Japanese?

I want to turn now to an analysis of Ri's story, "Kinuta o utsu onna" [The Woman Who Fulled Clothes], because I think it provides us one of his own answers to this question. By the time Ri Kaisei won the Akutagawa prize in 1971 for this work, he had already published a fair amount of autobiographical fiction. Most of it was set in Japan, told from the perspective of a young man, in language that was quite straightforward. Much of it also seemed to contain an admonition (to the Zainichi reader) to find pride in being Korean, and to do so in a personal way.[42]

"The Woman Who Fulled Clothes," like his other works, is a *shishōsetsu*, or personal narrative. It is told in flashback form; a young male narrator reminisces about the death of his mother. Many critics have followed Ri's own lead and read the story as the author's effort to come to terms with his mother's death. It is set in Sakhalin, where Ri grew up, and the familial details fit those of Ri's real life. The mother in the story is even given Ri's mother's name. Despite its simple plot, however, it is not a simple story. In it, Ri tinkers with language and themes to a greater degree than in his preceding works.

The story begins with not just a word, but a name, a concept we have come to see as fraught. The opening line, "Chang Su-ri died one winter day just ten months before Japan's long war wound to an end," is in Japanese, but beside the first three characters of the sentence (a woman's name) are katakana indicating an approximation of the pronunciation of her name as well as the fact that it is foreign.[43] The author's name of course also appears on the page, but although it is also an obviously foreign name, as was then the convention for those who retained their Korean names, the characters appear, but with Japanized pronunciation beside them. So although a reader might assume the story to be about the real author's mother, he would also sense a difference between Ri Kaisei and Chang Su-ri. The mother, she would surmise, is more foreign, even to Ri.

The title also evokes a foreignness, if a somewhat different one from the names. *Kinuta* is a Japanese word, surely, but not common in the current age. It also bears a phonetic gloss beside it, which, although a common device, in this case draws attention to the fact that this word, like the foreign name, is one with which the reader may not be familiar. What the word summons, then, is otherness, but not of another country but of an earlier age, because the fulling board is a common motif in premodern literature.[44] The reader wonders, then, how a romantic past when women beat clothes on fulling boards might be linked with Korean otherness. Might this indicate a shared past or pasts, found in Japanese literature and in memories of Korea, which are fused within the narrator's consciousness?

A sensitive reader will by this point realize that she must play close attention to the *furigana* (phonetics) beside the characters, for she may not know how to read them. Ri's strategy, then, has the effect of accentuating the oral/aural quality of language. But this opening is significant for several other reasons as well. Traditionally, married women in Korea are not referred to by their given names but by their title, usually as So-and-so's mother. The *ta* verb ending in the sentence is used primarily for past tense and, according to Karatani Kōjin and others, it similarly helps to bring about a "neutralization, or effacement of the narrator."[45] This neutral narration, accompanied by the third-person reference to the woman (which has a comparable effect) gives this line an air of historical or objective narration, as do the reference to the war and the dates.

In the very next line, however, we find ourselves with a new paragraph and a new narrator. "Boku" (a masculine first-person pronoun) tells us, "I distinctly remember that day. Probably that's because I was already nine. I cannot but think that having lost my mother during my childhood influenced the formation of my personality, but at that time I was still no more than a naive young boy" (318). "Boku" has no name; instead he is only the son of Su-ri, shaped to this day by her power. The text's masculine, Japanese-speaking, and confusingly Korean-Japanese–named narrator has been molded by a feminine and Korean past.

In the passage that directly follows the above, the narrator leads us to believe that important above all in this process was his mother's special naming of him. She called him by a nickname, "Jojo," the general meaning of which was "rascal," but the precise meaning of which the narrator has, until the textual present, been unable to determine. Here we see Ri pointing to the pivotal importance of naming not only for the child as an individual, but for him as a member of society.

This is a bit different from the Kim case, however, for what we see here is a mother not crushed or coopted by the state, but resistant to it. Kim's defense team, if not familiar with the work of Louis Althusser and his importance the importance of ideological apparatuses such as the family in making us all into national subjects, surely worked with similar ideas. Althusser famously argues that "before its birth, the child is . . . always-already a subject in and by the specific familial ideological configuration in which it is 'expected' once it has been conceived."[46] When the child takes the father's name, the child then reproduces (to use Lacanian terminology) the Name of the Father and thereby enters into the symbolic order of the patriarchal familial apparatus.[47] This model thus implies that the father represents the national patriarchal system. For Kim — or indeed for Ri or any other oppressed or colonized minority — inheriting the father's place in the symbolic order would of course mean accepting a subordinate place in the national community.

So when Ri Kaisei has the mother being the one who chooses this term of endearment for her son, he seems to be trying to find a place within the family that is apart from the oppressive politics of the colonial nation-state. When she calls him "Jojo," she is giving him the gift of Koreanness within the home, relatively safe from colonial authorities. Thus, even though the nation of Korea cannot exist and her son has no way of being Korean in the outside world, she can help perpetuate it through her actions in the home (which, if we follow the above logic, is not entirely "private").

Interestingly, the ability to circumvent the state's attempts to stamp out Koreanness seems to depend not only on who is doing the evading (a woman) but how (in spoken language). The narrator indicates that her name for him, "Jojo," is part of an orally transmitted ethnic conscious-ness: "in the dictionary there was no word of the sort" (318). He wonders if the nickname is from the dialect of his mother's hometown, which is "near Kyongju, the capital during the Shilla period" (318). For him, and for us, it thus evokes a true national Koreanness of the past.

Beverly Nelson, author of the most thorough reading of this story in any language, observes that it was during the Shilla period that the Korean peninsula was first unified.[48] Therefore, the reference to the Shilla period has a double nuance here. Within the narrative itself, the reference shows how "boku" is beginning to link his own life with a unified nation of the past; at another level, the juxtaposition of this reference with the backdrop of Japanese colonialism hints at the notion that were it not for Japan's actions, Korea would not be a divided land.

There is an additional way in which the particular significance of names in Korean history lurks behind this story. Chang Su-ri would have begun calling her son "Jojo" in the late 1930s (because he was nine in 1944). As we might remember from the testimony in the Kim case, the colonial command had compelled Koreans to take on Japanese names (in 1939). Making a similar argument to that advanced in the trial, Chong-Sik Lee observes, "Surname and clan origins were sources of pride, particularly for the *yangban* or gentry. Hence, the governor-general's demands forced all Koreans to commit a most unfilial act — denying their ancestors by assuming strange-sounding and arbitrary foreign names that bore no relationship to the past."[49] During the colonial era, for Koreans, names took on an explicitly political, ideological significance. To accen-tuate the Korean name Chang Su-ri is a sharp reminder of the implications of naming in a very specific historical past, and for her son to invoke her name an act of piety.

Of course, this piece of fiction is not only a musing about his family or even about the colonial era. Ri observes elsewhere that "No matter how small a family problem one writes about, one is not writing about some problem in the past, since depending on how it is read, it could instead be seen to be saying something about the relations [of Koreans] and Japanese today."[50] The presence of the adult "I" in the story also suggests to the reader that the events related here have ramifications in the present.

I have mentioned the way in which the name Chang Su-ri in "The Woman Who Fulled Clothes" takes on a double valence with the use of kanji accompanied by *furigana* with a Korean reading, forcing the reader to recognize the constructedness of his comfort with the language. Even more striking, perhaps, is that the narrator, in describing his attempts to locate the source of his nickname "Jojo," provides us, in Korean writing (*han'gŭl*), the four possible Korean pronunciations that that Japanized pronunciation could represent. The introduction of Korean words throughout the story is never more bluntly performed than at this moment. It is as if to impart shock — as if to say, I am taking your language and twisting into shapes which you will not be able to recover. I am polluting it, permanently, so that you will not be able to use it thoughtlessly again.

But the kind of uniqueness of style referred to in the above discussion refers also to dialogue, which, as Beverly Nelson recognizes in her analysis, "reveals a sensitivity to differences in the speech patterns of different people."[51] What is important here is that those people's speech is peppered with Korean: *oenom* (literally, "thief"; a derogatory term for Japanese), *aigo* ("alas," "oy vay"), *palch'a* ("fate"). And people are most often called by Korean appellations: accompanying the Japanese *otōsan* ("father") is the Korean *abŏji*, and so on. Such narrative contributes actively to the transmutation of Japanese.

Furthermore, twists of Japanese appear even in the frame narration, for example in his writing of the common word *kanojo* ("she") with a mixture of phonetic writing and Chinese characters that make it possible to read it as the classical form *kano onna* (or, even more classically, *kano me*) rather than the more natural *anno onna*, to indicate that woman ("far away"). This has the effect of accentuating an insurmountable distance between the narrator and the (Korean) women about whom he is speaking (his aunt, grandmother, even his mother) and evoking again the archaic aura of the fulling board.[52]

As I mentioned earlier, the story is in one sense a *shishōsetsu*. I spoke above of the "I" narrator, a young man reminiscing about his mother's death when he was a boy. The story also takes on certain characteristics of a form which is quite different. Certainly the *shishōsetsu*, with its unity of voice within a single narrator, is a modern form; critics have linked its emergence to the modern conception of an individual.[53] We shall soon see that in Ri's story, there are actually a multitude of voices. Within the frame of this narration of memory, for instance, there emerges another voice, that of the boy's grandmother, who, when performing the Korean custom of lamentation of fate, *shinse t'aryŏng*, a ritualistic mourning for her (step)daughter's untimely death, provides us with information about Chang Su-ri that the main narrator could not otherwise have known.[54]

The narrative, as I mentioned, begins with the simple statement of fact: Chang Su-ri died. From there, the adult "boku" takes us on a disorderly journey of memory, from before his mother's death through her death and funeral. In this description, the distance of the narrative voice from the narrated events seems to narrow. As Beverly Nelson argues, "The child's voice takes over and begins to wander off, picking up associations and expanding them, precisely as a child would tell the story."[55] But before we reach the grandmother's lament, the narration returns to the control of the reflective adult:

> Among the poems I wrote after entering middle school, there is one called "Reminiscence." It's a lousy poem, but for me, it's nostalgic.
>
> A boy is crying. The boy's sadness reaches the heavens, which sheds tears of sympathy. One day, when freezing rain is falling, the boy emerges from the crematorium clutching the urn of his mother's bones and ashes to his chest. The tapping sound . . . it's his mother. Such is the content of the inept little poem.
>
> This poem contradicts a number of facts. The boy, intent on completing this poem, has altered the facts to suit (323).

This passage illustrates how the text grants authority to a more stable-seeming voice, that of the reflective adult. In addition, this means that there are three, or perhaps four, voices, if we take the adult and child "boku" to be separate narrators.

What are these voices doing? They point to the fact of transmission, of the material passing on of history; both Kitada Sachie and Beverly Nelson point to the story as Ri's own *shinse t'aryŏng* for his mother.[56] Although I would hesitate to conflate Ri with the narrator (Ri's project is much larger, and it is not actually a *shinse t'aryŏng*, but a published story), I would point out that the narrator does lead us to the conclusion that he has taken his place in the succession:

> At a certain point, it began to seem that my grandmother, through her almost maniacal *shinse t'aryŏng*, was trying to raise me as the transmitter of the legend of my mother's life. It was as if my grandmother, who was already among the departed, was commanding through oral transmission to tell my mother's tale, to sing her praises.
>
> In fact, I had already sung my mother's praises openly. Of course, my *shinse t'aryŏng* did not possess the poetic rhythm of my grandmother's. It was just ordinary storytelling. (332)

Beverly Nelson makes an interesting observation about the tradition of *shinse t'aryŏng*: its secondary meaning (the first being one portion of the shamanistic rite) of *t'aryŏng* is the narrative line in *p'ansori*, a Korean ballad tradition.[57] Contemporary readers might not have known of *p'ansori* or that it developed out of shamanism. However, because references to spiritual possession are an obvious feature of the story, it would not have taken much for them to see that Ri was using the *shinse t'aryŏng* not only as a simple lament, but as a way to call up the dead or to bring the past into the present. As Nelson observes, the role of the Korean shaman is "to heal the rifts not only between living people, but between the living and the dead, the present and the past. The shaman is in communication with the spirit world, with the restless dead who have not been honored, with the unremembered, unappeased past. They do this by entering a trance or ecstatic state in which they can serve as the medium through which messages are transmitted."[58] And in this case — through the transmission of the dead mother's voice to the grandmother and from the grandmother to the narrator — we hear Korean history being told in the voice of Chang Su-ri. Indeed, in the passage just before the narrator's observation that he has taken up *shinse t'aryŏng*, we see that the historical narrator has prevailed. We are pushed to question whether the loss of self that would occur in a shamanistic trance has caused "boku" to call his mother by her given name, and to refer to himself in the third person.

The presence of multiple voices that sometimes conflict with one another is crucial, not only because it points to a contestation of meaning among Koreans of different generations but to the difference in emphasis that occurs when even the same person employs different modes of communication: written or spoken, lament or common speech, poem or story.

I have said something about the term *shinse t'aryŏng* within the text of Ri's story. It would be negligent of me not to point out its even broader implications, particularly in the era during which he was writing. As I mentioned earlier, *shinse t'aryŏng* is the name of one part of the Korean shamanistic ritual, or *kŭt*. In an essay on the *minjung*[59] or "folk" culture movement, Chungmoo Choi records the use of shamanistic rituals by students involved in political protest just as the treaty normalizing relations with Japan was being negotiated. She writes:

> In this moment of crisis, a form of folk culture was invoked to awaken the critical consciousness of the popular masses. The now-legendary Ritual to Invoke Native Land Consciousness (*hyangt'o ŭisik ch'ohon kŭt*) was performed as a part of the students' massive protest rally at Seoul National University in May 1964. The "funeral of national democracy," the symbolic funeral of the military government concluded the ritual, in which approximately fifteen hundred students participated. Such symbolic funeral processions have since thrived as a part of the protest movement.[60]

Choi further observes the way that the writer Kim Chi-ha developed a new theatrical form, the *madangguk*, out of the mask-dance portion of the shamanistic ritual.[61] These plays encouraged audience participation and dealt with political themes; many of Kim's own *madangguk* were banned under the Park regime.[62] In his work, Kim turned to "Korean millenarian religions" such as Chungsan'gyo, which "adapted shamanic ritual as a symbolic form of social transformation."[63] Central to use of shamanistic motifs was the idea of "collective ecstasy," which was seen by Kim and others as facilitating the formation of revolutionary energy and, it seems, a coming to consciousness of one's historical position.[64]

In her account, Choi carefully documents the rationalization of the adaptation of shamanism into revolutionary art in the 1970s and 1980s as a facet of the *minjung* nationalism movement. She shows the national character of shamanism in her text by emphasizing the explicitly historical and political content of the plays and rituals, and the way in which they further a sense of community. The movement's turn to shamanism in the first place — because it was looking for an indigenous culture that was free from the influences of Japanese colonialism, and one that was rooted in the people — can also be seen as nationalist, something in the mode of Frantz Fanon, who served as one of the inspirations of the movement.[65]

In 1972, after winning the Akutagawa prize, Ri went to South Korea and tried to go to see Kim Chi-ha, whose work had affected him deeply. In a discussion between the two in 1996, Kim says that he had read Ri's work and knew of his visit.[66] Later, in 1974 and 1975, Ri went on hunger strikes protesting Kim Chi-ha's imprisonment. He also published several collections of translations of Kim's poetry, the first appearing in 1974.[67] It would not be rash to assume, therefore, that even in 1971, when Ri wrote "Kinuta," he was already aware of the revolutionary potential some Korean intellectuals and students had found in the collective ecstasy of shamanism. Whether or not he was consciously manipulating such notions, we can read them into his work.[68] It is clear that he is appealing to *shinse t'aryŏng* as a non-Japanese art, a communal practice, an oral history (much harder for the state to censor); in addition, it is a way to register a complaint for past wrongs. Thus what might be mistaken for nostalgia for the premodern or for unhealthy nationalism, we can rather see as having revolutionary aspirations because of its open and unfixed form and its emphasis on specific historical oppression.

I hasten to observe, however, that despite Ri's apparent desire to appropriate the potential of such a genre, his own text is in fact written, and by his pen alone. I am compelled to raise once again the issue of his uneasiness with language, which I previously argued derived from a discomfort with Japanese and a recognition of the unnatural or constructed character of all language. Of course Ri's story is a written representation and is not itself a subversive oral or bodily act. Nonetheless, through its heightened sense of discomfort with its own (written) textuality, it constantly points beyond its own borders. Ri's attraction to ritual storytelling seems to stem from a nostalgia for an oral language envisioned as transparent — a language that, through the materiality of the voice, was capable of expressing something almost always left out of historical accounts but crucial for understanding their development: emotion. Yet couldn't this be a strategic use of nostalgia? Where would he find the impetus for revolution, after all, if not from anger, resentment, and the ecstasy of ritual?

In the 1990s it was pointed out that Kim Chi-ha did not author all of the works published in his name.[69] Even were this not the case, many have seen his works as the voice of a generation. Given that Kim was thrown in jail for his open criticism of the government, such an act might be seen not as one of stealing a fellow's work, but as protecting a colleague from punishment. But if Kim was brave in former years, in the 1990s, he backed down from his strongly confrontational stance. His earlier interest in Korean religion developed into an intense nativism. He came to uncritically accept, for example, the propriety of men's power over women, simply because it is part of the structure of East Asian tradition.[70] Nationalistic appropriations of native customs of course have the potential of turning into xenophobic rejections of all that is perceived as foreign.[71]

Perhaps for Ri the danger was less imminent than it was for the Korean national culture movement. For no matter how much he might be lacing his prose with Koreanisms, he wrote in Japanese. His acts could never replicate those of the South Korean *minjung* movement. We should recall that he said he wished to manipulate that which was good in Japanese culture and the global culture from which it had borrowed. This would distinguish him from the Fanon whom the *minjung* culture movement took as their guide, a Fanon who, in the words of Choi, "warns against the danger of creating a culture by utilizing techniques and language borrowed from the dominant other."[72]

Of course, Fanon's work is not so simple as all this; Homi Bhabha, who finds greater potential in a "hybridization" of minority and majority cultures than in a simple rejection of the culture of the dominant other, has claimed Fanon as a sort of forerunner of his own notions.[73] Perhaps neither characterization is entirely accurate. According to Henry Louis Gates, Fanon has become a "Rorschach blot with legs" — a phenomenon made possible by the fact that his writings are so filled with contradictions that they can be interpreted to many different ends.[74] Unclear though these conclusions might be, it is simpler to discern what he saw as the crucial questions. To what degree are colonial subjects determined by the representations of the colonizer? What role does language play? If our consciousness is indeed formed only through these representations (which is what he seems to be arguing in some places), then what is the way out (something he elsewhere affirms must exist)?[75]

Of course, these questions are the very ones Ri is exploring in "Kinuta" and elsewhere. In various essays and discussions, Ri refers to Koreans' presence in Japan (Zainichi) as a transitional stage and his literature as part of a temporary movement. Nelson argues against this notion, defining Resident Koreans rather as a minority group, and Ri's work as minority literature, the purpose of which is to "preserve a sense of community," "to restore pride and dignity" to the Korean people, to participate in a project of recovery of "myth" in order to stave off the loss of a shared heritage.[76]

My reading is somewhat different. Nelson of course did not have the benefit of hindsight; at this later date, I find this view limited.[77] I want to stress that his writing proposes not a single minority identity to be recovered by rather the possibility for Koreans in Japan to forge a range of self-definitions. For all his contentions to the contrary, the direction in which his characters are moving does not seem to be simply back to Korea. Nelson's claim that Ri's story is mythical, its characters archetypes, seems to me a similar effort to freeze his work into a single meaning. "Ri is not trying to create meaning but to find meaning that has been lost," Nelson further asserts.[78] I do not agree. Rather it is an attempt to depict his mother's life both as typical of the fate of Korean women in her historical time and as the singular life of a woman who held certain thoughts, beliefs, and choices that, although also historically determined, are not equivalent to those of any other human being who has ever lived. That is to say, I believe his work does provide a space for differences in the experience of "Zainichi."

Formal aspects of the story reinforce my suspicions that Ri was proposing that Zainichi Koreans had options other than simply recovering some static Koreanness. *Shinse t'aryŏng* does not serve here as a simple alternative to the oppressor's culture. Ri blends it with the (often meandering) *shishōsetsu* form, reinforcing his thematic concerns — difference of individual (Zainichi) experience, the possibility of human agency, and the issue of Resident Koreans' overcoming the legacies of colonialism. Indeed, through form, Ri articulates a philosophy of the individual subject's relationship to History with a capital "H."

Rhythm, motion, flow, and drifting are dominating motifs. As the narrative shifts from one voice to another, so does the place, and so do the characters. We accompany the narrator back in time, follow him to his aunt's for a scolding, go to school with him, to the hospital, to his mother's funeral, to her cremation, to his grandparents' house, through his recantation of his mother's journey home to Korea, through her earlier journey to Japan and to Sakhalin, and finally through her passage to the world of spirits.

Sentence patterns recur, particularly when marking the passage of time and when referring to the course of his mother's life. In fact, these are all part of the rhythmic *shinse t'aryŏng*, first of the grandmother and then of the narrator.[79] Nelson links the repetition to the voice of the child and sees it as providing a certain stability "for the son of homeless wanderers."[80] But as I argued above, in fact, the rhythmic language is found in the third-person narration, which I initially indicated as historical, but which we soon realize is in fact the voice of the "I" having lost himself in a trance, his performance of *shinse t'aryŏng*. It is within this narration that the main body of the tale of the mother unfolds, and as I implied in the previous paragraph, he recounts her life as a journey. Although syntactic patterns recur, their content — and their context — shifts. Repetition thus brings not more of the same but gradual change.

One could argue that the motion in the story is an imposed one, that the *nagare* ("current," or flow) of the story is not natural — that is, made not out of choice but rather out of desperation. We could then see the mother's journey to Japan as a result of poverty emerging from colonial rule, her following her husband northward a result of similar economic need, and so on. The story itself is not devoid of impulses in this direction; multiple references to *palch'a* (fate) are linked simultaneously with flow and with the motif of unjust appropriation.

The grandmother bluntly explains the reasons for daughter's fate, and her own. "It's all because the country's been overthrown. . . . Why did you decide to go to the country of thieves? My country stolen, and what's more my daughter!" (328). She blames Su-ri's journey to the northern-most tip of Japan again on forces outside of her control: "She was tricked by the man. No doubt about it" (329). Within his *shinse t'aryŏng*, how-ever, the narrator layers a complexity on to all of these terms. Ten years after leaving Korea, she returns to her hometown for a visit (with the nar-rator), and we overhear Su-ri telling her father that the real reason she left was not that she wanted to go to Japan to work, but that her birth mother had appeared. She confronts her father:

> "I was about the age my son is now. That is, when my real mother left, leaving me with you. Dad, you wouldn't let me go, would you? One time she came back to get me. She called my name quietly from under that persimmon tree. . . . By the time my current mother raised a fuss, saying Su-ri's been kidnapped, I was already far away. Three months later everyone came to bring me back. My mother went nearly crazy. . . ."
>
> The father and child remained silent for a while. Finally, the daugh-ter said reproachingly,
>
> "Why did you leave Mom? Men are all so selfish. Women are weak, you know."
>
> "She left on her own. I didn't do a thing. . . . But forget it. Don't ask about it again." (331)

Certainly we can read this episode as allegory. Su-ri's true mother (gone truly crazy later, we learn) has her role as transmitter of Koreanness (in the form of Su-ri) usurped by a (false) adoptive mother. Yet despite her pity for her birth mother, Su-ri decides to take her father and stepmother back to Japan with her, saying, "from now on I need to care for the mother who raised me" (332). In addition, of course, it is she who takes on the role of assuring the safe passage of Su-ri's spirit into the other world by crazily telling her woeful tale. This raises the question as to what constitutes a true mother, and indeed, true heritage. Is birth impor-tant? Or environment? Does one's bloodline make one Korean, or some-thing else? Can one's birth be stolen? Is the stepmother's craziness in any sense inherited from that of Su-ri's blood mother?

A nonallegorical reading of this passage allows me to return to Ri's treatment of the relationship between fate and choice. We see that Su-ri explains her reason for leaving Korea not as determined by the conditions of Japanese rule, but as one designed to increase her own happiness. Generally I am disinclined to trust authors' statements of intention, but in this case, Ri's words add to my sense that this story tries to negotiate between a view that sees human actions as being determined by material forces and one that tries to argue for individual agency.

> While feeling the temptation to layer the images of traditional Korean women on to my mother's disposition, I did attempt to write my mother as she was. For example, while there is no reason to suppose that she looked favorably on the violent colonial takeover which took place because of Japanese imperialism, she was the kind of woman who would quite casually wear a Japanese kimono. In addition, I tried to avoid reducing the reason that my mother had come to Japan to political relations. As a result, she did drift to the country of her dominators as a member of a cheap labor force; however, her reason for doing so was also a result of problems within her family.[81]

In Ri's "The Woman Who Fulled Clothes," I see ideas akin to those articulated in Fredric Jameson's discussion of Sartre in *Marxism and Form*. Sartre, Jameson argues, proposes a "biographical model" which he sees as enabling an "understanding of action not as the *result* of some larger entity (such as class being) which 'manifests itself' through the act in question, but rather as free invention directed toward the future, as essentially being a *project*."[82] In Jameson's perspective, this does not constitute a return to an earlier "historiography of intention" but a criticism of the hyperreductive character of what he calls "pseudo-Marxism."[83] Sartre's goal, says Jameson, is to recreate the intricacies of history "inside out, through the actions of individuals," enabling a complicated view of human beings as making conscious choices and yet being simultaneously unconscious of the ramifications (and causes) of their actions.[84]

It is this sort of project that I believe Ri is attempting to perform in this tale of his mother. I have been arguing that we cannot adequately explain the drifting in the story (the cause of being Korean-in-Japan) as being merely the effect of unjust actions, such as stealing (colonialism). Yet the story betrays a certain desire for stability and for justice — not necessarily of some natural, and thus legitimate, Korea (precolonial, governed by its birth parent/rulers) but of a Koreanness that encompasses elements of past culture and yet is somehow more righteous.

The narrator longs for his mother. He is mesmerized simply by watching her pound the laundry, which invokes a hazy memory of women pounding clothes in Korea, and draws him to that place (337). His desire for this ambiance thus is explicitly linked to a longing for the security of a stable Korean identity. He even says of watching her do housework, "I couldn't explain this spasmodic feeling. It made me want to fly in to her ear or something" (337).

Despite wanting intensely to be assured that he is the rightful descendant of mother and homeland, however, the narrator realizes that he has to earn the right to be his mother's child and thus to be Korean. The following example is most poignant: the narrator and his friends, on a whim, steal red bean buns. When she is scolding him for his deed, she says, "When did I raise such a greedy child? You're not my child. This is terrible. Get out. Get out of this house" (334). Many times in the text his mother taunts him with such words. The moral is evident: blood is not enough to make you Korean.

But there is more, I think, given that in Korean, "thief" was a derogatory term used for Japanese (remember the grandmother bemoaning the fact that her Su-ri had gone to the country of thieves). What does this say about Japaneseness? Is Japaneseness (at the time of the story's publication) locked in this stereotype? Is Japanese (oppressor) what you will become if you do not remember your Korean roots (victim)?

Restricting our gaze to this one small incident, it might seem so. What I have been trying to do, however, is to link this sort of detail with what seems to be the major motif of the narrative, *shinse t'aryŏng* — with its elements of oral history, lamentation, autobiography — and this motif, in turn, with the creation of a continually fluctuating Resident Korean identity in the late 1960s and early 1970s. What significance is there to the voice of the past in this story being feminine in this time (the early 1970s) and place (Japan)? Is Ri merely recapitulating a common idiom and portraying Japan (invader) as male who has ravished Korea the female? If so, in his formulation, does the present conquer the submissive past, or has the fiery vengeful female spirit of the common people returned to disrupt the deceptively peaceful present?

It is in some ways theoretically pleasing to me, as a feminist, to enter-
tain the latter notion—that Ri might have wished to suggest that the
oppressed, Korea, as woman, might disrupt the smugness of an increasingly successful capitalist Japan. Yet I do not think this is his point here.
Although Ri does not reproduce the stereotype of woman as the evil ghost
(for the mother in this story is anything but), he does use a version of the
virginal victim archetype. His mother remains morally blameless and
when she speaks, she is able to do so only in spirit. Therefore, I must conclude that in this story, a woman's voice is usurped by a man's; first generation Korean or Creole words erased by the fluent Japanese of the second generation. But are the power configurations always such that
speaking for one who cannot speak is reprehensible? Ri's gaze seems
frozen on the figure of an idealized mother—who lovingly called him
"Jojo," who suffered her husband's beatings, who thought always of her
children, and who mourned for her birth mother whose madness drove
her father away. Does this make her into a spectacle, forcing her into the
passive position of object? If mother equals Korea, does Korea then
remain forever in the past? Is his myth of a proud, strong, unified Korea
a justified tool of the present?

Fredric Jameson, in a controversial article, "Third-World Literature in
the Era of Multinational Capitalism," contends that "all third-world
texts are necessarily . . . national allegories."[85] In an essay on "Minor Literature," Gilles Deleuze and Félix Guattari put forward a slightly different, but still similar notion, that a "characteristic of minor literature is
that in it everything takes on a collective value," that "what each author
says individually already constitutes a common action, and what he or
she says or does is necessarily political, even if others aren't in agreement."[86] Such views have been attacked with fervor. Aijaz Ahmad's retort
to Jameson—in which he argues against the very term "third world,"
against the notion that oppressed people should all be nationalists, and
against the idea that somehow these third world texts' are important only
because of their third world status and not for other reasons—is by now
as famous as Jameson's original article.[87] Although I agree with much of
Ahmad's critique of Jameson, in contemporary discussions of Ri's work it
is painfully clear that his experience was usually taken to be representative of, and even as an allegory of, the experience of Zainichi Koreans.

Ri was highly conscious of this fact. In this light, I could read Ri's recreation of his mother's voice not as unethical or false but as inevitable, strategic. But rather than thinking in the abstract about the ethics of speaking in another's name, I want to think about the specifics of this case. Mightn't we evaluate this situation in the very terms it sets up for us; mightn't we try to believe that Ri's act in the present is to perform the filial act of telling his mother's fate, and by association hinting at the fate of many women, and furthermore, to provide a symbol of blameless oppression for Resident Koreans to share? By trying to write his mother into his own story, to reveal the manner in which she lives on within him, he called attention to a woman whose name would never have been spoken, who would never have been elevated to such a degree. In that sense, his narrative constitutes not so much an attempt to speak for women as an entreaty to heed their silent presence.

The gaze that Ri constructs for the reader, after all, is that of a son for his mother, and however sexual that particular gaze may be, it is not the same sort of erotic gaze of a man invoked by the writings of film theorist Laura Mulvey.[88] In addition, the very content of his narrative involves the travels not of a man (with the woman as mere landscape), but the *active* journey of a woman.

Or does it? We are beckoned to identify with the main narrator, after all. Is our journey therefore so ensconced in the imaginary world of the stable male narrator, speaking in our language, the language of rationality, of the present, Japanese, that we are not even motivated to identify with the mother? Or to return to my earlier question, does Ri's voice, that of the minor author speaking for an oppressed group, effectively mute a panoply of voices, and in particular, that of first-generation Korean women in Japan, such as his mother?

On one level, Ri seems to have actually been trying to point to the particular fate of Korean women, and to point to the variety of Zainichi experience.

> While I was writing "Kinuta o utsu onna," for no particular reason I recalled the photograph of some Korean "comfort women" I had seen in *Foto gurafu*. The photo-anthology shows Korean women crossing a muddy river, following the southward moving Japanese army. With their pants rolled up to their thighs, holding their luggage

on their heads with one hand, the women were crossing the river, smiling, somehow healthy-looking (!). But all that I felt from this scene was its tragedy.

At that time, I felt a chill. That my own mother, who had come to Japan, had escaped falling into the predicament of a "comfort woman" was one stroke of luck amidst great misfortune. In Japan, since Meiji, those women from farming villages whom we call "kara-yukisan" [Japanese women who went abroad as prostitutes — Trans.] have a similar sad history. The Korean women whose homeland was stolen and who drifted into the country of their dominators, as it said in a contemporaneous folk song "[if they] could bear even a single brat [they went] to the brothels."[89]

Not only is this passage about women, even Japanese women, after all, but, like his testimony in the Kim Hŭi-ro trial, it also reveals his recognition that things might have been otherwise, and that indeed that for others just as Korean as oneself, things were different. It thus leads me to conclude that his was a conscientious effort to engage with the complexity of history and the range of experiences among Zainichi Koreans, rather than a flattening of all into a simple victimization symbolized in women.

Chang Su-ri crosses a stream at the beginning of her journey to Japan, her belongings piled on her head, her skirt tucked up. Even without his direct reference to the images coming to mind as he wrote, it would be difficult for those reading his story now to (since the explosion of the comfort women issue in the media) to put our knowledge of the fate of those women out of our minds. But in the 1970s, the inconceivable tragedy of the comfort women did not attract anywhere near the attention that it has received in recent years.

Nonetheless, this scene is not the only reference in "The Woman Who Fulled Clothes" to refer to the specific oppression of Korean women. The story contains multiple passages, for example, where Korean men mistreat Korean women. They appear to indicate sympathy for the women and condemnation of the men. We see the tragedy of Su-ri's mother, left by her father (or did she leave him?), gone mad, Su-ri herself being beaten by her husband so badly that she almost leaves him. It is here, though, that we meet the unknowable; the father refuses to, or cannot, answer his daughter's question about why he and his wife separated. The mad mother, then, haunts the story. So, in a similar way, does Su-ri's ever-unreachable inner consciousness, her deepest feelings. "When she was pounding the kinuta, what could my mother have been thinking" (338), the narrator muses, and immediately proceeds to tell us of the worst of his father's beatings (338–39).

"Kinuta" closes with the narrator telling us that his father had spoken to his sons of their mother's death with "self-reproach." In addition he says that her final words, "Don't drift away . . . ," indicate the steadfastness for life she held even in her passing (339). The implication in this passage is that it is the father who has recognized his guilt in causing the misery of his wife. But given that this scene comes after pages of assertion of the individual's responsibility, there seems to be another message: that we should not let victimization (and the father, as Korean, is clearly the object of oppression) breed further victimizing.

It is not evident, however, that the father came to realize the evil of his deeds by imagining being in his wife's position. In fact, we only know that the narrator sensed remorse in his father's voice, and that it is the emotion he thought appropriate for him to have been feeling. His own access to this recognition was only made possible by his endeavor to imagine his mother's feelings, and his taking on a femininely gendered culture practice in his *shinse t'aryŏng*. I believe firmly that Ri Kaisei's fiction engages actively the question of Korean male collaboration in the oppression of Korean women; his tale points always to the unknowable, the unreachable, that which is not expressible in language.

Simultaneously, however, Ri's depiction of his mother does effect a silencing of the voices of Korean women about their history despite his efforts to give her a voice. She (as woman) does to some extent end up standing in for Korea as victim *and*, in her role as mother, the pre-Oedipal (precapitalist, precolonial) comfort to which we all wish to return — despite his efforts to represent her as a complex person. Would real women's voices, telling of horrors they suffered not merely because of their nationality/ethnicity but because of their gender, have been too much? If so, too much for whom? Was there really no way they could be understood, or incorporated into a Resident Korean identity? Were the articulators of this identity — even in the form of Ri — too much a part of some patriarchal power structure that the voices of Korean women would upset their views of Korean men as victims?

The Ri Kaisei I present here argues that Korean identity is something to be acquired. Ri himself based that identity in a shared experience of colonialism; the shared burden is the telling of that historical experience; revolutionary potential comes from joining in the struggle of speaking that history. Although it is not clear in this particular story that one need to forge direct links with the homeland in order to accomplish this task, Ri's later works are more explicit. His five-volume opus, *Mihatenu yume* [The Unfinished Dream, 1975–1979], for example, is based on the experiences of Resident Koreans who went to South Korea to participate in a movement for reunification of the country; it has been called a search for a native socialism.

It is this Ri — the Ri who turned to the homeland, not the Ri who opened up the possibility of defining Zainichi experience — who has been most sharply condemned. Most notable among his critics is Takeda Seiji, Zainichi author of one of the few book-length studies of Resident Korean literature (originally published in 1983) and now a prominent social critic and philosopher. On the one hand, Takeda is positive about Ri; he characterizes his work as providing a model of how one might turn Koreanness from something negative into something positive. On the other hand, he notes that in Ri's fiction, the characters move from recognizing their Koreanness only through discrimination and poverty and wanting to become Japanese, through a middle stage in which they are half Japanese, to a final stage in which they become Korean through a vision of the reunified homeland.[90] As a result, the "reality" of his earlier works gives way to the ideological dream of reunification. He adds, " 'discrimination' is dissolved, and this reality of Japanese society is reduced to the problem of the 'dream.' The true crisis of 'Zainichi' is that we will secretly bury the essence of our living as people who are discriminated against."[91] Takeda's assessment of Ri is not without truth: Ri's work does espouse a model of Zainichi that stresses a link with the homeland. I agree that this is a limited view — and perhaps one more palatable to Japanese readers, even, or perhaps especially, progressive ones. As I mentioned earlier, I also find problematic the fact that Ri codes Zainichi oppression in feminine terms.

Yet I would still argue that his earlier work, such as "The Woman Who Fulled Clothes," created an opening for people with a range of experiences to ascribe meaning to their own Zainichi, to conceptualize new ways of being, to see that there was such a thing as identity, and that they could have a hand in telling what that was.[92] After all, in this narrative, Ri grants a broader significance to the experiences of his mother; he also stresses the very importance of the act of telling. Ultimately, then, what this story proposes is that it is in the telling of history, in the telling of lives, that meaning is made. In this sense, it asserts that Zainichi themselves have the right to participate in the making of their identity.[93] As we shall see, this is a right that many other Resident Koreans will come to assert — and in very different ways.

3

Uncircumcised Ethnicity

In 1985, Kin Kakuei, graduate of Tokyo University and three times an Akutagawa prize nominee, took his own life. He was only forty-six. Takeda Seiji, the first critic to perform a detailed analysis of Kin's fiction, does not attempt to provide an explanation of why Kin Kakuei ended his life.[1] Nor will I. Yet his untimely death haunts the pages of his writing, pushing what is already dark into the realm of the tragic.

Depressing as it often is, there has been a resurgence of interest in Kin Kakuei, in large part as a result of Takeda's efforts. Takeda issued a collection of Kin's stories in 1986, and since then, articles about and references to him have appeared in a range of publications. While I was in Japan conducting research for this book in the late 1990s, I asked people which Resident Korean authors they thought deserved critical attention. Many came up with the name Kin Kakuei. Chŏng Yŏng-hae, a feminist sociologist particularly fluent in current postcolonial theory, credits Kin with being one of the few second-generation Koreans to criticize the oppressiveness of Zainichi nationalism, to expose its internal contradictions, including sexism, and to reject (her argument implies) the notion that Ri Kaisei-like notions of Korean identity are somehow redemptive.[2] In Japan in the late 1990s, Ri Kaisei was seen as antediluvian (Marxist and/or nationalist) and Kin Kakuei as a forerunner of the current main-stream (postmodern, postcolonial).

Kin was not always such a golden boy. Although he made his debut in the mainstream press before Ri Kaisei — his first story appeared in *Bungei* [The Arts] in 1966, when he won the magazine's new writer's prize — and continued to publish during the period of Ri's greatest critical acclaim, the late 1960s and early 1970s, contemporary sources often compared Kin unfavorably to Ri. "Kyōkaisen no bungaku — Zainichi Chōsenjin sakka no imi" [Literature on the Borderline — The Meaning of Resident Korean Writers], a roundtable discussion published in *Shin Nihon bungaku* [New Japanese Literature] in 1970, is typical in its evaluation of Kin.[3] The participants describe Ri's work as masterfully incorporating Korean humor (54), as revealing a flair for storytelling in the sense defined by Walter Benjamin (55), as speaking to a real audience (55), as showing that he has "absorbed the expressions" of all Resident Koreans (56). Kin's work, on the other hand, is seen as lacking this humor (54) and as being more similar to literature by Japanese writers: it lacks a purpose and does not seem to be written for any real audience (56). One member of the roundtable further proclaims that Kin's main problem is that he cannot speak Korean (61). Ri's work confronts the external world, he says, and finds its roots in a community; Kin's, in contrast, because it focuses on the internal, appeals mostly to the intelligentsia (55–56).

There is direct correlation between public opinion of literary texts and political matters. Indeed, the relative indifference critics showed for Kin Kakuei's work in contrast to the ardor with which they discussed Ri Kaisei reflects not only their aesthetic values (which are at any rate necessarily political), but also their awareness of the professed political beliefs of the authors. Ri Kaisei was one of several Resident Korean intellectuals who, in concert with Japanese literary figures, spoke out and engaged in a hunger strike in protest of the imprisonment and death sentence of Kim Chi-ha (in 1971), the South Korean activist poet. He also translated Kim's poetry.

In addition, Ri's *Mihatenu yume* [The Unfinished Dream], as mentioned in the previous chapter, tells the story of Zainichi Koreans engaged in a movement for reunification of the Korean peninsula under a new native socialism. Readers have assumed that he based this novel on the experience of the Suh (Sŏ) brothers, two Resident Koreans who became involved in the South Korean student movement while studying in South Korea and in 1971 were arrested under suspicion of being spies for the North. They were tortured in an effort to induce them to confess; they never did. They were nonetheless found guilty and jailed. The younger, Jun-shik, was released only in 1988 and the elder, Sung, in 1990.[4] When I met with Ri in 1997, however, he vehemently refuted any connection between his *Mihatenu yume* and the Suh brothers' experience, and he asserted that he had never subscribed to North Korean–style socialism as had the Suh brothers.

Still, Ri's fiction did have a decidedly political — specifically socialist — tenor, and over the course of the 1970s, he wrote numerous essays about current events and spoke out regularly about the Korean political scene. Kin was quite unlike Ri. Although he also wrote nonfiction, he did not speak out so strongly about political issues; when he did, he railed against the North-affiliated organization, Sōren. He visited South Korea, and even worked for the Republic of Korea–affiliated group Mindan's newspaper. His work "Kishū ga owatte soshite warera wa . . ." [Homesick No Longer] serves as quite a contrast to *Mihatenu yume*. In a style almost like a suspense novel, it tells of a Zainichi man and his Japanese lover being manipulated and subtly coerced by North Koreans to act in support of a reunification movement led by the North.

In many ways, Kin's fiction was similar to that of other contemporary writers of Japanese literature: it tended toward the psychological rather than the overtly political, focusing on questions of the self, and its form and language were virtually indistinguishable from non-Korean writers. Such were the reasons that critics maligned Kin's work, although at least one observer commented that because such features were rare among Resident Koreans writers, they did give it a certain "freshness" (56).

The historical event I will consider alongside Kin's literature, Pak Chŏng-sŏk's employment discrimination suit against Hitachi Software, likewise had difficulty garnering support, particularly from the Resident Korean community. Although surely few would have denied that Pak had indeed been fired for being Korean, many felt that this was not the right battle to be fighting: they viewed Pak as an assimilationist. After all, he was fighting for the right to work at Hitachi, one of the conglomerates involved in what were seen as neoimperialist endeavors on the Korean peninsula. Furthermore, he had misrepresented himself on his application, not only by using a Japanese name, but by putting his Japanese address in the space reserved for the place of family registration (which in his case was in Korea).

This case overlapped with the legal movements mentioned above, spanning from 1970, when Pak first filed his case, and 1974, when the decision was handed down. The members of the group supporting Pak ultimately founded the umbrella civil rights group Mintōren, a group identified for being the strongest force in establishing the notion that Resident Koreans should fight for rights in Japan rather than troubling themselves with the politics of the homeland. Twenty-five years ago, however, even those Resident Koreans who had left the South and North Korea–affiliated organizations, Mindan and Sōren, continued to assert that it was more important for Koreans to focus on the democratization and reunification of the homeland than on the eradication of discrimination in Japan.

Yet as I have said, now, quite the opposite is true. Some might still not advocate working for such a company, but the majority of Zainichi Koreans today probably would portray this movement as the first in a series of successful battles for Koreans' civil rights. Many in the core group that gathered around Pak, helping him in his legal battle and in directly confronting Hitachi, were young, and included both Resident Koreans and Japanese. They struggled over the gaps in their perspective of prejudice, and on occasion they lashed out at one another, but ultimately, their movement became a model of how Japanese and non-Japanese could work together. The prospects of future such movements were made to seem even brighter by the fact that the court ultimately awarded Pak not only his job but back pay and damages. Some of the fans of Kin Kakuei surely emerged from the ranks of this new generation.

The differences between earlier movements and this movement, and the work of Ri Kaisei and that of Kin Kakuei, however, have been overemphasized, leading interpreters to overlook what they share. I do not wish to fall into the opposite trap. However, I do find it significant that they both were placing their stakes in Japan. Additionally, this movement overtly, and Kin Kakuei somewhat more covertly, proposes that identity is a process, much as Ri Kaisei had suggested. Furthermore, despite a seeming affirmation of capitalism within Kin's work and the Hitachi trial, I perceive in them roots that are distinctly Marxist, or at least critical of single-minded devotion to economic development.

Kin Kakuei's fiction employs motifs familiar from Ri Kaisei. Much of his work examines domestic violence, and in particular, the son's effort to come to terms with his violent father. Moreover, like Ri, he adopts the metaphor of the gaze; he also probes the question of the relationship between speech and writing. Kin makes different points when he manipulates these themes. Not only do his storylines differ significantly, but he does not mix Japanese and Korean, and thus to read him is quite unlike reading Ri. Nonetheless, we would be wise not to adopt the erroneous assumption of contemporary critics that Kin's focus on the interior constitutes a rejection of the political. Even those motifs seen as distinctive to Kin the individual, such as the consideration of stuttering or of science and literature, act in service to an underlying argument about the meanings of human life within late capitalist society. In other words, what is interesting here is not only that various discourses of minority identity (ranging from nationalist to assimilationist) developed at this time, but that those narratives of identity furnish insights about a host of issues raised by Japan's particular experience of capitalist modernity.

As we saw in the previous chapter, the Kim Hŭi-ro incident and Ri Kaisei's early work concentrated in particular on the relationship among language, history, and ethnicity after colonialism. In the pages that follow, we shall discover that the Pak Chŏng-sŏk case and Kin's writing consider the place of technology and science in postcolonial or perhaps neocolonial Japan, and the effect of the dominance of scientific rationality on the human spirit. I structure my discussion around motifs from Kin Kakuei's fiction. I first address the way that he uses the metaphor of circumcision in one of his most famous novellas, *Kogoeru kuchi* [The Benumbed Mouth, 1966].[5] Then I consider the role of science and technology in his work, looking at *Manazashi no kabe* [The Wall of the Gaze, 1969] and other pieces. Finally, I come to the relationship between the gaze, violence, and gender, not only in *The Wall of the Gaze*, but also in "Ishi no michi" [The Stone Path, 1973]. I include my discussion of the Pak case between that of the stories.

The Benumbed Mouth opens with a quote: "And Moses said unto the

LORD, O my LORD, I *am* not eloquent, neither heretofore, nor since thou hast spoken unto thy servant: but I *am* slow of speech, and of a slow tongue (Exodus 4:10)."[6] This novella tells of a Resident Korean graduate student in chemistry who is tormented by a stutter. It is perhaps not strange that not only at the opening but on other occasions, citations appear from Exodus referring to Moses' stutter, his "uncircumcised lips" (Exodus 6:12, in *Benumbed Mouth*, 75, 97).

Critics have disputed Kin's use of the stutter in his fiction. Some have argued that the pain and the self-consciousness experienced by those who suffer from this affliction serves as a metaphor for the pain of living as Korean in Japanese society. Others, notably Takeda Seiji, contend rather that the motif serves the crucial purpose of allowing Resident Koreans to define themselves first and foremost in a manner that is not political: "Kin's distinctive contribution as a Zainichi author was to grasp the difficulty of living as 'Zainichi' by layering it upon the difficulty of living with a 'stutter,' being the first to question the categorizing of the problem [of Zainichi identity] as a choice between North and South."[7]

Interestingly, the interpretations I have read only touch briefly on the references to Moses and do not explore the fact that the citations are specifically from Exodus. Exodus is, of course, the tale of delivery of the children of Israel from slavery in Egypt and has thus long served as a source of inspiration for the possibility of liberation from oppression. Moses serves not only to lead the people out of Egypt, but he also serves as the mediator of the word of God and messenger to Pharaoh. Yet he is described as having "uncircumcised lips," which Kin interprets as meaning that he stutters.[8] Although Moses was born of Hebrew parents, he was raised and named by Pharaoh's daughter, who became his adoptive mother.

I do not wish to imply that Kin Kakuei is so self-aggrandizing as to imply that he (or his semiautobiographical alter ego), one raised in a alien culture, a stutterer, should be mediator of a covenant with God (or holiness in some form), or even between Koreans and Japanese, and is thus capable of helping his people to escape their state of oppression. In fact, on its surface, Kin's text is dark, as I observed at the outset of this chapter. Throughout, long passages in technical language, much of it in katakana, forces readers to stutter, as it were, as they read: we are slowed trying to decipher the sounds, and the phonetic writing provides us no ready access to meaning.

The present time of the story is a single (rainy and cold) day during which the narrator/protagonist has to give a presentation in front of his fellow chemistry students, although flashbacks dominate the text. The passage covering his presentation, however, stretches over an anxiety-inducing four pages. His report is interrupted several times by a phone call and the narrator's thoughts. Here we finally reach the moment when he stumbles over his words:

> Would I be okay? Would I say it okay? What should I do if I stutter? — I was reading the sixth and seventh pages aloud, but my mind was occupied with the "tetrahydroflan" on the eighth page.
> Then, finally, I approached that word on the eighth page.
> "The above applies to the case of solvents like pyridine cyclohexane, or pyridine chloroform, but next, for solvent II, in place of chloroform. . . ."
> As anticipated, I faltered there. I couldn't even say the "te" of "tetra." In general words beginning with the "t" sound and the "r/l" sound are difficult for me to say, but when difficult sounds are lined up as in "tetra," it's all that much harder.
> "In place of chloroform. . . ."
> I repeated myself, hoping that the momentum would enable me to keep speaking, but I still tripped up.
> I panicked. The more I panicked, however, the worse it got. The most important things for a stutterer to remember are to stay calm and to breathe regularly, but when you're on the line, all that collapses. As I said before, that is what makes a stutterer a stutterer.
> "In place of chloroform . . . that is . . . for solvent II, in the place of chloroform, I used tetrahydroflan, and in the case of solvents like pyridine tetrahydroflan. . . ."

The text stumbles along; elsewhere in the novella, long quotes from books the narrator is reading appear, and the present time is interrupted by memories of the past. Disorder and hesitation prevail.

The most fluid and informative passage we find is the sixth chapter, the twenty-odd pages of which are occupied by words of a different nature. Here we find written utterances of an Other in the form of a suicide note from the narrator's Japanese friend Isogai. Isogai's place in the symbolic web of the story is central. We learn his name before we learn the narrator's (Ch'ŏi). Ch'ŏi is currently dating Isogai's sister, Michiko, whom he met through his friend. Yet Michiko (whose name literally means "child of the way" or "child of the road") does not merely act as a mediator between Ch'ŏi and her brother in a homosocial bond, between the realms of the living and the dead, or between Resident Korean and Japanese. Instead, she becomes a possible route for Ch'ŏi to take in order understand the significance of his own life. Isogai's character acts not so much as a distinct character but as Ch'ŏi's alter ego (or, in less psychologically specific terms, that in himself which is other to him). Within the first few pages, Ch'ŏi tells the readers, "when he committed suicide, I felt not so much as if an other had died, but as if a part of myself had perished. Perhaps this is because he was a stutterer like me" (11).

The possibility of human understanding comes through a woman, and specifically through the act of sexual intercourse. The final scene of the novella, in which Ch'ŏi and Michiko have sex, enables us to glean more about the nature of that understanding, and it is the metaphor of circumcision that is the clue. Even though he comes to orgasm, he muses that even in this closest of acts, the experience of pleasure is ultimately separate (95). Then he ponders circumcision, the biblical references of which he first learned from Isogai. In his suicide note, Isogai had paraphrased Moses, saying that his heart is uncircumcised, that he has never "touched heart to heart with another person in a meaningful way" (75). Here the narrator builds on Isogai's observations:

> "[I], who am of uncircumcised lips . . ."
> Moses' words must not simply refer to Moses as a stutterer, but to him as a representative all human beings, including those who do not stutter. The only one who truly has circumcised lips, or who, in the words of Isogai, has a circumcised heart, is the Lord God himself. In front of God, are not all people, truly every one, of uncircumcised lips, lips that can never be circumcised? Do not their hearts remain uncircumcised as well? (97)

Human understanding, then, is not only an emotional endeavor, but ideally would be of a holy, or spiritual nature. Elsewhere in the Bible, there are multiple references to "circumcising the foreskin of the heart," indicating opening oneself to love for (and obedience to) God. We see here, however, that Kin is pessimistic about the prospects of realization of such bonds.

Still, Kin's later work (such as *The Wall of the Gaze*, which I will turn to presently) indicate that the act of confessing his stutter, although it did not stop him from tripping over his words, did help to alleviate his emotional pain. Observing this same point, Takeda Seiji likens Kin's work to that of early modern Japanese writers, whose narratives often revolved around the act of confession. In contrast to the novel, he argues, the genre of the early modern west, which tells of the coming to "maturity" of the protagonist, the *shishōsetsu* centers on confession, which enables the protagonist to overcome a "sense of misfortune" he feels when he acknowledges the confrontation between "'the world of real relations' (= the worldly) and 'the world of the relations of the human heart' (= the holy)."[9] The protagonist becomes upset when the material world rejects him or does not provide categories for self-understanding, but writing about the realm of human emotional relations and confessing his misfit status provide him (and the reader who identifies with him) a way to overcome his angst.

Takeda further suggests that although this approach was effective for Kin in his attempt to come to terms with his stutter, it ceased working for him in his later works, in which he directly confronted the matter of ethnic identity. Although writers like Ri Kaisei found meaning in the discourse of nationalist ethnic identity, for Kin, Takeda contends, "rather than liberating him from his 'sense of misfortune,' 'nationalism' was representative of another 'world' that declared to him the inevitability [of that misery]."[10] In a 1996 article, Takeda states retrospectively that one of the main points of his work in the 1980s — in which his analysis of Kin takes center stage — had been to point out the futility of conceiving Resident Korean identity in terms of a choice between ethnic consciousness (usually meaning affiliation with the North) and assimilation. At the time, he had predicted that nationalist tendencies would soon vanish.[11] Indeed, in those analyses, we find him coming close to attributing to Kin a decidedly nonnationalist (although ultimately not postmodern or poststructuralist) worldview; he sees him as possessing an intense desire for identity and meaning which for him is not fulfilled by the discourses of nationalism or Marxism.[12]

The feminist critic Kitada Sachie takes Takeda to task for his claims about Kin's perspective on Resident Korean identity. She quotes Takeda as saying that younger generations of Koreans are unable to find themselves through the issues raised by earlier writers, such as "ethnicity, the stolen language, and identity," that their sensibility resides in the recognition of the "impossibility of overcoming the difficulties of Zainichi." In contrast, she observes, Takeda sees Kin's literature as appealing because of its ability to speak to this younger generation. She then goes on to claim that his work is reflective of a broader trend in Japanese literary studies hoping to challenge the heavy Marxist influence of the postwar tradition in that field.[13] Whatever Takeda's motives in analyzing Kin's work, his writing style indicates a sympathy with psychoanalytic and poststructuralist literary criticism. For instance, his final conclusions about Kin in *"Zainichi" as Foundation* are as follows:

> The second generation of "Zainichi ". . . at some point must abandon an ideological desire for "society" and land themselves in the order of personal life. Then the impulse to appease that abandonment through the *narratives* of "the family," "history," "ethnicity/nation," is impressed upon them. What we must note is that the desire for "reconciliation" with the "father" or "history" at this time in reality appears as a conflicting discourse with those various "ideologies."
>
> That is to say, the adolescent libido is *denied (= repressed) for a moment,* and exactly the *reverse state,* that is being changed into its [libido's] precise opposite, moral standards, comes into being. These adolescents usually experience the struggle between moral standards and sexual libido as a psychological conflict, and in the same way "Zainichi" experience the rotation from a desire toward "society" to desire toward their "private lives" symbolically as the discursive conflict between narrative (ideological) and narrative (in terms of real life sensitivities).
>
> The path walked by Kin Kakuei was clearly a place where precisely these sorts of *narratives* of "Zainichi" intersected. However, it should by now be evident that as a result of his own particular nature, he continued throughout to be rejected by all sorts of narratives. What is important here is that the author Kin Kakuei in no sense came close to the notion of the "impossibility of narrative." That is to say, while continually desiring narrative, he nonetheless continually was rejected by it. As a consequence, his gaze painted the world as an incomprehensible scene, a scene of privileged truth from the place of a person who faced continual rejection, now sunk deep in the depths of the world. (emphasis in original)

I want to point out something interesting here. Despite the fact that Takeda's poststructuralist tendencies show through here and that elsewhere — including earlier in this same book, as I cited above — he draws the conclusion that Kin saw misery as inevitable because he saw "narrative" or "meaning" or "identity" as myths, here he argues the opposite. It is precisely this sort of slipperiness of language, and indeed thought — not to mention a tendency to overcomplicate — that makes Takeda such a challenge to read.

Perhaps Kitada is right in assuming that Takeda does see Kin as the forerunner of the postmodern antinarrative views of Resident Korean identity prevalent today, but she makes him into a bit of a straw man over this point. She is definitely on the mark, however, when she implies that he is so concerned with matters of individual psychology that loses sight of the effect of the historical place of Koreans in Japan on his work. I would add also that his arguments about Resident Korean identity rely on certain gender biased assumptions about psychological development.[14] I will come back to this question toward the end of this chapter.

At any rate, Kitada's main claim runs counter to Takeda's, and that is, that much like his contemporaries, Kin did develop a notion of ethnic identity in his work. His early (Zainichi inclined) fiction reflects a socialist influence, she says, but in his later writing, such as the "spy" story I mentioned above, he exhibited an animosity toward North Korea and Sōren. Therefore, while he was on the opposite end of the political spectrum from Ri Kaisei, he nonetheless ended up turning his eyes toward the homeland.[15]

My conclusions rely on the insights of each of these critics. Takeda is invaluable because he raises the matter of these authors' perspective on "narrative," as is Kitada for her recognition that both Ri and Kin ultimately do define an identity through delineating their stance toward the homeland.

Ultimately, however, I want take their insights to say something with a rather different nuance. I ruminate on what these authors have to say about Resident Koreans' changing self-definition, but I also will examine what their narratives of identity imply about Japan's capitalist modernity and the particular role of ethnic and gender discrimination within it.[16]

I now return to the work of Kin Kakuei to consider precisely such questions. His fundamental view of modernity comes through with the greatest clarity when he touches on science and technology. Although they are often thought of as contributing toward "progress," he portrays them as preventing human beings from leading a secure, fulfilling existence, in opposition to literature, which provides the opportunity for contemplating the significance of human life. In at least one story, "The Stone Path," he delineates the devastating effects of the desire for financial success and technological improvement. It is such motifs that make the pairing of his literature with the *Pak v. Hitachi* case so apt. The trial and the movement surrounding it, of course, reflect on such matters in much more explicitly political — and practical — terms, and it may seem strange to liken Kin's critical perspective with a struggle for a man to be allowed to work in one of Japan's most powerful corporations. Yet both focus on Resident Koreans' lives in Japan rather than concerning themselves with reunification of the homeland; they also share the view that although it is impossible, and perhaps not beneficial, to overthrow Japanese capitalism, they nonetheless wish to change it.

Kin's attitude toward science and technology should begin to become evident as I discuss *The Wall of the Gaze*, again a story of a graduate student in the sciences. In *The Benumbed Mouth*, Kin had already depicted scientific work as meaningless; for example, the narrator refers to his chemistry research as "empty" (14) because "life is for nothing if not the process of attempting to fulfill the self" (15), and the experiments he performs have no relation to these efforts. The somber ending adds further to the sense that nothing promises hope for ameliorating the pain of nothingness. Science rises no higher in this novella. The protagonist Su-yŏng finds only emptiness when he enters "T." (read Tokyo) University's Division of the Sciences (52). The hope for financial security that would enable him to rescue his mother from his father's violence first led him to this most prestigious of universities and to the sciences, although he claims that the choice was simply the result of his stutter, which gave him an aversion for language, the focal point of studies in the humanities (47–49). Still, implicit here is the ideology that science embodies the epitome of success within capitalist modernity. Science appears not as a gateway to truth, or even a means of escape from daily life, but merely the best means for getting ahead.

Science disappoints, in more ways than one. To begin with, it does not even insure a livelihood: Su-yŏng's professor has been unable to find him a position despite the fact that he has been trying for more than two years

(76–77). In addition, it does not provide the anticipated intellectual stimulation. The protagonist here echoes the thoughts of Ch'ŏi in *The Benumbed Mouth*: "I had begun to develop a great interest in human beings, and particularly in my own being, in the way that someone like me lives; when I realized that the experiments I did from morning to night had no bearing at all on this question, I came to feel immensely dissatisfied [with my work]" (63). What interests him is not so much the result of his experiments, but why he is standing there doing them at all. Science cannot answer this question for him, and in search of something that can, he begins reading literature (63–64).

By claiming that scientific experimentation is pointless, Kin intimates that human beings participating in what we think of as intellectual endeavor — regardless of whether they enjoy what they do — are necessarily also cogs in the machine of the capitalist state. It might be overzealous to make such conclusions were it not that the main theme of the story: the "gaze" of the title.

In the previous chapter, I considered the relation of vision with power and gender in Ri Kaisei. In Kin's work, vision is likewise intimately linked with the question of power, but here the dynamics are rather different. From the first lines of this story, it is evident that the gaze represents the discrimination against outsiders in Japanese society, and Kin writes from the perspective of the seen and not the seer. Here the main character reflects on the evaluation of a story he had written for a college literary magazine:

> The gist of the criticism from K., a member of the school magazine whom Su-yŏng did not know, was to concede that the gaze was commonplace. From what he had heard, K. was from Okinawa, so undoubtedly he was troubled by that very same gaze. Otherwise he wouldn't have gone to the lengths of raising Su-yŏng's piece just to criticize it so vehemently for having neglected to touch upon the gaze. (23)

The main storyline of *The Wall of the Gaze* consists of a one-night visit to an inn in the mountains, although as in much of Kin's work, memories and thoughts dominate the narrative. There is no action in the present of the story, in fact, for even this main action is indicated as having taken place "one month ago" (27). The narrative is propelled forward, however, not so much by action, but by the way that it reveals how Su-yŏng came to change his perspective on the "gaze," the existence of which he denied when he first received the criticism from K. In the story he wrote, Su-yŏng had focused on the pain of stuttering; as I mentioned above, he believed that "confession" had released him from his pain, that it had acted as a "catharsis" (26). Although he had at first thought K. was wrong, "the gaze to which K. had referred was now beginning to take the place of the stutter, [whose pain] he had forgotten. It was beginning to bother him more and more" (26).

The visit to the mountains, an "other" space, as is often the case in literature, serves as fertile ground for introducing the shifts in Su-yŏng's perspective. We learn that the story that K. had criticized had been about a visit to the mountains and was based on a visit to this very place five and a half years ago, after his girlfriend Fumiko had broken up with him. In addition, when Su-yŏng was very young, he had an aunt who lived near this place, and he had run away here with her on at least one occasion when her husband's violence had grown severe. Kim is thus able to use the various places Su-yŏng visits to trigger his memory, to allow him to show change in time, and to make not only Su-yŏng but the readers aware of how he has transformed. Furthermore, because the movement in space is one from Tokyo (the city, the center, the symbol of the modern) to the country (nature, the periphery, the traditional), Su-yŏng's observations on this trip thus bear on not only his individual development but, I would argue, on economic and sociohistorical development.

The following is a prime example. Su-yŏng calls the inn from the station to make a reservation. He remembers the old telephone number, but he realizes, when he puts in a coin to call, that the number he recalls is too short: the telephone has changed from operator to manual dialing and requires more digits. Then, for "some reason," he stutters when he tries to say his name. Finally, after several tries, he manages to say it (30–31). "When he heard that his name was Yi, the man had probably guessed that Su-yŏng had hesitated to say his name. That was not at all unreasonable, he thought. Yet it was unpleasant to think that the man had assumed that he was embarrassed to have it known that he was Korean. He felt that 'gaze' piercing him from F. Inn, beyond the mountains and trees" (32). If on the story about the previous trip, Su-yŏng had been obsessed with his stutter and oblivious to questions of ethnic prejudice or had linked the two, we see that it is now the latter that causes him greater grief. The question of the change in the telephone number seems unconnected to this event, a mere detail included to indicate the passage of time, or to endow the story with a sense of "reality." Yet might it not perhaps also suggest that rapid development brings with it a devaluation of memory, of the past?

When he arrives at the inn, once again Su-yŏng's ruminations on the gaze are juxtaposed with remarks that the countryside is no longer countrylike, giving further credence to my point that Kin connects the gaze with the social relations rooted in capitalist development. His first visual impressions are as follows: "At F. Inn, he saw that a splendid, but for that reason unsuitable, entranceway had been built. . . . When he got off the bus in front of F. Inn, and saw that, he doubted his eyes for a moment." He is disappointed that it is not the quiet and plain place it had been (34).

From this, he shifts to speaking about the new management:

> From the moment he saw him, somehow he had thought the man [at the front desk] was Korean. Perhaps it was slightly stern face, his overweight, flabby build, or maybe the fact that his unctuousness and greed made him seem stupid, or the manner in which he moved — such features somehow made Su-yŏng think, "Korean." (35–36)

> It is as if there were two types of Koreans: "me the Korean" and "that guy the Korean." But what kind of person was "that guy the Korean?" Greedy, pushy, a drinker, quick to get in fights, poor, dirty; in other words, uncivilized, an uncontrollable barbarian — these sorts of qualities came to Su-yŏng's mind. (36)

It is striking that Su-yŏng associates "inappropriate" development (what he later identifies as poor taste) with barbaric Koreanness.

Su-yŏng has internalized the gaze and the language of the oppressor. I mentioned in the previous chapter that names have served as the primary marker of otherness for Koreans in Japan. It is not strange, therefore, that Su-yŏng's first example of the gaze — the phone call — should be prompted by his having to reveal his name. I also discussed Resident Korean and Japanese intellectuals' debates over the question of language more generally speaking, and in that context, the name of Frantz Fanon soon surfaced. They called on Fanon for the notion that when the colonized use the language of the colonizer, they have no choice but to adopt the colonizer's perspective. Here Su-yŏng has indeed inherited the Japanese nuance of the term *Korean*.

Not coincidentally, one of the most commonly cited passages from Fanon's work is one in which he describes being looked at by — that is, feeling the gaze of — a mother and her young daughter, who says with horror, "Look, a black man!" Like Fanon, Kin portrays the manifestation of sociocultural power dynamics in the gaze and language, and the psychological pain these cause human beings. The particular dynamic Fanon is concerned with is racist colonialism (and sometimes gender).

In this story, however, the oppressive gaze and language are not simply based on race or colonialism but are even more pervasive. Su-yŏng recalls a story he heard from a friend; in an elementary school in Osaka, there were several Koreans and several "Buraku" students in a class; one would think they would play together (because Koreans and these descendants of Japan's former outcaste class were similarly discriminated against), but they did not. He bemoans the state of affairs: "Japanese direct the gaze of prejudice toward 'Buraku' people, even though they are Japanese, 'Buraku' direct the same gaze toward Koreans, and then Koreans direct it at other Koreans" (36).

Even if, as this statement suggests, prejudice is timeless in Japan (as elsewhere), Kin's persistently negative references to development and science suggest that the particular manifestation of bias against Koreans outlined in this story is uniquely modern, intertwined with Japan's postwar capitalism. The gaze he describes is likewise modern, reminiscent as it is of Michel Foucault's notion that the mechanism of surveillance lies at the center of modern society. Foucault suggests that while in the past, people were controlled by the central visible (but in day-to-day life, physically absent) force of the king, in the modern world, power is differently visual and omnipresent. His famous metaphor for this situation is the model of the "panopticon" envisioned by Jeremy Bentham, in which prison cells are arranged in a circle around a central observation tower in a manner allowing the guard to see all the prisoners while hiding him from their view. Earlier in the story, Kin makes use of a metaphor of crime to depict the feeling of surveillance:

> The gaze had become utterly disturbing to Su-yŏng. When he felt the gaze around him, he felt an unpleasant, uneasy feeling, almost as if he had committed some crime. If he had actually done something for which he was being looked down upon, for being looked at with that

gaze, then there would have been nothing he could do. But he had no memory of having done anything, and so it was that much more difficult to contend with, that much more unpleasant. (26–27)

In Foucault, such internalization of the feeling of being gazed on is a crucial part of the system, for it is this which enables it to work prophylactically.[17] Additionally, Foucault defines the transition to this particular visual power dynamic as dependent on the rise of the ideas of the Enlightenment, and particularly the modern human sciences, in which "man appears in his ambiguous position as an object of knowledge and as subject that knows; enslaved sovereign, observed spectator, he appears in the place belonging to the king."[18]

Kin's suggestion that Koreans are not merely objects but also subjects of the gaze reflects a perspective not dissimilar to Foucault's. Yet in his scheme, as in Fanon's, those who bear some mark of disempowerment (skin color, a name, poverty) are objects of the gaze to a greater degree. Perhaps, despite structural similarities, the gaze we find in Kin is different. It has often been pointed out that Foucault's excessive emphasis on an all-encompassing web of power forces us to overlook the fact that the web is not evenly spun, or that there are many webs, or that some of us play the spider more often, and others the fly.

We need to remember that an Okinawan pointed out the gaze to Su-yŏng, and that all who are caught in the snare of the gaze are non-Japanese. The most precisely historical example Kin provides is of a man we know from the previous chapter: "He thought that [the Kim Hŭi-ro incident] was the first time that the 'gaze' had come to the surface in all Japan and focused on a single place, a single person. Although the person on whom it was focused was Kim Hŭi-ro, Su-yŏng felt as if the aftershocks of the event fell upon him as well" (81). Su-yŏng goes on to say that he spoke publicly against Kim Hŭi-ro, echoing the opinion of other Koreans that Kim had done them a disservice. After doing so, however, he wonders whether he, who had internalized the gaze, had any right to level such criticisms. After all, "What had he hoped to shoot down with his rifle? What else could it be but that very 'gaze'? And if so, it was not only Japanese but Koreans like himself who had internalized that gaze at which Kim Hŭi-ro had been pointing his rifle. . . . Was it really fair to say that Kim Hŭi-ro had done something wrong?" (81). He answers this question in the negative and goes on for several more pages about the incident.

Next he launches into an explicit consideration of the question of "identity" in the sense implied by Takeda Seiji:

> He could not escape from the "Japanese person" within himself. Nor could he escape from his fate as a person who is neither Korean nor Japanese, or perhaps, both Korean and Japanese. But what was wrong with that? By coming to understand himself as a person who both was "gazed" upon and who pointed the "gaze" at others, wouldn't he be able to come to a more complete understanding of the "gaze?" Wouldn't he be able to think more deeply about the state, or the nation, or the human beings who had given birth to that gaze? And precisely by learning all there was to know about these things, or by attempting to learn about all these things, wouldn't he be able to find true liberation for himself (84)?

This passage makes particularly apparent the fact that Kin Kakuei's view of the gaze is modern in the sense that its origins are colonial, but that it is rather different from Foucault.

We could compare Kin's observations to those of Lukács, who argues that the proletariat can see what the middle class does not because "he feels himself to be an object, and this initial alienation within himself takes precedence over everything else."[19] Or we might perhaps draw on similar arguments made about the unique vision of African Americans (I think of W. E. B. DuBois's conception of "double consciousness"), or of a similar perspective some critics believe postcolonial peoples possess.

Such comparisons are surely as close to the mark, and they reveal that Kin's views are not necessarily parallel to poststructuralist thought. For all the ornery comments about the meaninglessness of modern science (and life) that Kin voices through Su-yŏng, I do not believe he would cast Enlightenment rationalism (and its wayward child, Marxism) into the sea along with the ills of modernity. His political stance is not as plainly socialist as Ri Kaisei's, but Kin is not a poststructuralist. Many of Kin's insights rely on Marxist ideas. The fact that he decries the usefulness of scientific experimentation, for instance, is derivative of the now classic view that in late capitalism intellectual workers, including scientists, have been subsumed into the working class.[20] In the final story I turn to, "The

Stone Path," we shall also see that although his definition of a proper Resident Korean identity is not identical to Ri's, he as vehemently affirms the importance of asserting an ethnic identity.

Furthermore, one might expect an author doubting the possibility of accessing (or even creating) meaning or truth through language to abandon or intentionally pervert standard language and literary form. There are no such tendencies in his work. For all his references to science, and for all his intellectual recognition of the "uncircumcised" nature of communication, his use of motifs, of character development, of plot, betray his confidence, or persistent hope, that written (rather than spoken) language and literary form can convey meaning.

How should we interpret such contradictions in Kin's work? However inclined it may be in that direction, Kin's work is not philosophy but fiction, and as such, the eradication of internal inconsistencies is not necessarily its highest priority. In fact, I believe that self-contradiction is one of the features making Kin's literature so compelling. Emotional, irrational desire — for meaning and identity, among other things — is the impetus driving his work forward.

Even within the text of *The Wall of the Gaze*, I find this to be so. The passages in which Su-yŏng reconsiders his relationship with a Japanese woman, Fumiko, which he had written about in the story criticized by K., are revealing. He is in part upset over their breakup because it is through Fumiko that "he felt as if he had first come into contact with the outside world" (55). In addition, although he had formerly denied that it was the case, he now admits that their union was doomed because they were "unable to overcome that gaze" (67). He concludes that a love that conquers the gaze may be impossible (68). He had come to the mountains "hoping to put himself in nature not as a Korean or as a Japanese but as an individual human being," but even at the mountain peak, there are people, and thus the gaze as well (80). He acknowledges only a single relationship in which the gaze did not interfere: that with a child whom he tutored (74–75). Critics like Takeda have observed that what gives Kin Kakuei appeal is not his conclusions but his adroitness at conveying what it feels like to be a Korean in Japan. This story creates meaning more in its process than in the conclusion that in the adult world (particularly the adult sexual world) meaningful human relations are unachievable.

The final scene is memorable less for what it says than for the atmosphere it conveys. Arriving at the train station to go home, Su-yŏng comes upon a stone statue of a Korean girl and boy, commemorating the return of Koreans to North Korea.

> He was faintly surprised that this sort of thing had been built even so far away in the mountains. Wiping his face and neck with a handkerchief, he looked up at the statue for a while. No doubt the people who had built it had done so out of the joy they felt knowing that they would be able to return to North Korea. However, when he looked at it, Su-yŏng felt he saw not their joy but the countless "gazes" that had poured upon this statue. . . .
>
> There were just a few taxis standing in front of the station. Nothing moved in the square, eerily quiet in the bright direct sun. When he looked around, he noticed multiple eyes staring at him standing there in the center of the square. The people standing in front of the station garage, the people sitting on the bench at the bus stop, the people lined up on the sidewalk in front of the shops, even the people sitting by the window of a second-floor cafe on the square, the faces of countless people were directed toward him. . . .
>
> He felt ashamed. Normally he would have fled, but now he did not want to do such a thing. He pulled himself together, deliberately putting his handkerchief in his pocket, and looked around once more. A few people were glancing absently in his direction — that was all. The scene about him was not unlike that in front of any other ordinary station. (85)

His detractors may have found such writing apolitical and overly concerned with emotion, but his admirers did not. Those involved in the movement supporting Pak Chŏng-sŏk, to which I now want direct my attention, should be counted among those devotees. In a panel discussion held not long after the conclusion of the trial and published in 1974, one young Resident Korean central to the movement refers to the fact that many second- and third-generation Koreans feel "much like a character in a Kin Kakuei story, in the sense that they feel neither Japanese nor Korean."[21] It is crucial here that his emphasis is not on Kin's politics as exhibited in his writing, but on the fact that he imparts a certain feeling. This is true despite the fact that this story, as we recall, explicitly mentions employment discrimination.

As I have mentioned, the mainstream of the Resident Korean community viewed Pak Chŏng-sŏk with the same disdain as it did Kin Kakuei. Ch'ŏi Sŭng-gu, a Resident Korean student at the center of the movement supporting Pak, recalls that he first went to visit him after reading about him in the newspaper. He was involved in a church youth group and attempted to enlist the other members for this cause. They argued, however, that fighting for Pak meant endorsing assimilation and refused to help. It was only because Pak did not possess "ethnic subjectivity," they contended, that he had met the fate he did. Furthermore, they insisted that it was more important for them to figure out their relationship to Korea and explore questions of their own ethnicity than to work against discrimination in Japan. Eventually, the group kicked him out.[22]

The main group involved in the Hitachi struggle, Paku-kun o kakomu kai [The Committee to Protect Pak], was formed not by Koreans, but by Japanese students from Keio University's Beiheiren, originally an anti–Vietnam War organization, who were approached by Pak as they distributed leaflets protesting Immigration Law changes. These students managed to elicit the help of several prominent Japanese activists involved in the Kim Hŭi-ro trial.

Ch'ŏi had also appealed for support from an experienced activist. When he approached Reverend Yi In-ha (a Korean involved in the Kim trial), minister of a church that he attended, in a neighborhood of Kawasaki where many Resident Koreans lived, his request fell on receptive ears.[23] In the panel discussion cited above, Reverend Yi says that he did not hesitate to become a founding member of the organization aiding Pak because he did not feel that Koreans themselves were responsible for their inclination to assimilate. He had spent time in the United States, where he had observed that in the course of their struggle, African Americans had come up with the slogan, "the black problem is really a white problem," and eventually with the motto "black is beautiful." The struggle for rights led black Americans to refashion their "subjectivity." Resident Koreans similarly need to "recover their ethnicity" and should not be blamed for the inclination toward assimilation.[24] If at the outset many had disparaged Pak Chŏng-sŏk and Ch'ŏi Sŭng-gu for being assimilationists, after several years of the movement and the influence of figures like Yi In-ha, this accusation could be levelled at neither. Pak had gone from using a Japanese name to using a Korean one, and Ch'ŏi had studied in South Korea.[25] Indeed, much like the Kim Hŭi-ro trial, the moral of this story was that Zainichi Koreans should hold on to, or rather find, an identity. The difference was that this one enabled them to do without any pretense that they would some day return to Korea.

In 1970, when Pak Chŏng-sŏk had sought employment at Hitachi, he had been only nineteen. He had gone by the name of Arai Shōji and barely knew his Korean name. He was indignant about the fact that Hitachi would not hire him even though he had passed their exam; the notion of assimilationism was completely unfamiliar to him.[26] Even after the trial began, he continued to use Arai except with people involved in the movement.[27] By his own admission, he was ambivalent about the entire process, feeling uncomfortable speaking as the representative of 600,000 Resident Koreans.[28] He also felt resentful of the Japanese students, wondering what they could possibly understand of the difficulty of what he was confronting.[29] They, in turn, were critical of Pak's passivity — for example, his reluctance to brainstorm about trial strategy.[30]

Toward the end of the trial, however, Pak began to change. In much the same fashion as the Kim Hŭi-ro trial — and perhaps as a result of the overlap in participants — Pak's lawyers called a good many scholars and public intellectuals to the stand to speak about the history of Koreans in Japan. They also were able to convince the judge that the testimony of ordinary Koreans and a tour of the areas in which they lived (including Osaka and Nagoya, near Pak's parents' home) were necessary in order to convey the fact that Pak's experiences were the norm rather than an exception. Pak tells of the experience of hearing the testimony of people his age in Osaka:

> [They] spoke calmly of their upbringing and about how they planned to live their lives with a sense of their ethnic subjectivity. I was shocked, but also moved.
>
> I had faced all kinds of discrimination, but it wasn't just me; the experiences I had faced were faced by all Koreans. This gave me courage, I suppose you would say, and I moved to Sakuramoto, in Kawasaki, where the Korean church is.[31]

In addition, he began to use his Korean name in his daily interactions, and he began to study the Korean language at Yi In-ha's church.[32]

Pak's legal team raised two major questions: the first was whether a legal contract had been concluded, and the second was over Hitachi's reasons for denying Pak employment.[33] Hitachi asserted that the letter sent to Pak was notification of a decision that was not yet official and that it had ultimately not hired Pak because it had discovered that he had "lied" on his application, an indication that he was untrustworthy.[34] Pak's lawyers, on the other hand, insisted that Hitachi's letter should be construed as a legal contract, something they needed to prove in order to make demands for back pay. They saw Pak's dismissal as proof of ethnic/national discrimination. They pointed to the fact that as soon as Pak had called and informed Hitachi of his Korean name, they had held off the offer of employment but had said nothing about the reasons; crucially, they had not inquired about the matter of the name and address he had supplied on his application. They had not found out he was Korean, investigated the documents, found the discrepancy, and then fired him. Rather, they had fired him based solely on the fact that he was Korean. These facts, they concluded, constituted ample evidence of the fact that Hitachi's real reason for firing Pak was his nationality (/ethnicity).[35]

Although the clarification and interpretation of such factual details was of course crucial to the plaintiff's case, they also attempted to use the suit to campaign against discrimination in employment and more generally in Japanese society. Other Koreans had accused Pak and his supporters had been of being assimilationists. Although the objective of Pak's legal team in this court case was not to counter the criticisms of the Zainichi community, one of its primary goals was nonetheless to place the blame on Japanese society for forcing Koreans into the difficult position of assimilating or being excluded. Scholars they called to the stand testified that the historical origins of Japan's current assimilation policy could be traced back to Japan's colonization of Korea, and particularly to the late colonial period, after the beginning of the war with China. At this time, Japan had realized that it might be compelled to draft Koreans into the military, and that if Koreans were to be given guns and expected not to turn them against Japanese, Japan needed to do as much as it could to crush their consciousness as Koreans and to make them aware of their status as subjects of the Japanese empire. As was mentioned in the previous chapter, Japanese law required Koreans to use Japanese names, prohibited the use of the Korean language, and so on. Assimilation did not mean equality, however, as Koreans continued to work under inferior conditions for inferior wages.[36]

Pak's lawyers further asserted that Japan's postwar position toward Koreans should be seen as in a continuum with the prewar. They cited the fact that although there was a tendency within Japanese schools to treat Koreans as if they were the same as Japanese and to encourage them to downplay their difference by using Japanese names (a policy of assimilation), Koreans still faced discrimination in employment (a reality of exclusion).[37] Thus they concluded that Japanese society had forced Pak to believe that he had to cover up his Koreanness if he wished to obtain employment at a company like Hitachi.[38] Pak's supporters interpreted Hitachi's particular actions, which resulted in his ultimate exclusion despite the fact that he had assimilated, as a "symbol" of the way discrimination worked in Japanese society at large.[39]

Pak had grown up in an area where there were few other Koreans, so his parents did not teach him Korean customs or pride in his Koreanness. He had gone to Japanese schools and had incessantly worried that his classmates would find out he was Korean. As a consequence of both these personal factors and the pressure of society at large, he therefore had been uncomfortable with his Koreanness.[40] Although probably none of these facts could have redeemed Pak in the eyes of those who had originally seen him as a traitor to his kind, his ultimate "discovery" of a Korean identity, referred to briefly above, may have mollified some of his critics.

Not only Yi In-ha but nearly every other commentator on the Hitachi case referred to Pak's transformation as the most meaningful outcome of the trial. In his final decision, the judge accepted the arguments put forward by Pak's side and even expressed his admiration for the changes that Pak had implemented in his personal life:

> [Pak learned that] when Resident Koreans face employment discrimination and the economic poverty that it brings—not to mention the disdain with which Japanese people view them as a result of their dire circumstances—most are robbed of their hope of leading [normal] hard-working lives, and some even have breakdowns. He has said that he has come to believe that in order for Resident Koreans to recover their humanity, they must have a Korean name, act like Koreans, respect Korea's history, and live with pride in the Korean people. I

must say that I overflow with sympathy toward the plaintiff for his psychological suffering.[41]

Most poignant, however, was the fact that this was true for Pak himself. On the stand, he said, "I don't know if I'll win or lose this case. However, the result isn't the issue. This trial allowed me to recover the ethnic spirit that I had lost and to make the decision to live as a Korean. For me that is the ultimate victory."[42]

For certain critics of Pak and the movement, however, that he had come to be proud of his Korean ethnicity was not enough because their negative view of assimilation derived at least in part from their perspective on Japanese capitalism. The notion of becoming Japanese offended such people not only because of the history of colonialism in Korea or the persistent discrimination and prejudice within Japanese society, but also because of Japan's contemporary economic and political relationship with South Korea.

We have seen that the 1965 treaty between Japan and South Korea had important ramifications for the Korean community in Japan. Its direct legal effects included the possibility for Koreans in Japan to attain "permanent resident" status in Japan if they took South Korean citizenship. A second repercussion of the treaty, crucial for us here, is that it unleashed a wave of Japanese economic expansion into South Korea. The 1970s, by most accounts, are retrospectively considered to mark Japan's emergence as a major global economic power.[43] There can be no doubt that its activity in South Korea helped it rise to that status. The treaty provided South Korea money not in the form of reparations, but $800 million in public loans, grants, and commercial credits. Although such aid certainly helped the ROK to develop its economy, it meant that Koreans were forced, for example, to buy equipment from Japan. This situation then paved the way for massive direct investment by Japanese companies in South Korea. During much of the 1970s, Japanese invested more in South Korea than did any other country.[44] The situation, of course, benefited Japanese industry as much as it did Korean industry. Furthermore, the aid let the state off the hook in terms of the question of war reparations, or so the Japanese government has continued to argue in every lawsuit demanding compensation since (as we shall see in particular in the case of the "comfort women," in Chapter 6). Such factors left Korea dependent on Japan economically, and with little room for political bargaining, and many scholars therefore described the relationship as "neoimperialist."[45]

Members of the *Committee to Support Pak* were not oblivious to the debates over this matter. In the course of the above discussion, one of the Japanese members of the group asked Ch'ŏi Sŭng-gu what his feeling was when he heard of the plans to confront Hitachi directly. He responded that he had not aggressively supported this effort because "it's not just Hitachi." When he went to South Korea and saw with his own eyes the extent to which Hitachi and other firms were engaged in business there, he finally came see the term *economic invasion* as appropriate, and he felt that it was essential to link their movement to the broader issue of Japan's economic activity in Korea. The Japanese students with whom he was speaking make it clear that they were not entirely convinced of the importance of including this issue.[46] Ch'ŏi does not elaborate on why he became so upset but does comment on the fact that Japanese industry had found cheap labor and an environment that they could exploit without the protests they increasingly faced in Japan. The year 1970 has been given the appellation, after all, of "Kōgai Gannen," or "Year 1, P.C. (pollution calendar)."[47] Although not everyone in the movement shared the view that Japanese capitalism was neoimperialist, Ch'ŏi could not have been the sole participant who subscribed to such a view. As was the case with Kin Kakuei, then, we see that Pak's supporters were not as disinclined to think about the homeland as their critics charged.

A few final comments. It is not coincidental that the industry concerned was computer software and not, say, publishing. This is not to suggest that nontechnical businesses were free of prejudice, but rather to make clear the degree to which Japanese economic development depended on technology, and consequently the success of people within that economy was based on an ability to work in technological fields. In fact, in documents submitted to the court, Pak's legal team bemoaned the fact that because Koreans are well aware that an academic degree alone will not guarantee them a job, regardless of their interests, they tend to go into engineering and the sciences in order to acquire concrete, saleable skills. We see in this lawsuit and in Kin Kakuei's works that science and technology are perceived as tools of industry, detrimental to human beings and, although not expressly indicated, to the natural environment as well.

However much this lawsuit may have contributed to spreading the notion that it was possible to live with a Korean identity without sacrificing one's livelihood for the cause, in real terms its effect was of course limited, and employment discrimination persists to this day. In addition, even in terms of the matter of identity formation, it paved the way only for men.

In speaking of his family, Pak refers to the violence of his father against his mother and to the fact that two of his sisters work as bar hostesses.[48] If matters regarding women's employment and sexual exploitation of women would need some time before coming into the limelight in Zainichi and Japanese circles, the matter of domestic violence was central to most discussions of second-generation Koreans' upbringing. This is as much the case in Kin Kakuei's literature as it was in Ri Kaisei's.

Takeda Seiji conceptualizes this problem as one of the son's coming to terms with his relationship with an authoritarian, violent father. In Ri Kaisei, he says, the contact with society (and, as he further implies, its narratives of history and society, not to mention the separation from his family) enables the characters to come to excuse their fathers' behavior.[49] This factor makes Ri's not unlike early modern Japanese literature, in which "the problem of the 'father' mediates the adolescent self's double-edged feelings towards 'society' and 'life' in that society, and appears as a part of the *link* enabling him to mature as a social being (Shiga Naoya serves as a typical example)."[50] On the other hand, in the case of Resident Korean fiction, the father mediates the son's relationship not only to society in general but to the Zainichi community, and thus in order to come to terms with his identity as a member of that community, he must reconcile with his father. In Ri's case, Takeda tells us, acquiring a knowledge of the "'masses' or the 'ethnos' or the 'history' in his father's past" is what enables him to do so.[51] In other words, he ceases blaming his father for his violence because he now understands that it is a product of his own oppression.

For Kin Kakuei, in contrast, such knowledge never permits the luxury of forgiveness. His depictions are raw. The mothers do not protect the sons; rather, the father serves as both purveyor of and protector from violence "in exchange for being the guardian god protecting the family against the discord of the outside world, he entraps the family with his tyranny, preventing their escape."[52] Ideology helped Ri's characters come to terms with their fathers, but in Kin, even after reconciliation comes with his father (only when he is old and weak), no narrative (and, the implication is, authority) can take his place.[53] Takeda thus conceptualizes the Zainichi father in Kin's work within his more general framework of understanding.

Takeda's analysis of Kin depends on his depiction of violent fathers in his earlier stories, including the two I examined. In *The Benumbed Mouth*, for example, we learn that Isogai's father beats his mother horribly. "To my father," he tells Ch'ŏi in his suicide note, "my mother was a wife only when he wanted to fulfill his sexual urges" (70). She had begun an affair with one of her husband's fellow workers, but when her husband discovers the affair, he beats his wife and her lover. Isogai's mother then commits suicide by throwing herself in front of a train. Isogai, however, sees her death not as suicide but as murder at his father's hand (72–73). Isogai had originally sought out Ch'ŏi's companionship because his mother's lover, the only man who had been kind to his mother (as well as to him and his sister), whom he had seen make his mother laugh as his father never had (71), was in fact also named Ch'ŏi. Isogai's father is Japanese, but Kin Kakuei stated publicly that he had modeled this character (and not Ch'ŏi) on his own father, a fact most critics take to be significant.

In *The Wall of the Gaze*, we learn of Su-yŏng's father's violence, his "once beating [his] mother over the head with a stick with all his might, so hard that the stick broke." (An almost identical scene appears in *Tsuchi no kanashimi* [The Sadness of Soil], published one month after Kin's death in 1985.) In Su-yŏng's house, this sort of scene is common, occurring once or twice a month. The children's fear leads them to hide in their futons, to embrace each other and cover their heads with quilts (47). Such is the violence from which Su-yŏng wants to rescue his mother.

In the final chapter, I will come back again to the question of witnessing violence; however, I do wish to acknowledge here that the experience certainly must come into any attempt at psychological analysis of Kin's literature. A wealth of studies on survivors of trauma indicate that seeing violent acts can be as devastating as experiencing them directly. One of the best-known, not to mention the most prevalent, effects of posttraumatic stress disorder is dissociation, one element of which may be depersonalization, the feeling that one is watching oneself from the outside. I do not wish to diagnose Kin Kakuei, but I do think considering such factors allows us to further ponder the ultimate meaning of the "gaze" in Kin's work.

I do not wish to limit my own discussion of domestic violence in his literature to a contemplation of the way that this experience influences the son's struggle with his father and then in turn affects his maturation and acquisition of "identity" in the psychological sense. Rather, I want to explore the ways in which this violence both serves as a literal comment on oppression of women (and, because they are forced to watch it, against children) in the Korean community, as well as — much as was the case in Ri Kaisei — how it works as a metaphor of the exploitation of Koreans. "The Stone Path," a seemingly nonautobiographical story, is inhabited by archetypal figures with quirky details of character that enable Kin to speak on these two levels at once.[54]

A woman is walking up a hill. Three weeks ago, the "sky she had glimpsed between the buildings had seemed more expansive, brighter" (278). That had been her first visit to the women's clinic. She is trembling, hopeless.

> She had come back to where her mother had given birth to her. One might assume that just as her mother had grown to adulthood and given birth to her, naturally she had now grown into a childbearing adult. Instead she felt merely that she was embarking on a foolish path tread by countless women. One thing was decidedly different in her own case. While her father had been at her mother's side, she had no one. When she considered that ultimately this was because she had no parents around to protect her, the misfortune of having lost her parents at such a young age welled up painfully within her. (278)

The structure of this piece is similar to the earlier two in that the story covers only a brief moment of the "present" and summons its depth through the use of flashbacks. There are four sections, each of which begins in this present time. Thirty or so pages after the above, less than an hour has elapsed for Pang-ne, but we have traveled with her memories through the two decades of her life. In other respects, however, this story departs dramatically from the previous works I have examined. The central character is a woman, and the work is not directly autobiographical. Moreover, although it is a tale of "coming to adulthood," this young woman's story does not have the meandering feel Kin cultivated in his *shishōsetsu*; that is to say, he gives each element of the plot, each image, a purpose. If one is never sure quite what led Su-yŏng to develop to the point of perceiving the significance of the gaze, we see Pang-ne catapulted into adult life by the monumental events the narrative is built around: her rape by Sang-il, the man who has cared for her since her parents' death, and her abortion of the pregnancy caused by this rape.

From the initial flashback, a moment from Pang-ne's youth, we sense that something will go awry. One night during the war, there is an air raid. Pang-ne's father and Sang-il, a distant relative and their current neighbor, had built a shelter in Sang-il's yard, and the two families are gathered there. When the bombing lets up and it is clear that the target is the nearby city and not their village, her father and Sang-il go outside. Sang-il climbs an oak tree and begins shouting, "Look! Look! Everyone come out! Look!," watching the city ablaze. His wife scolds him, telling him it is dangerous. When he finally starts to descend, he makes a wrong step, and a branch gives way beneath him. He falls to the ground. Everyone laughs except Pang-ne, who, "glancing up at the alarming red glow of the sky, instead could only tremble" (279–80).

The names of the two male characters likewise indicate what their fates will be. Pang-ne's father is called Myŏng-sun, an ideogram for light followed by one for obedience, whereas Sang-il's name is composed of those for prosperity and the number one. The women—Pang-ne, her mother Ok-sun, and Sang-il's wife Ch'ing-gang—have names denoting fragrant civility, jewelled obedience, and the quietude of a river, respectively.

The recollection that follows further reinforces our immediate impressions. Pang-ne, being cared for at the house of Sang-il and Ch'ing-gang after the death of her mother, witnesses a terrible fight culminating with screaming and a bowl of rice grazing Ch'ing-gang's head before it smashes against the wall. The six-year-old Pang-ne runs out in search of her father, who works far away at the base of the "white-capped mountain," the exact location of which she does not know. As she travels, we are led even farther into the past, to her hospitalization from whooping cough, during which her mother "as if she were trying to suck Pang-ne's illness right out of her, brought her face close and opened her mouth too, and rubbed her back firmly" (284). Only a year later, we then discover, her mother died of tuberculosis (284). Meanwhile, Pang-ne continues to walk toward the mountain, and the scene ends after she "returns to her self as if awaking from a dream" (285), begins crying, is found by a couple (286), and loses consciousness (287). At this close to the first segment, a daughter, a mother, and a wife appear as victims to the vagaries of fate and the violence of men.

In the second section, Pang-ne feels the weight in her stomach and then recollects that her father died just five years after that. Her father and Sang-il had opened a Korean barbecue restaurant together. As a consequence, they kept pigs, which they then killed, robing themselves in clothes "suggestive of army uniforms" (287). Myŏng-sun's name implies that he is different from Sang-il, but both "got a bloodthirsty look in their eyes, and an angry look on their faces as if they were going to kill a person and not a pig" (287). Sometimes they slaughtered other animals as well. On one occasion Pang-ne peers in as they kill a mountain sheep she had played with: "Pang-ne gasped for air, thinking, 'that cute sheep. . . . ' She felt pain as if her own body were being cut, and her shoulders shuddered out of her control. She ran out of the shed to escape" (288).

The episode is prescient, for indeed Pang-ne will become a sacrificial lamb of sorts. But sacrificed to what? And by whom? Given that the sentence that abruptly follows reads, "The shop seemed to be prospering," it is apparent that her sacrifice will be for prosperity. Yet the army uniforms and the murderously enraged faces remind us that these events are taking place not long after a colonialist war that brought these men to Japanese land in the first place. Might not her suffering come as a consequence of that violent militarism? Violence, we can infer, forms a necessary component of prosperity. As to who is responsible for the perpetration of violence, the answer seems to be Sang-il, who appears even more frightening (287), and whose later crime is foretold here. Yet we do see that even a pure man is capable of terrible things, indicating that it is not so much the men themselves at fault, but avarice, that is making prosperity (*sang*) one's number one (*il*) priority.

Sang-il ends up being responsible for Pang-ne's father's death. While speeding along on the motorcycle he has just bought, they come to a narrow bridge. The noise frightens a cow that is just then crossing, and it stops short. Myŏng-sun is thrown into the air, falls to the ground, and dies instantly (290–91). Pang-ne observes that his death is "cartoonish" (292). It is ironic, of course, that a cow — an animal as peaceful as the sheep — should cause this death. Kin portrays Myŏng-sun as proudly Korean and nonmaterialistic, in contrast to Sang-il, and perhaps we can only assume that Kin wants to create a character innocent in his death.

We come to the penultimate section, the longest. It tells how economic success alters Sang-il's life, which becomes "just like that motorcycle charging forward" (291). It closes with a harrowing scene in which he rapes Pang-ne. He expands his business beyond the restaurant to *pachinko* and mah-jongg parlors and trades in his car every few years for a new and flashier one. When Pang-ne starts high school, he comes to her opening ceremony as her father, and on the way home kindly tells her that he will put her through college, because that is what her father, who as an elementary school graduate was an "intellectual by Korean standards, would have wanted for her" (294). Then suddenly, he starts speeding, saying, "Look 100 kilometers an hour!" And so on. "He's forgotten. He has already forgotten the terror of the accident. Pang-ne was overcome with the urge to vomit, and could not help covering her face. Sang-il just went faster and faster" (295). "His character changed," Pang-ne then quips, "in proportion with the growth of his businesses. Sang-il suddenly started to dislike Koreans" (296). Finally, he decides to apply for Japanese citizenship, saying he has no prospects of returning to Korea. The center of his concerns, however, is actually business, because his lack of citizenship prevents him from getting loans and renting buildings (296).

This decision annoys his wife: "'Anyway,' she said sharply, as if there were no room for consideration, 'it isn't as if naturalizing changes anything. Once a Korean, always a Korean, you know'" (297). She has not changed with him. She continues to serve Korean foods, and she always performs the Korean rituals honoring their ancestors. She convinces someone they know from the "organization" (clearly Sōren) to dissuade him, to explain that it is not even certain he will succeed (298). He gives up, but not before the fellow Koreans in the town find time to beat him (299–301).

This experience changes him even more, and his violence against his wife grows to a new intensity. It used to be that he would come out of his anger in a day, but no longer. Soon, "Pang-ne began to notice a certain look from Sang-il" (303). She runs into him several times as she is emerging from the bath, so she begins changing into her clothes before leaving the room. One night, she stands in front of a mirror, gazes at her body, touches her own breasts, and realizes she has grown into a woman: "thinking of that look of Sang-il's, she felt at a loss over what to do with her own body" (304). She had begun working at one of his mah-jongg parlors part time since high school, and since graduation, full time. One Saturday night he shows up drunk, at 2:00 A.M., when the last customers have finally left. As she is cleaning up, suddenly he is standing over her with "an empty gaze" (306). She pushes and yells when he grabs her, but to no avail, for "he was looking at Pang-ne as if he could not remember that he was the one grasping her. It seemed as if his attention had been captured by something behind her. In his eyes she saw, for the first time, a plainly disturbing animal look" (307). Finally, he hits her across the face. "Everything went black. For a moment, the room returned to silence, but soon the sound of the rain came rushing in. Then, as if she were falling into a large dark hole, she was assaulted by a feeling of ruination" (307).

Song Mi-ja, in her analysis of the story, in the vein of much criticism of Kin Kakuei, focuses on the relationship of the author with the two fathers in the story. She thus argues that Sang-il serves as a variation of the fathers found in earlier works.[55] She then sees the fathers as representative of the second-generation child's access to Koreanness. She contends that the origins of Sang-il's decline (which of course results in the rape, although she does not mention it) lie in the "loss of the homeland"[56] and rails against the fact that the depiction of this character through the eyes of Pang-ne results in "ideological criticism of him." Moreover, she bewails the fact that as she sees it, Kin provides no practical alternative vision of how to be Korean in Japan, because, as we shall see in the final section, the path he has Pang-ne follow is heavily dependent on images of Korea such as "rows of poplar trees," which, in Song's words, "are not cultivatable within Japan."[57]

My interpretation diverges significantly. In simple terms of plot, we witness here the rape of a young girl by her adoptive father, a man who has "changed" as a result of his financial success. One facet of the change is that he has come to hate Koreans. At the base of that hatred of course lies internalized discrimination, which in turn can be traced to colonialism (the loss referred to by Song). All the main characters in the story, however, have lost their homeland, but only Sang-il's character metamorphoses. Not only does he want to become Japanese, but he betrays his companions, violently beats his wife, and rapes his adopted daughter. What distinguishes Sang-il from the other Resident Korean characters — his wife, Pang-ne, Pang-ne's parents, the other Korean shop owners — and thus transforms him, is avarice. We do not have to read this as a parable of what will happen to those who forget their Koreanness, although it is that. It is also the tale of a rape of a not-quite-adult woman by a man overcome with desire to possess things, and we can interpret it as a lamentation of the abuse of women and children within the Resident Korean community.

This point is reinforced by the use of the metaphor of vision within the rape scene. In earlier scenes in this story — and of course in *The Wall of the Gaze* — eyes, vision, and looks are linked with power and violence. When slaughtering animals, the two men have bloodthirsty eyes, as if ready to kill not a beast but a man; similarly, now, Sang-il's gaze is bestial and empty, as if he is as much victim as he is perpetrator. He does not *see* what he does or whom he does it to. It is as if Kin wishes to depict the unbridled violence resulting from long-term victimization by the "gaze" (in the sense of his earlier story). Song Mi-ja implies that Kin paints Sang-il unsympathetically; his later works, she says, are those of an ungrateful, spoiled boy who does not appreciate how hard his father worked to put him through college, and she instead harps only on the bad in him.[58] Yet who is more pathetic here? Sang-il, whose eyes are empty, or Pang-ne, who felt at a loss looking at her own reflection, for whom everything goes dark as she descends? It is hard to say; might not we conclude that this is a lamentation for Resident Korean women victims and their victimized victimizers as well?

In the fourth and final section, Pang-ne finally arrives at the clinic. We learn that a month and a half after the rape — and just the same amount of time before the present — she moved in with a friend in a city in the next prefecture. After the rape, she had felt like it was a "dream" and had to lie to Ch'ing-gang about her swollen face (308). Sang-il became cling-ing, sweet. She is sickened and informs the family that she is leaving. Sang-il's gaze grows even emptier (309–10). Back in the clinic, looking at the ceramic basin placed beneath the table where her legs will go, she recalls the urn in which her father took her mother's ashes to Korea; he had gone there in part to take the ashes, but also to see if there were prospects for them to return. Her father later told her about the rows of poplar trees; perhaps, she muses, Sang-il's misery is a result of forgetting that scene. Her own, however, perhaps came from not knowing how to get there (311–13).

The story ends with Pang-ne drifting into anesthetic unconsciousness, running down a hall in school, chasing children who have stolen from her a precious piece of gauze. She yells, "It's important! Give it back!" (314). Then suddenly, she is by a small river with her mother; two cars on the nearby road collide; her mother is hit and does not get up (314–15). She is on the road alone. The cars have disintegrated into fragments of metal, making noises like the welding shop she passed on her way to the clinic. She hears the voice of a snowy heron, as she did walking on the path to see her father long ago. Finally, she notices that this is the white stone road leading to the mountain and says, "Ah, this is it." On both sides of the road are poplar trees. "She sighs 'this is it' again and again, and walked toward the path as if swimming" (315).

An embryo formed of violence in turn produced by avarice and for-getfulness is aborted. It is sent, perhaps, in its own urn, the way of ashes, to Korea. Pang-ne's own empowering act sets her once again on the path to her father's place, a place with the shade of poplar trees, again to Korea. But what is killed here, really, and what is brought to life? Song Mi-ja finds poplar trees and herons too imagistic to serve as a symbol for Koreanness. What Pang-ne discovers here, however, is not merely a Korean scene, but a road. She does not come to the mountain, her father, Korea, but instead to the process of searching itself. It is significant she accomplishes this by means of repossessing her own body, by murdering the Sang-il, and therefore the gaze, within herself.

I have consistently argued that the avarice found in Sang-il is the par-ticular result of the impulse to develop and expand that is found within

Japanese capitalism both in its prewar and wartime colonialist form and in its postwar manifestation. It may be something of a stretch to contend that Kin Kakuei is criticizing Japanese capitalism here, and even more of a stretch to propose that his anticapitalist stance is socialist. One could argue, for example, that he is rather attacking something much less specific, that is to say, the human foible of greed. I believe, however, that when we read this story in the context of both his other works and the historically contemporary Hitachi trial (itself imbued with overtones of Christian humanism), we can justifiably categorize his stance as anticonsumerist humanism.

Critics see a turn in Kin's work at roughly the time of this story. As I have mentioned, not only did he travel to South Korea many times and begin attacking the North, but he began publishing a regular column in the South-affiliated newspaper. Not surprisingly it went by the name "Poplar." Still, Kin was no apologist for South Korea's political and economic system; although he may have lost some of his earlier socialist inclinations, he had not lost his hope for a decent life for all people. The ink of his pages bleeds for those whose quest for dignity and inner peace has been stifled by the cruelty of discrimination that is specifically based in colonial and postcolonial economic systems.

What Kin so marvelously conveys in his literature is not precisely his political views or even an abstract male-gendered struggle over Resident Korean identity. Unlike the early Ri Kaisei, his main objective is not to explain the tenets of, and perhaps foment, revolution. Rather, the beauty of his work lies in his nuanced portrayal of the thwarting of the desire for holy communication, of the sorrow that violence brings to both perpetrator and victim, of an intense emotion that is a blend of hope and despair. Perhaps it is this very complexity that has led those inclined to interpret his work by means of logical theories to speak in such ambiguous language.

Even so, one thing is certain: his works had a significant influence on the Resident Korean narratives to succeed them. In the following chapters, we shall see that the writings of women in the 1980s and 1990s build on and sometimes challenge such metaphors of the gaze in relation to both the power of the state and to the violence of men against women. When we read those later authors alongside contemporary grassroots struggles, many of which emerge directly out of the Pak movement, we perceive that their literature, like Kin's, is deeply concerned with the role of literature in a society dominated by the control of a discriminatory, technologically based state capitalism. The struggles, like Pak's, represent people's attempts to assert their legal rights within Japan and to define themselves through affiliations with groups other than the nation-state.

4
Ikaino the Homeland

Ikaino has almost iconic stature. Although not quite a Zainichi Harlem, this Korean neighborhood of Osaka has served as a center of both political and literary activity. Certain non-Osakan members of the Korean community even speak of an Ikaino nationalism — that is to say, some people believe that to be really Zainichi, you must be from Ikaino and speak a fluent Osaka dialect.

My visits to Ikaino in 1996 and 1997 were prompted, however, not by a fascination with the mainstream of Resident Korean culture, if such a thing could be said to exist, but rather with its margin: in particular, the works of Chong Ch'u-wŏl and Kim Ch'ang-saeng, two relatively obscure writers. They have not won prominent prizes, nor have they appeared in mainstream literary journals or pocket-size paperbacks. Instead, they publish out of small presses or in literary publications in or near Osaka, where they are based, in left-leaning journals and in magazines devoted to Korean issues. Their names (never mind analyses of their works) appear only rarely in criticism on Resident Korean literature. They have never supported themselves by writing, and neither is college educated. Chong fled to Osaka at age sixteen and worked at small factories and at odd jobs until she opened a bar she ran for many years. After graduating from high school,

Kim worked as a waitress. Now she owns a used bookstore, in which, she reports, she is forced to carry mostly what sells: comic books and pornography. As with most women of their era (both are second-generation Koreans; Chong was born in 1944, Kim in 1951), they are mothers, and they have been responsible for nearly all aspects of child-rearing.

It is not my point here to claim that the oppression of women both in Zainichi life and in the Japanese literary world has meant that these writers have been treated unjustly. Rather, I wish to draw attention to the fact that they write under conditions and for reasons vastly different from the men of their generation, such as Ri Kaisei and Kin Kakuei, who graduated from elite universities. The content of their writing reflects these dissimilar conditions. They also differ from Yi Yang-ji and Yū Miri, younger women writers who came after them (and who are from the Tokyo area), who have both won the Akutagawa prize, in 1989 and 1996, respectively, because these latter women's works have become big sellers, literary commodities marketed at least in part as testament to Japan's multiculturalism.

The literature of Chong Ch'u-wŏl and Kim Ch'ang-saeng is self-consciously nonelitist and locally situated. It almost invariably focuses on Ikaino, which they use to various ends in their works: as background, as metaphor, as character. They stress material aspects of existence in this Korean neighborhood, focusing in particular on the experiences of women. In their work, the concrete, the bodily, the local, the margins, Koreanness, and women's lives are woven into an intricate web.

Much of their work appeared in the 1980s, and I read it as entrenched in the discourse of the *chiiki undō* (local or community movement), of which the antifingerprinting movement I read about in 1986 was a crucial part. This is the best-known Resident Korean movement, and one of the more successful: the fingerprinting requirement was repealed for permanent residents (including Koreans) in 1992. The protests against this law attracted international attention, and even the support of well-known figures like Jesse Jackson. Yet if in one sense it was a mass movement, the actual resistance took place at local government offices, where foreigners registered. In addition, many of the movement's leaders were engaged in community-building efforts and justified their actions within this context — as part of a struggle to wrest power from the controlling state and put it into the hands of local communities.

In the 1980s, Japan's status as an economic superpower became an incontrovertible fact. The decade simultaneously saw major shifts in the structure of global capitalism, which, many have argued, gave rise to what we know as postmodern cultural forms.[1] As elsewhere, the question of whether the world had indeed entered a postmodern era and whether a modernist public sphere was viable in such a time drew the attention of scholars in Japan.[2]

Some of the most salient features of the new stage of capitalism, sometimes called "disorganized" capitalism, are flexible, just-in-time production; globalization (including a division of labor across rather than within nations); and decentralization. The postmodern cultural forms seen as concomitant with these economic changes are characterized by fragmentation and an emphasis on difference, and a schizophrenia of sorts, in which, in the words of Fredric Jameson, "the interlocking syntagmatic series of signifiers which constitutes an utterance or a meaning" breaks down.[3]

Many have observed that such economic and cultural shifts — as well as "space-time compression," the feeling of time being faster and distances closer that we experience as a result of new technologies that have helped to bring about these shifts — have left many people groping for their bearings in the world. Thus, the argument goes, there is a renewed interest in place. We find increased correlation of spatial positioning and identity, particularly among feminists, postcolonial peoples, and minorities, who play with notions of the home, the margin, and the local.[4] Some critics, such as Harvey, have characterized the emphasis on region, place, and otherness in politics as reactionary in their nostalgia and desire for stability; others, notably Doreen Massey in a criticism of Harvey, have proposed that it is possible to perceive of place in a more dynamic manner, with an identity that "is always formed by the juxtaposition and co-presence . . . of particular sets of interrelations . . . [and] a proportion of the social interrelations will be wider than and go beyond the area being referred to in any particular context as a place."[5]

The renewed interest in local community among Koreans in Japan concatenates with this global trend, and when I began this research, I thought that my main conclusion would center on precisely such issues. However, the longer I have pondered the literature of Chong Ch'u-wŏl and Kim Ch'ang-saeng and texts from the antifingerprinting movement, the more

I have begun to feel that to make only such an (albeit satisfying) argument would be to make a great mistake. The dialectic between the fictional realm and the arena of grassroots politics is complex and sometimes messy; Resident Koreans used these discourses to form identities that are in turn complex and messy. My objectives in this chapter are to delineate and decipher that jumble and, in so doing, to explore the ways in which the literary and political acts of individual Zainichi Koreans have trans-figured the Japanese social landscape.

In 1973, the name "Ikaino" disappeared from the map of Osaka, split up and renamed as parts of Ikuno Ward (*ku*). The oldest and largest Korean neighborhood in Japan, however, was not so easily excised from the consciousness of its residents. The popular first-generation poet Kim Shi-jŏng memorialized it in his *Ikaino shishū* [Ikaino Poems]:

> Everyone knows it yet
> It's not on the map
> It's not on the map so
> It's not Japan
> It's not Japan so
> It might as well vanish
> It doesn't matter so
> We do as we please.[6]

Legend has it that Koreans began to settle in Ikaino with the beginning of the construction of the Hirano Canal in 1923.[7] More likely, however, Koreans came to live in what became known as Ikaino because of the pre-ponderance of small and midsize factories there.[8] A ferry began running between Chejudo, an island off the southern tip of Korea, and Osaka in 1922; Chejudo had been hit particularly hard by Japanese colonial rule, and by 1934, nearly a fourth of its population had headed to Japan in search of work.[9] Contemporary accounts describe living conditions as wretched—crowded and smelly; some people are described as living in "shacks made of [salvaged] logs, scraps of wood, and fragments of brick."[10]

Resident Koreans did not benefit from Japan's postwar economic growth to the same extent as the majority of Japanese residents. In the

1950s, boom years for the Japanese economy, Koreans faced unemployment rates of up to 80 percent.[11] In the 1960s and the 1970s, they continued to lag behind Japanese economically. Even in the 1980s, legal discrimination persisted and poverty had not vanished: in 1986, 42.6 percent of Korean families in Ikuno-ku received public assistance.[12] Still, Ikaino was not the slum that it once had been.

Relative economic equity with Japanese, as well as the passage of time, meant that as in the rest of Japan, Koreans in Ikaino were becoming assimilated. The vast majority was Japan-born and spoke little or no Korean, attended Japanese public schools, and, even with kimchi sold nearby, ate predominantly Japanese food. At precisely this moment when the culture that bound Koreans in Ikaino together was threatening to disappear, these women held up the "ghetto" as their primary referent for Korean identity. But what was that community? Why was their Ikaino inhabited particularly by women who not only retained markers of Korean culture such as eating Korean foods and using Korean names, but spoke an accented and Creoled Japanese, and even practiced shamanistic religious practices from Chejudo? Does this merely represent an attempt to find a form of affiliation that is not national but is firmly ethnic?

It will be helpful to locate the discussion of Ikaino and local communities within a debate over Resident Korean identity that surfaced at roughly the same time. For the first time, some began to argue that there was a "third way," a way of life involving neither assimilation nor returning to the Korea. Three camps of Koreans were identified: those with *doka shikō* (inclination toward assimilation), *sokoku shikō* (inclination toward the homeland, even if they did not plan to return there), and *Zainichi shikō* (much like the "third way"; the literal meaning of *Zainichi* is "residing in Japan").[13]

To the participants in this conversation, assimilation was simply not an option, and it was thus the other two camps that received their attention. These men (they are all men) argued in lofty language about which of these stances was better, as if one way or the other reflected a more honest way of being Korean. The divide between them is particularly prominent in a 1985 debate opposing "Zainichi as method" to "Zainichi as fact." Kang Sang-jung, the proponent of the former, places emphasis on the fact that unlike other minorities in Japan, Resident Koreans have a homeland. In fact, he sees the position of "straddling the national border" between Japan and Korea as the most significant aspect of their existence. He refers to this as their duality. This duality, he argues, compels them to orient themselves toward the homeland (whose history their own fate depends on). In addition, because it places them outside the system of modern nation-states, it enables them to see the pitfalls of "Japanese-style modernization" (and potentially a Korean modernization modeling itself after Japan's) and puts them in a unique position to critique such modernity and its concomitant national ideologies. In order for Resident Koreans to be capable of such critique, however, they need to maintain a certain distance from Japan's "value system" and thus to assert their place as "marginal," rather than fighting for the right to be integrated into the national community.[14]

Yang Tae-ho, in contrast, believes that Kang, in his effort to stress this concept of duality, "attempts to make a method out of [Resident Koreans'] foreignness." Yang sees this attitude as dangerous because it reinforces the equation of ethnicity with nationality. Yang stresses that it is not entirely accurate to call Resident Koreans foreigners, thus implicitly questioning the determination of Japaneseness or foreignness based on "blood." He fundamentally disagrees with Kang's sense that Resident Koreans are "straddling the national border," that their lives are as tied to the fate of the Korean peninsula as Kang claims. He calls for recognition of "Zainichi as fact." For better or worse, he contends, most Resident Koreans have made and will continue to make Japan their home, and this needs to be acknowledged, even if it seems as though it will lead to the eventual dissolution of the community as they assimilate. The emphasis therefore needs to be placed on finding common ground with — and, the suggestion is, fighting for the same rights as — other members of Japanese society. Even if this struggle stresses Koreans' right to the same treatment as Japanese residents based on a common humanity, the process need not necessarily entail sacrificing a sense of their identity as ethnically Korean.[15]

Yang Tae-ho was a member of Mintōren (Minzoku sabetsu to tatakau renmei, The League to Fight Ethnic/National Discrimination), an umbrella organization of Resident Korean civil rights groups. Although

Mintōren did not initiate the antifingerprinting struggle, it did play a central role disseminating information and bringing together "refusers" (as they were called) from various regions of the country. Yang Tae-ho in fact participated in the antifingerprinting movement. Even though Mindan and Sōren, the organizations affiliated, respectively, with the South and North Korean governments, spoke out in support of refusers, the philosophy of the movement as a whole locates it staunchly within the "Zainichi as fact" camp.

Other scholars have argued that the effect of Japan's postwar economic development and of the high-growth economy on Resident Koreans is as responsible for the shift to *Zainichi shikō*. Although Koreans did not reap benefits equal to Japanese, many grew richer, and all were influenced by social changes spawned by the country's newfound affluence, such as so-called my-home-ism, intense competition in education, and the declining birthrate.[16] Japanese activists had begun to focus their sights on local society rather earlier (so-called residents' movements emerged in the late 1960s); by the mid-1970s, a small number of Resident Koreans began to do so as well. Only in the middle to late 1980s, however, when Japan had become a major player in the global economy and laborers flowed to Japan from the Middle East, South America, and Asia (including South Korea), do we find the peak of the local movement among Koreans. This influx of foreigners who had quite a different relationship to Japan from Resident Koreans — who were not at all assimilated and made for a much more visibly diverse community — no doubt contributed to Resident Koreans' increasing tendency to recognize the degree to which they had a stake in Japanese social and political life, and which gave them the courage to participate in the antifingerprinting struggle and to assert that Ikaino was their homeland. We can thus see the increased inclination toward *Zainichi shikō* (and sometimes toward assimilation) as tied to Japan's particular experience of the transformation of global capitalism.

As I stressed at the outset, however, I do not see Resident Koreans' "turn to the local" as simply a reflection of or reaction to generational change or particular experiences of disorganized capitalism and/or postmodernism, but rather as entrenched in many different discourses at the same time. Let me now begin to unravel the internal dynamics within and dialectical relationships between texts focusing on the local. Because it was literature that lured me in the first place, I begin my analysis by looking at works by Chong Ch'u-wŏl, and I end with those of Kim Ch'ang-saeng. Between these, I will sandwich my discussion of the antifinger-printing movement, focusing on the case of a prominent (male) refuser and community activist from Ikaino.

Resident Koreans today are more likely to flee Ikaino than to gravitate toward it, but in 1960, at age sixteen, unable to find employment after graduating from middle school, Chong Ch'u-wŏl ran away to Ikaino. The Koreans who gathered at her family home in Kyushu, in southern Japan, had often talked about the neighborhood, and both of her parents had lived there when young. Her first job was for a Korean-run clothing man-ufacturer; the employees lived on the first floor and worked on the sec-ond. She was provided meals and tickets to the public bath, but she made so little money that it took her two years to earn enough to visit her par-ents. Later she worked pasting heels on shoes (and wrote a memorable poem about her experience of growing light-headed from the glue); for many years, she ran a bar. Today she is in semiretirement, writes when she can, and spends much of her time helping to raise several young grand-children.

Both in print and in person, Chong tells this and other details of her personal history with candor. She began writing poetry while working in Ikaino's small factories, and as Norma Field has recounted, she would often write in the bathroom — the only place where she could find peace. The tale of Chong's move from the country to the city and of her creating art amidst hardship has immense power, yet what is most distinctive about her work is rather her persistence in showing how her own life is entwined with those of the various people with whom she has come into contact, and how their lives are together entrenched in broader histories. If modern Japanese fiction has tended to border on autobiography, her work comes closer to ethnography.[17]

The particular community at the center of her work is that of Ikaino, and especially women in Ikaino. From the 1970s onward, she depicts the repetitions of daily life, maintained within the home and by women. Women are thus granted respect for their role in the reproduction of Koreanness. Food is of particular importance in this regard:

When morning comes
To the waves of tiles
The woman takes out kimchi from the jar
And cuts it, chop chop
As from long long ago
Women have always done, day after day
The green smell
Of a clump of soil in the field
Of garlic
The white leaves, dyed with red hot pepper
Crimson kimchi
Even for her mouth-rinsing son
Her gum-chewing daughter
The kimchi on the table
Even then
Incites an appetite
Dyeing them crimson
To their stomachs
The sting! Dyeing also
The woman's fingers, crimson
When morning comes chop chop
From the point of the knife
She cuts in the home town
"C'mon guys,
Time to get up!"[18]

Here the less literal reproduction of the *furusato* (translated here as "home town," but which could also mean "homeland"), "day after day, from long long ago," is linked to food. And food, which produces the odors associated with Koreans in stereotypes of them by Japanese, is turned into lush imagery of reproduction and desire—kimchi crimson like blood, the green smell of soil and garlic, kimchi stimulating appetite, which, as in English, can also signal desire.

Yet if the bloody images here are linked with the giving and maintaining of life through food, they are also violent: we hear and then see the chopping of the knife; we feel the woman's fingers sting. The reproduction of culture, at least on this embodied level, then, is a fraught matter; as that of human beings, it is inherently painful. These aspects of the poem seem implanted in a cyclical, productive space and time, like the folkloric chronotope described by Bakhtin,[19] yet the presence of gum-chewing and mouth-rinsing children situate the action of the poem firmly in the present. The final line (literally, "wake up!") can be read as a clarion call to the reader — and perhaps the narrator herself — to snap out of a reverie.

In an essay contemporary with this poem (1973), she credits first-generation women with giving life to Ikaino by creating the market at its heart, setting up shops and tables selling Korean goods to ensure that they could "pass on to their children all the Korea that they possessed — the flavors, the customs, the conventions." If they had "fended off persecution with [their strong] bodies," however, it was a "strength that almost appears to be stupidity" which enabled them to do so.[20]

In this and other essays and stories also originally published in the early 1970s, the traditions of Chejudo shamanism provide a source of seemingly superhuman strength for these women. In one story, she says, "women who give of themselves as mothers, wives, daughters, women of Haengja's generation, when they have been sapped of inner strength, recharged their power by tying themselves to the gods and to the spirits."[21] She even calls shamanism the only orgasmic ecstasy that these women will experience (124). In addition, she repeatedly utters the phrase *san'i ittai* ("three statuses, one body," referring to the dead, the living, and the Korean woman rolled into one), mentions the transmigration of souls, and juxtaposes her own pregnancies with the death of others, intimating just such a transmigration. In so doing, she evokes a premodern, or perhaps antimodern, time, linking birth with death, biological reproduction with cultural reproduction.

If exploring shamanism allows her to find value in what has been debased as feminine, she is simultaneously blunt in her criticism of the Ikaino women's dependence on shamans. For example, she tells of her mother-in-law, who is dying from Parkinson's disease and yet demands that she call a shaman (again) despite the high price and the fact that the shaman herself admits that some people simply will not get better.[22] She likens the habit of first-generation women in Ikaino to hire shamans to the gambling engaged in by men, a sign of their desperate hopes for a better life (202). They did not have the ability to control the course of their own lives, and their illiteracy left them no choice but to grasp for the help of gods (211).

In Chong's work, women's efforts to propagate Koreanness — and the strength that empowers them in this task — cannot be understood apart not only from such religious notions but from their role in the material reproduction of human bodies. As we saw in the kimchi poem, she stresses both cultural and material functions of food. The interlacing of the cultural and the biological in her literature, however, is most palpable in her portrayal of motherhood.

I suggested earlier that much of her writing verges on anthropology. In one piece that very much fits this description, "Waga aisuru Chōsen no onnatachi" [The Korean Women I So Love], first published in 1974, the act of giving and sustaining life is at the core of the connections she makes between her own experiences and those of other women in her community, and thus in her interest in relating their stories:

> In Ikuno-ku, Osaka, where I live, there are sixty thousand Resident Koreans.
> Let us suppose that ten thousand of those people are women who are related by their very flesh to the transmigration of souls. My days, those of these ten thousand women, are exhausted by the unrewarded love that is motherhood, by the manners of mothering. But we have no regrets.
> . . . Men are born from women's bellies; for this reason alone, women embrace men with their mothering, and therein protect the normalcy of the everyday.
> In Japan, these women's preservation of normalcy in the everyday becomes, in a word, beauty.[23]

The tone of this passage, in the opening few pages, is literary. Here and in the conclusion we find a plenitude of emotion and the aesthetic. Assumptions such as whether all women really embrace their role as mothers are left unexamined. The series of flesh, transmigration, mothering, and preservation of the everyday somehow result in "her days" being not similar to, but the same as, those of ten thousand other Korean women who are mothers.

The body of the text, however, tells the stories of seven women in a voice that is more matter-of-fact, even ethnographic. We learn of Yong-hwa, whose husband drinks himself into a stupor every night and becomes violent. She understands that his days of high-pressured but repetitive labor with dangerous machines, which turn him into a human vegetable, cause him to act this way. Her comprehension does not lead her to be passive, however: "When her husband, consumed by alcohol, begins to hit and scream, Yong-hwa isn't silent. She believes that hitting back and screaming back are an expression of fondness."[24]

In most of these tales, economic strain is a major cause of hardship. We hear of a woman buried by a cruel system of moneylending prevalent among women in the Korean community, with interest of nearly 100 percent, a pregnant young woman doing piecework in a cramped apartment so that her husband can participate in grassroots activism, a woman whose husband was born in Japan but lived in Chejudo for some time and is thus technically an illegal alien and can only work under the table. She sometimes refers directly to the way that Japanese capitalism affects these people: the woman with the activist husband, Chong notes, thinks that "it is difficult for the grass to exercise the subjectivity of grass in Japan, which overflows with commodities."[25]

In her closing passage, Chong asserts that one thing has the power to turn these women's lives, which are indeed tragedies, into "divine comedies." That one thing is their speech (*kotoba*).[26] She praises the humor, the roughness, the crudeness, the bluntness of their words, their intonation and timing. So too the unique blend of Korean and Japanese, the masterful analogies, the jests. She cites one woman: "Try making my life into a novel. You'll win the Nobel Prize for sure!" This language, she opines, enables them to turn sadness into laughter and to "weave together the everyday."[27]

Ultimately, she declares that these women's speech is the true art of the people. What a contrast, she remarks, with the dignified words of a Japanese writer on learning that his hunger strike urging commutation of the death sentence imposed on South Korean poet of the people, Kim Chi-ha, had achieved its goal. Of course it's better that they protest, she goes on, but have they ever thought about why it is impossible for women like me to act as they do? Have they ever thought about the relationship between Japan and Korea and why people like me are here?[28] She closes with, "I imagine that of the approximately ten thousand Korean women in Ikuno-ku, fewer than half know Kim Chi-ha's name. For this I love these Korean women, heroines of divine comedies yet to be written."[29]

Chong does sometime slip into a romanticization of these women's suffering. They are beautiful, yes, but trapped, as we see in her references to domestic violence. On one occasion, she describes women as putting up with their husband's beatings because their maternal nature allows them to be giving enough to let men be the humans — that is to say, to express their pain of "the life of *Zainichi*, with no exits, no escape."[30] Elsewhere she describes her own husband's violence as the most direct form of communication.[31] I doubt that humor and generosity can obviate the physical and psychic pain of abuse.

It may have been radical to assert that it was the power and mothering of Korean women that assured the continuation of Korean culture, but at what cost? Such a perspective, in which women's positive qualities are linked so closely with their biology, like certain types of feminism in the United States, is "in danger of solidifying an important bulwark for sexist oppression: the belief in an innate 'womanhood' to which we must all adhere lest we be deemed either inferior or not 'true' women."[32] In this case, it does not even seem feminist: maternal nurturing will condemn them to a lifetime of suffering.

Chong published three books between 1984 and 1987, with the last two coming from Tokyo presses. This might be unremarkable for some writers, but she had published only one book before this, in 1971, and has issued nothing since, although when I met with her in 1997, she was writing. These books for the most part contained material that had been printed previously, but it bears noting that her work was considered worthy of attention at this precise moment.

The burgeoning of the antifingerprinting movement clearly not only contributed to the success of her work but served as an impetus for it. Each of her books from these years touches on the matter. *Saran he/ aishite imasu* [*Sarang hae*/I Love You, 1987], gathers essays she wrote for two journals put out by the labor unions of local government employees actively participating in the movement; *Ikaino taryon* [Ikaino Lament, 1986] includes the transcription of a talk she gave at a national conference of one of these unions. Even the earliest collection, *Ikaino•Onna•Ai •Uta* [Ikaino/Woman/Love/Poetry, 1984] contains a poem addressing the fingerprinting system and Resident Koreans' use of Japanese names.³³ In 1985, Chong herself refused to be fingerprinted. Within less than a year, however, she gave her prints "of her own will." The police threatened her with losing the bar she ran, and so, in order to "protect her family," she conceded.³⁴ She nonetheless continued to write and speak out against the system.

Rather than delving into texts directly considering only the fingerprinting system, however, I wish to examine a piece which explores issues that form the intellectual underpinnings to Resident Koreans' objection to this requirement of the Alien Registration Law, or ARL. In a 1985 story (essay?) entitled "Mun Konbun omoni no ningo" [Mun Konbun Ŏmŏni's Apple], we find further development of themes from her earlier work: references to the fleshly connection of mothers to the transmigration of souls, the setting of Ikaino, old women's masterful speech.³⁵ Yet what sets it apart is the degree to which she draws these together to contemplate the relationship of the individual, and particularly female, body in space and language with the politics and history of the nation-state. This theme lies at the base of the antifingerprinting movement because the system, designed by the Japanese nation-state during the colonial period, kept Koreans in check not only by holding written records of their presence, but by marking their existence in a more material manner by retaining an imprint from their physical bodies.

The story beings with a discussion of Korean apples. There are two sorts, the narrator tells us: *sagwa*, the commercially cultivated type, and *nŭnggŭm*, the wild and smaller variety. And then, she says, there is something in the "fluent Japanese" of first-generation Korean immigrants, something superior to even the *nŭnggŭm*: the *ningo* (15). *Ningo* is technically a mispronunciation of *ringo*, the Japanese word for "apple." However, in Chong's story, there is no mispronunciation, only "living language" (16). Living language, or *seikatsugo*, more literally the language of daily life, is not mistaken, but "delicious" (14), for it bears the traces of history: "The taste of the *ningo*, only guessed at when biting into the western breed of apple known as a *sagwa*, is the taste of passion of the aged immigrants, already waiting only to vanish, a clear taste, clear after being filtered through their flesh" (14–15). The text then jumps immediately to a poem entitled "Ningo," which begins "I bite the flesh of an apple/The dripping blood/So clear" and ends with the lines "Apples/One basket a hundred yen/Get your apples here!" At the start, the shift in tone to poetry is minimal, because the prose itself is poetic, breaking sentences in the middle as if lines of poetry or adding commas to break sentences into the rhythm of a verse, but by the end of the poem itself the language is not "poetic" per se, but that of Osaka dialect, words no longer about, but rather in, living language.

Chong is not the first or only writer to include the living language of first-generation Koreans in her work, nor is she the first to play with form. Other Resident Korean writers have done likewise in a desire to twist Japanese language and literary tradition into shapes of their very own. For example, we remember that Ri Kaisei, in his Akutagawa prize–winning story *Kinuta o utsu onna* [The Woman Who Fulled Clothes], infuses the common *shishosetsu* (I-novel, or personal narrative, a form associated with Japan's modernity, and in which perspective is for the most part limited to a single point of view) with elements of the Korean *shinse t'aryŏng*, a form of lamentation of life linked with both the Korean storytelling tradition and with shamanism.[36] Their motivation was founded in the conception that language (and by association, literature) structures and limits the way we think. The Japanese language was the language of the colonizer, and its words for Koreans and their culture were all imbued with negative nuances. To incorporate *living* language (that is, oral, not written) was to make visible the control that had been wrought by written Japanese, by the treaties granting them control over Korean land and treatises affirming that Koreans were backward and dirty.

The living language inhabiting the pages of second-generation writers' works is characteristically the language of the first generation, and often of the writers' parents and parents' friends. In Chong's case, that language is almost always that of women, and this story is no exception. Of particular importance is that by repeating certain phrases throughout the narrative, she develops a sense of the "home" as the site of the living language. For example, after a query about the meaning of language for Korean women, she says: "After having parted [once] with language, my encounter with true language began. In the home, there was the language of everyday life" (16). In describing what she means by this language of everyday life, she speaks of the language her parents used at home and the similar language her children now use (16) and cites the speech of the women in the neighboring homes (17).

It is not coincidental that the people in whom she finds vital language are women and the site where she locates it is the gendered space of the home. We have seen that a perception of women as more bound to their biological existence than men is consistent throughout Chong's work. The home (*ie*), although manipulated so often by the abstraction of the Japanese state that it is permeated by it, is nonetheless also the place of material reproduction of bodies—of eating, of birth, of nurturing. Like language itself, it serves as the location for twisting that very abstraction. In Chong's words,

> I couldn't see the meaning in writing poetry, that is the meaning of words. . . .
>
> At some point I had been programmed to become of the kind nature (/sex) that is the mother, unable even to stand on the side of the people and say "Death to those who use words!"
>
> The personal histories of *Zainichi* (residing in Korea), the painful history which is the very history of Japan, the stormy conditions, which women's history could not even begin to grasp, was perhaps a history of human resistance within that deepest place, the home, but even though they did not possess an understanding as Confucian the men they lived with and the sons they popped out, they cared for them warmly, and as they rubbed their bodies, and put their hands together in prayer, Korean women, who had hoped for their good health just for a single day, just for that day, while they killed themselves, for these Resident Korean women, what meaning could words, could language, have?
>
> I decided to live my poetry with my flesh.
>
> How painful to write poems on one's body. (15)

The resistance here is fleshly, however, in speech and not in writing. She has just mentioned that the comment "Death to those who use words!," however, is from a farming woman in Narita, where a struggle developed against the building of Tokyo International Airport, which had led the government to push farmers off the land. Many students, members of a

strong and violent "New Left," joined this movement — and this statement is undoubtedly a response to their hyperintellectualizing their
actions. She implies that this sort of abstract understanding is male and is
of no use for women, who are ensconced in the material world by virtue
of the fact that they give birth.

Yet she says that writing "on her body" was painful, and she sounds
regretful that she has been "programmed" to be so kind. We thus begin
to get the sense that she also feels that writing can be, or perhaps should
be, important. The rest of the story indeed explains how she came back
to writing, and it argues that even writing from the home can serve as
resistance. This shift in her thought is most apparent when she talks
about writing again after a decade of near silence. In 1984, 4,000 copies
of a collection of her poems, *Ikaino/Woman/Love/Poetry*, were released
by a small publisher. The incident she credits with spurring her to write
this book draws attention to the political nature of her writing. She could
not simply stand by and watch, she notes, "the epoch-making event of
Chun Doo-hwan's visit to Japan and the emperor's apology" (17) — that
is to say, the first visit of a Korean president to Japan since the war and
the apology of the emperor for the colonization of Korea.

In addition, several times, she refers this act as a "solitary rebellion";
Osaka she designates as the "periphery" of the "state" (*kokka*, a com-
pound composed of the characters for "country" and "house/home/
family"), and her "home" (or house or family) she calls the "deepest part
of the periphery" (17). *Solitary rebellion* was the term used again and
again to describe the act of the first fingerprint refuser in 1980, before the
broader movement emerged. Tellingly, the covers of the volume feature
vastly enlarged fingerprints, sky blue and lime green on an off-white
background. Which better confirms my unique existence, she teases, my
fingerprint or my poems? Even a home in the hinterlands, she declares,
can be a site for political action. Not such a revelation, perhaps, to those
of us living in the United States today, but certainly not a common thing
for a Resident Korean woman to assert. What is evident here is that writing achieves politicality through recognizing that personal histories, in
cyclical time, are what form the grander narrative of the history of
nations, or linear time.[37]

In the culmination to the first section, she has a revelation. When she reads her poetry aloud, she feels that the rhythm her parents gave her has permeated her Japanese (19). Earlier she had mentioned having felt shame at her parents' speech when she was a child; yet now knows that "the memory of that shame . . . was proof that I have lived, and to lose that memory would be to deny my very existence" (16). She says that she has found meaning in writing poetry: "The poems I write," she says, "are proof that (I/we) lived in Japan" (19). Two points are crucial here. First, she comes to see both the memory of feeling ashamed *and* the process of overcoming that shame as part of who she is (her history), and second, she determines that the meaning of writing poetry (history) lies in by the context in which it is heard/transmitted, notably from generation to generation. The latter point is even more evident in the second half of the story, to which I now turn.

In this section, entitled "My encounter with *ningo*," we (and Chong herself) are at last introduced to the *ŏmŏni*, or mother, of the title.[38] Last fall, she tells us, the morning after reading her poetry in a mixed-genre performance, she received a phone call from a friend who had come to hear her. Her mother, who learned to write by attending middle school at night, also writes poetry and would like to meet Chong, the friend tells her. Thirty minutes later, Chong's encounter with this woman begins.

I pointed out earlier that Chong sometimes incorporates elements of ethnography into her work, but as is manifest in the passage about apples, it might be more accurate to say (at least in this story) that she blends multiple genres. In this story, she strategically uses structure and style to enable her to explicate her vision of the relationship between space, gender, language, and history. She intersperses analytical prose, lyrical prose, stream of consciousness, poetry, storylike dialogue, and even a transcription of a tape of Mun reminiscing about her life.

The first part of the story is limited to Chong's voices: poet, explicator of her own work, anthropologist (she records multiple examples of typical Creoled speech). In the second half, she cedes the title of poet to Mun Konbun and becomes annotator; we also hear from Mun's daughters, and others they run across. We read a poem of Mun-*ŏmŏni*'s; we read Chong's interpretation and reaction; we hear of how they agree to meet weekly, of more poems and more interpretations, and of further meetings and further reactions. Finally, she asks Mun-*ŏmŏni* if she will speak about her life, and the transcription she provides, Chong notes, was performed by a bedridden friend. The piece ends with a final poem by Mun, and a final interpretation and emotional reflection by Chong. The effect is a web of conversations, and the shift performs the function of leading the readers to see that the act we have been undertaking is not passive, but an active and integral part of the making of meaning. The multiplicity of voices is resonant with the Bakhtinian notion of the novel as composed of diverse language.[39]

Let me provide a simple example, one I have chosen for obvious reasons:

The *ningo* that permeates her [Mun's] life and that of my own mother is proof of their humanity.

> *On Fingerprinting*
>
> They said, you're Japanese
> They said, stop being Korean
> I came by boat
> When raising my children
> I wore a *kimono*.
> To rent a house
> I wore a *kimono*.
> I put my *chogori*
> away in the dresser.
> I will give my fingerprints
> for alien registration
> I'll make my children give theirs
> But
> I don't want to make my grandchildren give theirs
>
> — Mun Konbun

Every Friday when we part, I give Mun-*ŏmŏni* homework.
She did this poem for homework, too.
"Mother keeps going around to all of her daughters' houses, saying, teach me history, teach me history. I think she's even having indigestion. Do you suppose she really should study history properly after all?"
It was just about then that I got the call from my friend.
"No, I think *ŏmŏni* is just fine the way she is. All she needs to do is to put her life into poems without worrying too much," I answered. (26)

In just a half a page, we see the voice shifting from Chong's analytical voice, to Mun's poem, to a descriptive tone from Chong, to Mun's daughter and Chong in conversation on the telephone. Much is lost in translation here — we do not feel the difference in texture of written and oral, or formal and informal, language, nor do we see that the poem is littered with mistakes, including one that turns "alien" into "monster." Nonetheless, we get a feel for the rapidity with which such fluctuations in tone occur. This pace is not unique to this passage.

Takeuchi Yasuhiro, who published an analysis of the story a few months later in the literary journal in which it originally appeared, indeed calls on notions from Bakhtin to make grand conclusions. The "polyphonic" character of the narration, he argues, enables this story to "overcome differences between Japanese and Koreans" without "dissolving the problems," by which he presumably means unresolved historical and political issues.[40] How could this be? I am not confident that merely granting oneself the ability to imagine the abstract other could bring about such an effect. Even the more specific point that the Japanese language is constituted by Koreans in Japan as well as Japanese probably does not have such expansive ramifications. However, as Takeuchi suggests, this work does stand apart from the majority of fiction in Japanese, in that it proposes a new form of "linguistic action," one that affirms the possibility of communication with others even in a consumer society where most "so-called literature has transformed into mere entertainment."[41]

Saussure's discussion of linguistics, he tells us, precludes any consideration of *parole* (individual utterance or speech act) and *langage* (language-speech, or perhaps living language), focusing rather on the system of language, or *langue*. Bakhtin, on the other hand, urged that *parole* should be at the center of any philosophy of language and that "the principle organizing all utterances, all expressions is not internal but external, that is in the social milieu which surrounds the individual."[42] We have seen that Chong Ch'u-wŏl's work places its emphasis on the importance of the utterance of individuals (in the form of living language), and that it is intensely novelistic in the sense that Bakhtin used the word. It is inhabited by many different voices, thereby monopolizing on the fact that language is on "the borderline between oneself and the other,"[43] that it is "overpopulated with the intentions of others."[44] It accents the "dialogic" character of communication, to borrow another term from Bakhtin. To elaborate, it points to the fact that its meanings are necessarily imbedded in an ongoing social process, that it too is "living" and will attain new meanings each time it is read. Therefore, Takeuchi stresses, as did Bakhtin, and would I, that language and literature must be studied in its sociohistorical context.

I have drawn extensively from Takeuchi's observations about Bakhtin not only because I agree with some of what he says, but that he is part of the context necessary for understanding Chong Ch'u-wŏl's texts. He also helps to locate her place vis-à-vis Japanese literature and not just Resident Korean identity. As he tells us, in Japan at the time of the writing of his essay, 1985, the effects of structuralism (based on Saussure) had led literary critics away from actually thinking about what specific works do. Marxists were stuck in old theories of culture as superstructure, and others bandied about theories of poststructuralism and postmodernism as if they were brand-name clothing.[45]

Aside from the presence of a strong old-school Marxist camp, the sight is not unfamiliar. I raise his point that Chong's work poses an alternative to structuralist (and poststructuralist) notions of language because I want to raise it, too. I have consistently referred to the "I" in this piece as Chong (Takeuchi does not) because I want to reject a poststructuralist tendency to refer to the narrator of an ostensibly nonfiction text as being somehow unrelated to the living being of the same name. Rather than placing emphasis on the fact that the "I" in the text who authored *Chong Ch'u-wŏl's Collected Poems* cannot be identical to (or even an identical reflection of) that living, breathing human body who originally wrote the words constituting the book of the same title sold in the "real," material, world, I want to stress the fact that the multiple voices in the text (the "I"s) and the ranges of forms of expression that she uses in her daily life all emerge from a single, biological being who (sometimes) goes by the name Chong Ch'u-wŏl. People reading this and other pieces with this name on them have written to her, visited her at the bar she used to run, and (as in this text) called her up on the telephone. Her writings function intertextually within broader discourses about Koreans in Japan and about Japanese literature, and their circulation in turn changes the way that she lives (and the conversations she has) from day to day.

On the basis of such observations about her texts, it seems fair to say that her vision of Ikaino and of the home approaches the reimagining of place provided by Doreen Massey, one that acknowledges not only its dynamism but its connections with other places. Part of the objection of people like David Harvey to place-based politics, Massey contends, is that they confound them with place-bound politics, and they thus see them as never being able to counter the oppressive power of global capitalism.[46] We see in Chong, however, that her focus on the local and on women does not prevent her from understanding the way that global capitalism holds us down, or from believing that class-based politics are also important.

Yet at times she aestheticizes motherhood and Koreanness to a degree I find vexing. This is no less true in this story than in her earlier works. The final poem in "Mun Kon-bun Ŏmŏni's Apple," in fact, is one by Mun recalling the safety and connection she felt snuggling under her mother's skirts as she worked. The poem ends simply: "That mother's child has become a mother/Now I have become an old grandma" (30). Chong accepts, even builds upon, Mun-ŏmŏni's nostalgic portrayal of the mother-child relationship. She sees the skirt connecting Mun and her mother as Mun's "own maternal nature," and, by using terms similar to those in her Kwangju poem and elsewhere, she perceives the last lines to indicate Mun's perception of the smallness of each of us "in the cycle of transmigration and reincarnation" (30).

In addition, we remember, in this story she called the flavor of the uncultivated, oddly shaped apple, whose flavor is reflected in the speech of first-generation women, "clear." Here and elsewhere, Resident Korean women, and in particular, first-generation women, most of whom are illiterate or only semiliterate, occupy a distinctive position in her formulation of the margin. Why should Mun be held back from learning about history? I feel as though I am hearing familiar old binaries, women and nature and oral language pitted against men and culture and written language — not to mention proletariat versus the rest, colonized (Koreans) versus colonizers (Japanese), the former being pure, the latter corrupted.

Is motherhood the only vehicle through which we can understand other's pain, through which supranational affiliation can be forged? Or only minorities (or immigrants or formerly colonized peoples)? Can women only contribute to the lessening of others' oppression through reproduction? Is written language only valuable when it approximates the oral? For all these shortcomings, to affirm that the margins (women/the home and Ikaino) are important and to say that the simple acts of Resident Korean women's lives are beautiful turned the dominant ideology on its head. Even within the discourse on Resident Korean identity, the attempt to integrate women's experience, and to link it with the more properly historical, was distinctive.

We have seen that the *chiiki undō* (local community movement) and antifingerprinting struggle are an important context to Chong Ch'u-wŏl's literature. Like these movements, she finds inspiration in the idea that people can live more humanely if they respect people's differences and identify with and pour energy into local communities. Not all fingerprint refusers, however, shared Chong's concern with the particular plight of women, although more women participated than had in any such movement in the past. From its very beginnings women were prominent in the struggle. Approximately half of the first thirty refusers (September 1980–February 1983) were women.[47]

Several of the earliest women refusers were from Osaka and formed an organization called Shimon ōnatsu seido ni hantai suru naze naze shimon? onnatachi no kai [Why Fingerprints, Why? Women Against the Fingerprinting System]. One of the members, Pak Ae-ja, in the founding statement for the group, relates that she opposes fingerprinting for the same reason that she objects to Japanese family registration laws: both systems are examples of the excessive control of people by the state. Hence, she refuses to enter her name or her children's in her husband's family registry. He is Japanese — and Japanese law requires women to take their husband's name and become part of his family. In Korea, women's fate is equally bad: they are not even considered worthy of taking the man's name or being put into his family records. In both cases, children are entered only in the man's family's register and "belong" to him. "My children belong to *me*," she says, and she thus refuses to enter them in his registry.[48] She further inveighs against the ways that these systems have been used in the modern nation-states of Japan and Korea to discriminate against people by caste or place of origin.[49] She perceives the Japanese system of managing its populace — going online as she wrote — as worthy of the concern of not only Resident Koreans, but all members of the Japanese community.[50]

Although her feminist views were decidedly not mainstream, this essay found its way into a book sometimes called the bible of anti-ARL activism, the 1984 *Hitosashiyubi no jiyū* [Freedom for the Index Finger]. Another woman activist who contributed to this volume, Yang Yŏng-ja, uses gatherings of refusers as a forum to speak out (sing out, actually) about the oppression of women within Resident Korean life. Her earliest memories, she reveals, are of her father beating her mother. When she performed a song about this violence at gatherings of ARL protesters, however, several other Koreans castigated her, she recalls, arguing that men had done what they could, given the circumstances. They never blame the men, only Japanese imperialism, she bemoans.[51] Unlike Chong Ch'u-wŏl, she speaks bitterly of the image of "'strong, kind, powerful' maternalism . . . forced upon these women on the lowest rungs of society."[52] Resident Korean women should use the movement as "training" for expressing their pain, their sadness, their hopes. "Freedom is not one's own," she declares, "until one feels it for oneself."[53]

It is no doubt a distinctive feature of this movement that women like these were able to manipulate it to their own ends. In all likelihood, the local character of the struggle made it easier for them to do so. The struggle attained relative success (the fingerprinting requirement was repealed in 1992, but only for permanent residents) at least in part because of the ability of the umbrella group Mintōren, the founders of which were mostly Christian, to mobilize Christians worldwide. However, a more direct source of power for the movement emerged from the collaboration between Resident Koreans and Japanese living in the same regions. The act of alien registration, including fingerprinting, took place at the office of local government, at city town, or ward offices. The first Japanese to join in were employees of those local government offices, who first garnered the support of their union branches and eventually that of local officials (such as mayors) against the Ministry of Justice, the body controlling immigration and alien registration. In addition, the fact that many refusers were already active in community-building efforts when they committed their acts of civil disobedience made it easier for them to organize, and more difficult for the courts to paint them as criminals.

The case of one such community worker, Kim Dŏk-hwan, who was (and is) based in Ikaino, is illustrative. In May 1985, the same year "Mun Kon-bun Ŏmŏni's Apple" was published, Kim Dŏk-hwan refused to give his prints at the Ikuno ward office. Although he was not a member of Mintōren, he was a Christian, and he worked for a community center run by his local church. Osaka, like several other local governments, had decided not to cooperate with Ministry of Justice demands, and he did not at first face prosecution. However, after he neglected to appear for questioning at the local police office, he was arrested.[54]

He was brought to trial in March 1987. He used the time granted him in the courtroom to make a case not only against the specific law, but more generally for the inclusion of Resident Koreans within Japanese society, particularly at the level of the local community. To this end, he described his own experience of poverty and prejudice, relating it to the broader exclusion of Koreans in Japan over history. He argued that the fingerprinting system was the legacy of blatantly racist colonial system of control, one that had been adjusted rather than eliminated in the postwar period.[55]

Kim clearly did not see legal changes as sufficient to provide Resident Koreans an atmosphere in which they could live with dignity. Hence he sees his involvement with the *chiiki undō* (community movement) as part and parcel with his efforts to eradicate discriminatory laws. His interest in this movement began when in 1977 he began teaching at an *ŏmŏni hakkyo* (literally, "mothers' school"), where first-generation women came to learn to read and write Japanese. It was run by the Osaka Seiwa Church, which he attended. In 1978, he had joined in the struggle against housing discrimination in Ikuno-ku; in 1979, he was appointed manager of the Ikuno Local Action Committee (which was formed by a coalition of eight area churches); and in 1982, he began working full time heading the Seiwa Community Center. The *ŏmŏni hakkyo*, he reports, is "not only a place to learn to read and write, but a support for these women in their lives, or, in the terms we use today, a site of community."[56]

His first efforts in the community, he says, were depressing. Ikuno-ku had a higher rate of juvenile delinquency than other Osaka wards, and 70 percent of the cases of youth misconduct involved Koreans; yet not a single Korean group was included in the ward office's list of organizations working on social issues. In addition, despite the fact that one-quarter of the population of the ward was Korean and one of the elementary schools 85 percent Korean, not a single Korean parent was an official in the PTA.[57]

When he became head of the Seiwa Community Center, his main objective, he says, was to facilitate *deai*, or "encounters." He stresses that this word is at the very core of his activism, that the coexistence of Koreans and Japanese in Japanese society depends on it.[58] To this end, the Seiwa center ran a nursery school, as did Korean churches elsewhere in Japan.

Perhaps its (and thus Kim Dŏk-hwan's) most successful endeavor, however, is one unique to that locale: the Ikuno National/Ethnic (that is, Korean) Cultural Festival (Ikuno minzoku bunkasai)—featuring music, food, dancing, games, and so on—held each fall since 1983. In his trial, Kim reports that initially, he had a lot of difficulty garnering support for this event, both from Koreans, who were strongly divided into camps affiliated with the two respective governments of the peninsula, and Japanese, who at first did not want to let them use schoolyards or public parks.[59] The police had a hard time believing that this was a cultural festival and not a political demonstration, and they did not want to supply the permit needed for a parade through the streets; the parade was delayed to allow a "purifying" by the local shrine scheduled to go first.[60] In the end, however, the event went on, and ever since, not only have schools offered their space, but local Japanese people have even begun to contribute money for the event.[61]

Some people continued to find the open display of Korean culture as an obstruction to the creation of community. Kim argues, however, that this rather is a step toward true "internationalization."[62] It was still a move in the direction of coexistence (one buzzword of the movement), because in order for Koreans to be full participants in a community, they needed to have pride in themselves. At the time he founded the cultural festival, many Resident Koreans had become aware of their identity in negative ways—that is to say, through discrimination and poverty. He and other community activists proposed that in order for children to gain a more positive view of Koreanness, they needed to be exposed to Korean culture. Increasingly, culture became the point of focus for Resident Koreans exploring their identities.

I went to this festival with Kim Ch'ang-saeng in 1997, and she told me that she had attended nearly every year. Her work bears the influence of both the community movement and of Chong Ch'u-wŏl's literary world. She professes that she was so moved by reading Chong that although she couldn't get her own copy of her first collection of poetry, she transcribed a borrowed copy word for word into her notebook.[63] She then went on to articulate her own Ikaino in the essays in *Watashi no Ikaino* [My Ikaino], published in 1982, and "Akai mi" [The Red Fruit], a 1987 short story. Kim is a friend of Chong's, and their work shares many themes, but Kim's prose is more critical of women's oppression and more direct in proposing ways they might overcome it. It differs stylistically as well. At times searingly funny, it renders the details of life, work, and death in language somewhat simpler than Chong's, all accented with dialogue in Ikaino dialect. As a consequence, she introduces us to a gritty reality not always visible in Chong's literature.

The figure of Kim's bitter mother looms large in *My Ikaino*. Two essays in particular trace Kim's attempts to come to terms with her mother. One of these pieces, originally published in 1977, is the story of her mother's death. Unlike the writing of most earlier Resident Korean writers, there is no resplendent maternal sentiment here. In one passage, we find a perspective rare in its frankness. She watches as her sister-in-law bathes her invalid mother:

> It was a cruel sight. Would I have to gaze upon the hole from which I was born as my mother had once yelled at my brother that he must do [when he was changing her diaper]? Her pubic hair all fallen out, it was the hole from which I was born that gazed at me. From between my sister-in-law's legs [who stands above her as she lies on her futon], she had trapped me, and would not look away. I'm being tested. This mother was testing her own daughter.[64]

The mother is not passive; the very body of this naked woman is transformed from that which is gazed upon and has violence done to it to that which does the looking and inflicts the violence. Indeed, at every turn, her mother is cursing her children. Kim says that as a child she had rejected everything about her — her Koreanness, her poverty, her lack of education. She yearned for a mother who would make her a lunch to take to school; she was jealous of the very Japanese word for "mother." Although she could cry for the fate of the Korean people she read about in books, she says, she could not do so for her own mother; she spoke filthy Korean (36).

She tells us that only when she transferred from a Japanese school to a

Korean school, run by Sōren, the North Korea–affiliated organization, and began to learn Korean did her feelings for her mother begin to soften (36–37). From the early 1970s, many had stressed learning the Korean language as the key to attaining Korean identity. Although clearly no Resident Korean was ever going to recover some true Koreanness (or even become the same as a Korean-born Korean) by virtue of learning Korean, it is important to acknowledge that learning the language has provided a great number of people with a sense of empowerment.

By the time of this essay, Kim has come to see her mother's life and death as similar to that of many other first-generation Korean immigrants, and "the dark days [her] mother," born in 1907, had led as "the very history of [her] homeland, Korea" (41). By the publication of a second essay reflecting on her mother's death four years later, she even embraces the ways she is similar to her mother (49). She now imagines listening to her mother's ceaseless complaining not with the thought "not again," but with eager ears. It now seems to her a plaintive cry for "the life she tried to but was never able to live" (56).

If she saw her mother's history as much the same as other first-generation Koreans, she indicates that her mother saw her suffering rather as the result of a "bad fate" (42). Not long after, she wonders whether her mother's life might have been different if she had been literate. Would written language alone have accorded her the broader perspective necessary to see how her own life was the consequence of that broader history? In the next essay, she says that her mother's illiteracy meant that she was "never, in her whole life, able to look at herself objectively" (49). She thus proposes that written language gives people the capacity to perceive themselves with detachment as participants in world history. For all her acuity at transcribing dialogue, then, Kim's work evaluates the written more positively than Chong's. She in particular finds useful the separation from self that writing permits, perhaps because it remains as an object after the fact as opposed to disappearing into air, as does speech.

Kim's works more directly express the notion that literacy is a practical tool not only for personal affirmation, but also for social change. In a 1980 essay, she tells of teaching at the *ŏmŏni hakkyo* in the Seiwa Church in Ikaino. Before she began teaching there, she had seen a sign for the class and simply assumed that the women were learning to write Korean. She peeked in one day, and to her great surprise, it was Japanese. Then again, she muses, "In Ikaino, empty theories have no meaning" (113). The women are most proud of being able to read the station names on the train and, ironically, being able to write their names when filling out documents for alien registration. Learning to read and write had helped the women to be practical in a quite different way, however: it gave them the confidence to protest housing discrimination in Ikaino, to speak out against the Japanese state.[65]

If her conceptions of language diverge from those we saw in Chong, so too does her Ikaino. She claims it as her "homeland," but it has taken her awhile to be able to do so with a sense of peace.[66] In a discussion in 1987, she observes that her view of Ikaino is quite different from Chong's. When someone credits Chong with developing the notion that Ikaino is Korea, Kim responds: "Ikaino is Korea, all right, but for me, that's not enough. The *ŏmŏni* are sure strong and they sure raised us well through that era. . . . But can't we get beyond that somehow? That's what I think we should be focusing on now."[67] She further suggests that the difference between their approaches is a result of the fact that she had grown up in Ikaino and wanted to run away, whereas Chong (whom she sees as having an internal sense of herself as Korean) had come in search of a Korean "community" to run away to, a place where she could just be Korean.[68]

Whatever the reasons, Kim's Ikaino is not a romanticized margin, but a place rent by conflict. Political differences sometimes bring members of the community to spar. She tells the story of a woman who reports that while in South Korea as a student, she was raped by an intelligence agent interrogating her for antigovernment activism. At a demonstration in her support, one woman shopkeeper brings her Chinese medicine, but the Mindan (South Korea affiliated) women's group says she has no proof and calls her a whore.[69] Nonetheless, she believes that if Korean reunification is to come from anywhere, it must come from Ikaino. In Ikaino, unlike Korea itself, those supporting the North and those affiliated with the South live side by side and must deal with each other every day simply to get on with their lives.[70] She thus seems to find hope that the recognition of conflict will impel people to acknowledge the necessity for change.

In addition, the daily life of mothering and working in Ikaino, which seems only a pleasure in Chong, is oppressive here. In the first essay on her mother's death, she describes with painstaking detail the moments after she has heard that her mother has died:

> With tears streaming down my face, I put another load of dirty clothes in to the washing machine, ran upstairs, took the clothes in from the line and folded them. I was angry at myself. I was angry at this stupid busy life that deprived me of even the time to cry. I had thought before that when the time came that my mother died, I would leave my daughter with my husband and go hide away somewhere. But in the reality of my daily life, even the death of my mother is dissolved into the routine of everyday life. All my time, minced and cooked. Even when I tell myself "my mother's died, I have no home and no embrace to return to," my hands move on their own. My daughter is fussing and crying, and I change her diaper. I stuff a change of clothes in a bag. When my husband finally comes home and I tell him, he brushes me off, telling me not to lie. I guess my tears had dried and my expression was blank. (38)

The contrast with Chong is striking. The rushed tempo of her life, the mindless repetition, afford her not even the opportunity to mourn, never mind to protest. Elsewhere, in a manic, almost manifestolike essay in which she describes her busy life working and raising a child, she calls daily life a "massive mechanism" (89). "I want to go to the mountains! I want to read a book!" she cries (89). Unlike Chong, then, she is not speaking from the home or Ikaino as an abstract border; the places she speaks from feel more like trenches.

She fantasizes of escapes from this misery. She finds it with knowledge attained not from fellow Resident Korean women (who tell her to have children young and to put up with whatever comes), but from reading books. After talking of her despair, her tone shifts suddenly and she quotes Ibsen's Nora and a Japanese feminist, whose words, she says, "saved" her (88–91). Waiting and forbearing should not be women's only virtues, she argues: "let's use that [notion] back against men. In our very day to day lives, let's develop the will to change." She finally concludes, "my reunification of the homeland lies on the same faraway line of the horizon where women's lives and their sex are fused into one" (93).

The personal is made political here in a manner consonant with 1970s U.S. feminism. If this is also romanticization of a sort, it is patently divergent from the ideas we saw in Chong. Women's attainment of written language is not a positive thing merely because it allows them to communicate what they have to say, but because it enables them to hear the voices of people outside of the small community in which they live. The act of reading is preeminent here in a new way.

In her 1987 "The Red Fruit," Kim further affirms both female writing and female sexuality. The text is complex. It tells of a Korean woman character's oppression (including rape) by her husband *and* his complicit mother and her eventual divorce from him. At the same time, the protagonist ponders her childhood shame of being Korean and fantasies of being Japanese and its relations to the fantasy world of her own young daughter. The narrative is laden with rich imagery of childbearing (seeds, fruit, apples) and of transmigration (circles, a crematorium, ashes, Buddhist chants). It uses this imagery to a specific hopeful end, contrasting the woman's experience of rape (by her husband) and unfulfilling masturbation with the possibility that her daughter will not merely repeat the same cycle as her mother but will perhaps find sexual satisfaction through her acquisition of literacy in Korean:

> On the next exposed page, the boxes were filled with apples. The Korean "o"s — written darkly with a practice pencil — the strength left over from writing the circle made a line extend beyond it. The measured boxes were filled with mismatched apples that hadn't been pruned.
>
> Would they possibly ever ripen?[71]

Within the lines escaping their bounds, the escape from the uniformity of the circles of Korean letters, she locates the opportunity, I believe, for an escape from the circularity of Buddhist transmigration and the repetition of oppression of women.

The fact that she builds on symbols and imagery from Chong's writing makes it easy enough to contrast them. We might identify Chong's romanticization of orality and repetitive cycles of childbearing and culture (or more spiritually put, the transmigration of souls) as almost antimodern, and Kim's grasping onto the power of the written and of progress as affirming the linear time of history and a positive view of modernity. Likewise, we might assume that Chong is, in the manner of much postcolonial theory, hoping to fight colonialism by rejecting all that it is tainted by association with the colonial, including rationality and narratives of progress, and that Kim is engaging in a more classic modernist, "nationalist" sort of anticolonialism that merely hopes to overturn the balance of power (after all, it is Korean and not Japanese her daughter is learning).

If this is true, they nonetheless both find value in the community (particularly of women) in Ikaino. Kim volunteers as a teacher in that community and talks about being happy to live in a place where there are other Koreans, in a place overflowing with Korean language, food, and culture. Descriptions of bodily functions also have a prominent place in Kim's work, although more often it is the body dissatisfied: one exhausted, pained, sexually frustrated. For Kim, the critical task is not only to find value in Ikaino and Korean culture, but to acknowledge their dark side as well, so that everyone's quality of life may be bettered. In the roundtable discussion quoted above, she says that she has been reading a collection of African American writers, and has found striking the way that they all talk about the support of the "community." In her reading, what they dread is not so much discrimination or lack of education, but "severing themselves from the traditions of their race/people."[72] As simple as this notion may be, we must remember that even as these works were being published, ideas affirming the importance of identification not with Japan but in affiliation with the homeland (such as the "Zainichi as method" argument) still held a great power for people, and that even with the "Zainichi as fact" camp, feminist voices had barely begun to be heard.

When I first decided to consider Ikaino literature and the antifingerprinting movement, I anticipated that they would neatly fit into my preconceived notion of what "Zainichi as fact" was all about. I thought that they would simply show how Resident Koreans had used identification with the local regions where they lived to enable them to perceive of their identity as residents in Japan without forcing them to identify with the Japanese state. The essential objective of the antifingerprinting movement is to deny the modern nation-state system (in the form of Japan) the ability to control people, to make them into abstract units, and to instead assert the right to determine their identities apart from such a system. Kim Dŏk-hwan's narrative was one of many such individual stories to make that point. To stress, as Chong and Kim do, the importance of the daily experience of being female in Ikaino seems to teach a similar lesson. Clearly they find subjectivity in spaces somehow not entirely controlled by Japanese language and ideology. Their portrayal of first-generation women provides an antidote to the exoticization found, for example, in a 1987 collection of photographs, *Onnatachi no Ikaino* [Women's Ikaino], in which the photographer says, "The women, more than the men, were people of an alien culture."[73] It also challenges the sexism of earlier male author's romanticization of their mothers' forbearance. When I met them, I felt that writing had empowered them both.

I suggested at the beginning of this chapter that their philosophies of writing (found in both form and content) were interlaced with the very turn to the local. It is perhaps easier to see in Chong's case how this is so because she rejects standardized written speech in favor of "living language," just as the community movement attempts to establish a life of dignity outside of the control of the centralized state. In addition, her emphasis on the production of meaning within the writer-reader relationship seems a response to the increasing commodification of literature. Her concept of the margin, if at times nationalistic, ultimately seems a broader appeal against the homogenization of culture and the oppression of minority voices in Japan. By 1987, she was calling for collaboration not only with the labor unions of local governments, but with other minorities — Okinawans and Ainu and descendants of Japan's former outcaste class, referred to as *hisabetsu buraku*.[74] When I spoke with her in the summer of 1996, she told me that for her, Ikaino was wherever oppressed people are found. She said she wanted her next book to be about the Filipina women she had met while working in a *pachinko* parlor in the countryside outside Tokyo. "The deepest part of the periphery," it seems, is no longer populated by only Koreans.

Kim's work, on the other hand, although it does contain a good dose of dialogue in Osaka dialect and thus makes good use of Bakhtinian dialogism, still finds meaning in using the standard language and literary form of the Japanese nation to argue against the ideology implicit in them. Her stress on reading works of long-dead authors appeals to a different sort of relationship between reader and writer, but still one no less opposed to the mere consumption of texts. Kim Ch'ang-saeng also lives between and sometimes clings to vestiges of nationalism — her family still works in the North Korea–affiliated organization, and she did not hide her delight that I spoke Korean and loved Korean food. Yet she is more openly critical of Korean women's oppression of other Korean women. It makes no difference if feminist ideas come from the west or even from Japan. Her Korean culture is one creatively assembled of those elements she finds useful. Much the same might be said of the women activists I cited.

Even the community movement, associated so closely with the idea of *Zainichi shikō*, which taught older women to write Japanese, the language they needed for practical purposes, believed that Koreans should identify with Korean "culture." Therein lay the purpose of events like the Ikuno ethnic festival. It might rather have proposed ways for them to find value in the culture that was theirs to begin with, a culture that is an amalgam of Korean and Japanese, a culture borne of the history of Koreans in Japan. The antifingerprinting struggle likewise did not argue, as perhaps it might have, that not only the requirements of the ARL but the fact that people from Japan's former colonies had not been granted the choice of Japanese citizenship was utterly unjust. Even today, when a great number of Zainichi Koreans become Japanese citizens each year, when people whose parents or grandparents were naturalized have earned the right to use Korean names, and when there are significant movements fighting for Koreans' rights to be employed in management positions in local government and to vote in local elections, not a soul is to be heard arguing that immigrants from the former colonies and their descendants should be offered the choice of becoming citizens. And ten years ago, at the height of the antifingerprinting movement, this was all the more the case.

Perhaps I have been too critical, stressing the de facto nationalism of cultural activities or learning Korean language rather than acknowledging the ideology of multiculturalism put forward here. It is evident that the conceptions of the local addressed by these authors and activists are not simply reactionary nationalism or conservative postmodernism; they do not dismiss global capitalism as a useful rubric for understanding what happens in their local area. Each tries to depict the dialectic between the local and the global, both materially and in terms of discourse. Less thoughtful entreaties for coexistence, in Japan as in the United States, tend to rely on the assumption that there are people who hold culturally distinct identities. Joan Scott proposes that a genuine multiculturalism would perceive identities as relational, historically defined, and engaged in an "ongoing process of differentiation, relentless in its repetition, but also . . . subject to redefinition, resistance and change."[75] I sense here an increasing inclination to characterize both Resident Koreanness and Japaneseness in this manner.

It is important to realize that in the 1980s, and even now, many Japanese have had trouble coming to terms with even the more ordinary version of multiculturalism. There has been great resistance to seeing Resident Koreans as "Korean Japanese" — that is to say, Japanese of Korean descent, even though by American standards of ethnicity of course many such people exist. "Go home" letters sent to fingerprint refusers attest to this fact; how can someone go home to a place he has never been? All this on top of the fact that discrimination in housing, employment, and government benefits persists. It thus takes a great deal of courage, or, some would say, foolhardiness, to propose making that leap to primarily identifying as one who belongs in Japan, the ultimate sign of which would be to become a Japanese citizen. Until Japan's wartime history is taught in a way that explains and justifies Resident Koreans' presence in Japan by acknowledging the fact that it was Japan's colonial policy that forced them to come in the first place, no such view even has soil from which to sprout. Even then, there is no guarantee that people will become accepting of such notions. In the late 1980s and the 1990s, however, as we shall see in the subsequent chapters, Koreans holding Japanese citizenship begin to reclaim cultural Koreanness and those holding Korean citizenship to affirm their cultural Japaneseness, putting a firm slash through the equal sign so often found between citizenship and ethnicity.

5
Words that Breathe

Yi Yang-ji was unquestionably the most prominent Resident Korean writer of the 1980s. From the time she published her first work of fiction, *Nabi taryon* [*Nabi T'aryŏng* (A Butterfly's Lament)], in a major journal in 1982, her work garnered considerable critical acclaim and sold a large number of copies for a work of "pure" literature.[1] Her fiction was also translated into Korean, making her one of the few Resident Korean writers to attract a readership there.[2] In 1989, she became only the second writer of Korean descent to win the Akutagawa prize; however, she died just three years later, at the age of thirty-seven. Her prize-winning novella, *Yuhi*, was her final published work.

By the 1980s, authors like Murakami Haruki, whose books contained multiple references to pop culture and name brands, not only sold millions of volumes of their work, but garnered critical acclaim. In the eyes of detractors, however, this fiction was merely stylish fluff.[3] Although the same could never be said of Yi Yang-ji's literature, one critic, writing in *Mintō*, a journal sponsored by Ri Kaisei, placed her and another young Resident Korean writer firmly in Murakami's camp. He claimed that their fiction was devoid of the political consciousness seen in earlier Zainichi fiction (such as that by Ri Kaisei) and that it was headed in a dangerous direction:

Like the young generation of writers such as . . . Murakami Haruki . . . they do not direct their attention at the world, society, or revolution, but rather correspond strikingly with a reality conspiring with an inner vacuousness. By depending on a sense of "difference" to define their own existence, or in other words, by placing "ethnicity," one of the *raison d'être* of Resident Korean literature, at the center of their works, their literature manages to escape falling into "literar-ism." However, contained within it is the danger that it may — who knows when — assimilate itself into the misguided mainstream of the contemporary literature of "Japan." In reality, in her recent work *Rai-i* [Arrival] (*Gunzō*, May 1986), Yi Yang-ji has exacerbated this tendency toward existentialism. Not a single iota of "ethnicity" is to be found.[4]

Yi Yang-ji's work indisputably strives to say something about matters beyond ethnicity in a way that that of Ri Kaisei, or even Chong Ch'u-wŏl and Kim Ch'ang-saeng, does not. Although I share this critic's concern that contemporary Japanese literature has become vapid, it seems ridiculous to me to assert that all literature need focus on social issues, and even more so that Resident Koreans need restrict themselves to writing about ethnic identity.

Nor is it fair to claim that Yi Yang-ji did not write about ethnic identity or was unconcerned with the history of Koreans' discrimination in Japan. With the exception of *Arrival*, Yi Yang-ji's works are about women struggling to come to terms with their being neither wholly Korean nor wholly Japanese. She makes many references to discrimination in both Japan and South Korea. In one of the works I analyze in this chapter, she depicts a character thrown into a state of anxiety because her class is about to come to the page in the text where Korea is discussed. This is a poignant scene given the prominence during the 1980s of historian Ienaga Saburō's efforts to get the government to approve his textbooks, which include frank (if brief) descriptions of Japanese aggression in Korea and Asia more generally. Indeed, readers of her work disagree about whether or not her work addresses matters of ethnic identity, often, it seems, on the basis of whether or not they agree with what she is saying.[5]

As pointed out by literary critic Kawamura Minato, Yi Yang-ji's conclusions about the matter put her more in the camp of a writer like Kin Kakuei than that of Ri Kaisei. Drawing on Takeda Seiji's interpretation, he argues that because Kin saw his stutter as being as fundamental a component of his sense of self as was his ethnicity he was compelled to acknowledge the "impossibility of identity," by which he seems to mean the impossibility of identifying simply as Korean. For Yi, he goes on, her gender (literally, her womanness) served an identical purpose.[6] Takeda himself says that he feels her to be a "woman writer" more strongly than he feels her to be a "Resident Korean writer."[7] Kim Ch'ang-saeng makes a similar observation.

Incorporating gender into ethnic identification, however, was a characteristic of the writers I considered in the previous chapter, although nary a soul would characterize their work as apolitical disavowals of Korean identity, or as more "women's writing" than "Zainichi." What distinguishes Yi's work form the earlier authors is that she persistently depicts her ethnic in-betweenness as an insurmountable source of pain. Not Korean womanhood but sexuality as experienced by women is one of the most prominent features of her work. Almost all of her characters reject motherhood and are promiscuous, sometimes even selling sex or living off the patronage of married men. In this respect, she certainly does overlap with mainstream Japanese writers, or at least women, many of whom had written works focusing on sexuality at least since the 1960s.

Nonetheless, Yi's work shares many preoccupations of the Ikaino women. This is not surprising because Yi Yang-ji started on a path not dissimilar to theirs. She dropped out of high school, ran away from home, and worked in an inn in Kyoto. She began going to night school there. Later, like Chong Ch'u-wŏl, she was drawn to a Korean neighborhood (a rather smaller one in Tokyo) and worked in a sandal factory, just as Chong had in Ikaino. She too wandered in search of Korean identity.

By this point, however, Yi, whose family was more affluent than Chong's or Kim's, had already begun studying Korean and had attended and dropped out of Waseda University, the prestigious institution from which Ri Kaisei had graduated, and which she had chosen for its active Korean students' organization.[8] Yet none of this satisfied her desires. For one thing, the student group was not accepting of the fact that she was a Japanese citizen. It is not clear that disappointment with this group was her main reason for leaving college, but soon after her death, an acquaintance recalled that when she met Yi at age twenty, she had said that she wanted to "renaturalize" — that is, take on Korean (presumably South Korean) citizenship.[9]

Her choice to work in a factory, then, was different from Chong's.

Surely she also needed to make money and also wished to be near
Koreans, yet it also seems to have been part of a self-conscious effort to
deny herself some of the privileges her Japanese citizenship, her class, and
(if she had graduated) her educational status would have afforded her.
Once living in this neighborhood, she became involved in the effort to
free a Korean man who had been jailed for a crime he did not commit.
None of these activities, however, provided her with the sense of identity
she had sought.[10] While working at the factory, however, she began learning the *kayagŭm*, a Korean stringed instrument, and in this at last she
found something Korean about which she felt passionate.[11] Yi, who had
originally studied Japanese traditional music and dance, seems to have
had some talent with the *kayagŭm*, for she gained an introduction to a
famous teacher in Korea. After going there to study in 1980 — the year of
the Kwangju uprising and well before it was popular to study there — she
first saw *salp'uri*, a dance derived from shamanistic rituals. She was cap-
tivated and eventually turned her efforts to learning Korean dance.

She began writing fiction after she went to Korea, and Korean culture
and arts — particularly language, shamanism, music, and dance — have a
prominent place in nearly all of her works. She stated openly that she had
gone to Korea to learn Korean language, music, and dance in an attempt
to "become Korean." In a conversation with the critic Kawamura Minato
not long after she was awarded the Akutagawa prize, she says that the first
time she heard the *kayagŭm*, she had felt that she had heard it in an earlier life; when she first danced, she felt she had done so in a previous incar-
nation; "in the end, there isn't really anything to be done about blood or
whatever it is inside one."[12] She grows irritated, however, when Kawamura
casts her work in terms of identity, proposing that in it, dance or shamanism appears as a "place to go home to/identify with" in the way that
North or South Korea, Sōren, or language appears in other writers (seemingly making quite different conclusions about Yi's work, although per-
sisting in his use of a simplistic concept of identity).[13] Your reading is too
schematic, she says; it's too general; I think that Zainichi Koreans are a
diverse bunch; I do not feel able to represent them; I can speak only for
myself or my characters.[14] For whatever reason, by this point, she had
come to reject the simplistic brand of identity put forward by Kawamura.

At the same time, she refuses to dismiss outright the idea that Resident

Koreans share certain experiences as a result of having been brought up in Japan. Later in the same conversation, she refers to the emotional difficulty "most overseas Koreans" have when they learn the Korean language, presumably because they think they should be able to speak it like a native but find that they cannot. She talks about how "Japanese" her motions were when she began Korean dance and admits that she had hoped her study of Korean dance and music would allow her to express a "dogmatic nationalism." Ultimately, however, her body's resistance had made it impossible for her to be a nationalist.[15] It is evident that she saw place of upbringing as being as important as blood in constituting cultural identity. She goes on to say that she sees language and the body as the fundamental forms of expression in life.[16] It therefore seems that the fact that we learn subtle sounds of the voice and movements of the body — things usually associated with a national or ethnic culture — from our environs rather than inheriting them by blood was of great significance for her and ultimately led her to reject the notion that Resident Koreans could simply claim Korean identity.

Yet Yi Yang-ji did not want her work to be read as being only about the question of identity and her characters' lives, as representative of all Resident Korean lives. She might as well have been angrily refuting Fredric Jameson's claim that all third world writers' works are national allegories.[17] Rather, she aspired to write literature about aspects of existence at once much narrower (that is to say, about unique personal experiences of particular historical conjunctures) and much broader (about universal aspects of human interaction) than ethnicity. Thus when she includes interludes about school textbooks (in the first story I examine) or a Korean teacher's misunderstandings of Zainichi history (in the second), her point seems less to draw attention to the fact that history is being taught poorly than to probe the way that such a state of affairs affects a person's life experience. It's not surprising, then, that what stays with me from her literature is not conclusions she comes to about what it means to be a Korean in Japan, but rather repeated motifs, fleeting images, and an intensity of emotion: self-hatred, terror, and irritation, mostly; but on occasion, joy. Her fiction is not so much about where the characters end up (which is not at any time Korean identity, strictly speaking), but about their journey to that point, about their feelings, their interpretations of images, their often frustrated attempts to communicate with others.

In this chapter I will examine two short pieces by Yi Yang-ji. The first, "Kazukime" [The Diving Maiden, 1983], tells of a Resident Korean woman's feelings of persecution in Japan; the other, *Koku* [Koku, 1984], tracks a single day in a Japan-born protagonist's struggle to come to terms with her feelings of alienation in Korea. They do not provide simple models of how to overcome such feelings of persecution or alienation, and necessarily, my interpretations will thus comment on what her refusal to propose such models might mean. The bulk of my readings, however, will revolve around the motifs that lie at the center of the works.

Shamanic contact with a spirit world is one such theme that punctuates the two pieces. Shamanism is familiar, of course, from the writings encountered in the previous chapter, yet Yi manipulates it in a markedly different manner. If Chong Ch'u-wŏl and Kim Ch'ang-saeng at times used shamanism as a literary motif, for the most part, they reviled the way women in the real community of Ikaino placed false hopes on shamanic ritual. Yi Yang-ji, in contrast, seems to have been genuinely attracted to the connections with a spiritual realm offered not by shamanism in practice (either in Japan or in Korea) but in the abstract. In particular, she was inspired by the arts connected with it—dance and music. In 1982, she wrote retrospectively, "the image of the long white cloth used in the *salp'uri*, the traditional shamanistic dance that is said to release *han* [grief, resentment], became for me the symbol of life itself."[18]

Although Kim and Chong had connected religious beliefs of transmigration—often from Buddhism rather than shamanism—with motherhood and thus with the continuation and renewal of the community, Yi's characters, despite great interest in the world of spirits, invariably reject reproduction. The narratives dwell on bodily function and sensation, on menstruation and cramps, on unwanted pregnancy, on rape and subsequent masochistic desire. Her very different manipulation of shamanism and sexuality, based in a literary style that is also quite different, leads certain critics see her as having an ambivalent relationship to ethnic identity, whereas they see Kim and Chong as properly nationalist writers.

Her development of these themes in "The Diving Maiden" is particularly provocative. It is set in Japan and lacks any direct reference to Korean music, dance, or shamanism.[19] The narrative, divided into eight discrete sections, alternates between two distinct voices. The first, although in the third person, gives us access to the thoughts of the unnamed Resident Korean protagonist; the second is from the perspective of the protagonist's estranged stepsister. The story told in the sections by the first narrator follows the meandering path of the protagonist's memory; that by the second narrator recounts her discovery of her stepsister drowned in her bathtub and her interviews with a number of her friends in an attempt to make sense of her life and death.

The structure draws attention to itself. After all, we can interpret the lines of narration as being in the voice of the dead. I like the effect of this contrived scheme, particularly because by the end, we are led to see that it reinforces the thematic content of the story. But I am getting ahead of myself. In the first section of the piece, the unnamed protagonist, known throughout only as *kanojo* ("she") or *onēsan* ("[my] elder sister"), is a young child. Only a year before, she moved to a new town when her mother married a Japanese man, and no one there knows she is Korean. Since entering her new school, she has been dreading the day that, in fourth-period social studies class, they will reach the page on which Korean history is introduced. She imagines all sorts of escapes:

> There will be an outbreak of an infectious disease and school will be closed, there will be a massive earthquake, the night before lightning will strike the school and it will burn down, Sakai [the teacher] will suddenly fall ill. . . . She thought of all sorts of possibilities, yet these unreal imaginings actually made her more uneasy. After all, even if there were no class on Monday, the time would still come when they would open the text to that page. (64)

Any contemporary reader surely would have thought, on reading this, about the vociferous complaints in the 1982 by the governments of Asian countries (including the Koreas) about the representation in textbooks of Japan's military aggression in Asia.[20] In addition, Japanese historian Ienaga Saburō filed a third lawsuit against the state in 1984 appealing the revisions demanded of the textbook he submitted for approval to the Ministry of Education in 1980. This included references to the actions of Koreans resisting the Japanese during the Sino-Japanese War.

The story is set, of course, years before these events, when no such direct references to the truth of Japanese aggression could be made in the textbooks. We see the devastating effect of the glossing over of history on the physical body of a young girl. She so associates Korea with something shameful that she wants to stay home to avoid the encounter, yet she ultimately decides not to do so because being there, where her stepfather is always beating her mother, is just as unpleasant. When the day comes that they are going to reach that page in the text, and horrifyingly (and yet in the context of the narrative, miraculously), she breaks out in a fever the moment the class begins. The teacher suggests she go to the nurse's office, but instead she goes directly home. Her mother calls the doctor, but he is unable to figure out the cause of her illness. He only gives her medicine to quell her fever. Then, fearing that the building ceremony that they had performed that day (they are building an apartment building on their land) was improperly performed and has brought bad luck, she calls an old woman who dispels curses (*harai no rōba*), that is to say, a shaman.

The shaman's ritual consists of waving a *gohei* (an implement used on such occasions, usually made either of linen or folded paper, often white, attached to a stick) over the girl's body, at which point the girl feels she is sinking in a pot of boiling water; she tries to get up but finds she cannot move; finally, "after peering into her face, the old woman hit her chest and head repeatedly with the white clump [*soku*] of the *gohei*." At this moment, there is a flash of light, and her eyes burn. Then

> the face of the old woman and those of her family, which had gathered around her as she slept, disappeared. Her eyes were covered with a bright white film, which began to shine so brightly she thought it would pierce her eyes. She could not blink, and so with her eyes open, she stiffened her body. She felt her blood vessels begin to send waves from the tips of her toes; her ears felt blocked from all sound as if she were in water. Somewhere far off she heard a low groan. Each time she heard the drone of that voice, the white film covering her eyes wavered slightly and cast shadows in tandem with the waxing and waning of the voice.
>
> "Go out, go out into the water."
>
> The same words repeated three times. She heard the words distinctly, and ruminated upon them. (65)

At this moment, the film disappears, her eyes begin to focus, and her fever at last breaks.

It is worth noting here that in Korean shamanism (and, incidentally, in such traditions elsewhere), those who are to become shamans are usually acknowledged as having special powers after undergoing either severe trials, such as the death of a family member or an illness that doctors cannot diagnose.[21] Only through undergoing a ritual are they cured of their illness; for many, this simultaneously serves as their initiation as shamans.[22]

I read the scene of the girl's illness as suggesting that she is a person destined to become a vehicle for the gods. I believe so not simply because her illness, which lacks a cause (unless we count the Japanese government's), is finally cured by the act of a shaman, but also because of the narrative details of the passage: she sees a bright light, and she feels that her body is sinking in a pot, as if being boiled. Mircea Eliade, in his study of shamanism around the world, notes the significance of light in various religious traditions, including shamanism, and the commonness of symbolic death in the form of dismemberment or boiling in the initiation ceremonies of certain other shamanic traditions.[23]

The subsequent narrative of the girl's life, gleaned both from the sections with her memories and from those sections in which her friends tell their memories of her to her stepsister, we find subtle but persistence references to things of a spiritual nature. If on one level the story is simply about the life of a woman who dies an untimely death after surviving a number of adversities and, as I mentioned above, about her mostly unsuccessful efforts to come to terms with her Koreanness, reading the character as a shaman of sorts elevates her life. Its tragedy becomes tragedy for a purpose. The original cause for her sickness, we may intimate, is the Japanese government's burial of its history of aggression, and the potential cure lies in unearthing and spreading the knowledge of that history.

But this level of meaning lies below the surface. The story is one of an individual woman. The first section continues with the little girl running away after she recovers. It begins to rain and she gets drenched; hearing water sloshing in her shoes, she thinks a frog has gotten in them, and she throws off her new and beloved sneakers with cosmos flowers printed on them. The scene ends with her walking along in the rain.

At the beginning of the second section, we note the shift in voice to a third-person narration focused on a character named Kyōko. It does not take long for us to see that this woman is the younger stepsister of the character in the first section; we first see her cleaning out her sister's apartment. Before long, we learn that their relationship had always been difficult, that Kyōko had been jealous of her sister, who had been beautiful and intelligent, that Kyōko was often mean to her sister because of this. We come to know that the sister's mother had died of cancer; that not long after, she had stolen money from her stepfather's company, where she had been working; that she had then disappeared; and that her name had become taboo in the family. Yet Kyōko also recalls that her stepsister had showed up at her college dorm with a gift, and that this is the reason that Kyōko knew where her sister was living and had come to her apartment. The scene ends with Kyōko reflecting on the meaning of the mere ten years between the time her stepmother and stepsister came into her life and now. For what reason she does not know, she cries, feeling "burning pain" in her eyes.

In the four sections that follow, two of which are further memories of the protagonist and two of which comprise the recollections of her life by friends as spoken to Kyōko, a portrait of this woman gradually forms. In the first of these, we witness her as a teenager at the dinner table, gorging herself amidst a tense atmosphere, running down the hall to the toilet to vomit, returning, and eating even more. We also see her musing about why her mother remarried a man just as violent a drunk as her father, and finally, we watch a scene in which, in her shame on realizing that her kindness to a male teacher has been answered with lecherous gestures, she once again sticks her fingers down her throat and forces herself to vomit.

In the subsequent sequence, we hear that as an adult, her self-destructive behavior had escalated. Kyōko meets Morimoto, a man with whom her stepsister lived for a time two years earlier. He first met her at a bar where she was working. He heard rumors of her promiscuity, which he did not believe. But one evening when he and his friends (all of whom fell in love with her at first sight) invite her to drink with them, she ends up making advances toward, and then sleeping with, one and then the other of his friends. Here he describes this night:

> I'd known several women who were so starved for stimulation that they would just sleep with any man. But with her, it wasn't that sort of detachment. It didn't even seem like it was done on a whim or for fun. It was like she was challenging something, or trying to get through something; there was that much force in her actions.
>   "Come here, Icchan."

She called to me as she fondled my friend's crotch. Her almond-shaped eyes glistened. Her voice was also a bit raspy and agitated and I absentmindedly thought that she seemed like a shaman; I somehow felt as if my arms and legs were separating from my body, but I felt no pain at all. (78)

Morimoto is disturbed and repels her advances, but it does not stop her from moving in with him a few days later. She quits her job at the bar and begins working at a local bookstore so that she can spend time with him.

From the way that Morimoto recalls his life with her, we ascertain that her self-destructive tendencies are related to her Koreanness. He begins by talking about the fact that when she first moved in, she would sometimes eat hurriedly and rudely (much as we saw her eating as a teenager); he tells her to slow down. A few nights later, she says that she learned something important from him: that she does not need to laugh or talk or do anything when she does not feel like it. That same night she first tells him she is Korean and, when he tells her his (positive) impressions of Koreans he met when working on a fishing boat, she finally says that she is going to "give [him her] virginity" (80). After this, she begins to deteriorate. She develops a tic, he comes home to find her sitting on the veranda naked and cold as ice, and another night he discovers that she has self-inflicted bruises and cuts covering her body.

At the end of the section, he describes one of their final nights together before she leaves. They take a bath together and Morimoto gets out first. She is taking a long time, and when he goes in to ask if he can wash her back for her, he finds her passed out on the tiles. She notes that there was an earthquake, and then begins speculating in a paranoid manner about what would happen if there were a great Kantō (Tokyo area) earthquake as in 1923. Here again, history — or the popular understanding of it — intrudes, but her point is less about the way that history ought to be taught than to complicate our understanding of what its legacy might mean for the lives of real people. Would Koreans be killed, stabbed with bamboo spears as they were then?, she wonders. She goes on:

No, this time I don't think that would happen. The world is different now from the way it was then. Not to mention that now our pronunciation sounds almost exactly like Japanese. Hey, Icchan, if I were to be killed anyway, would you hold me, would you stay together with me,

saying you're my love? But no, this time we definitely wouldn't be mas-
sacred. But that's no good — I have to be killed. . . . It will hurt, a whole
lot. You know that knife you sharpened? I grabbed it. Then my whole
body tingled and got excited, like the feeling when you have sex. . . . I
tried cutting myself all over with the knife. . . . Hey, what happens if I'm
not killed, does that make me Japanese? (81–82)

In this passage, we see that for this woman who grew up in an entirely
Japanese environment and who speaks Japanese "almost exactly" with
the pronunciation of a Japanese, the only affirmation of her Koreanness
that exists is physical pain, a pain self-inflicted but imagined to be the persecution of vindictive Japanese. This closing leads us to believe that all of
her self-destructive behavior — from her childhood bulimia to her eating
without tasting, her promiscuity, and her cutting and bruising herself as
an adult — as an effort to define her ethnicity through victimization. In
this delusional world, it matters little that the suffering is self-induced.

Morimoto says at the end that by the time he found her in the bath, he
had already become overwhelmed with her problems and was thinking of
leaving her, but that before he could, she took the initiative and left him
(81). Yet as he speaks, Kyōko sees his eyes glistening, and not from
drunkenness. He thanks her again and again for getting in touch with him
(75). Although he is now married to someone else and had forgotten
about her, he admits to Kyōko that after receiving a brief phone call from
her half a year ago, he had begun to think about her obsessively (like
falling in love for the first time, he says (76). Despite the fact that he says
he "frankly could not handle her" and that "in the end there was no place
for" him because he could not give her all the help she demanded (76), we
are left with the impression that she had remarkable power over him. We
recall that he and his two friends fell in love with her in an instant and
that he had noted something shamanlike in her as she made sexual
advances to them. Her sexual power, then, is depicted as part of her
shamanic character, and his obsession, therefore, might better be named
possession. It bears noting here that in Korea, the majority (roughly 80
percent) of shamans are women[24]; the initiation ritual, in which the gods
are said to "descend" into the body of the chosen woman, has been
likened to a sexual encounter.[25] Yi's creation of a character whose overwhelming sexual power over human men is proof of her connections to

the spiritual world seems a barb directed at the more typical view of women who act as the protagonist does.

Whether or not we accept the depiction of this character as possessing spiritual powers, however, we must acknowledge that in a mundane sense, she suffers from psychiatric symptoms, including a self-destructiveness evidenced by her alcoholism and her self-inflicted wounds. Interestingly, the pair of sections that follow lead the reader toward two simultaneous analyses of her character: one that is entrenched in a rational, earthly world and another that sees her as shaman in at least a symbolic sense. Scientific analyses of shamanism do note that some of the characteristics of what is perceived as spirit possession bear a likeness to the symptoms of certain psychiatric conditions.[26]

Being a survivor of incest, for example, could have led her to exhibit the symptoms she does.[27] This first of the next segments focuses on the protagonist's rape by both of her stepbrothers and her impregnation by one of them. The scene opens with her sitting in her room feeling as if the walls and then the ceiling and floors are closing in on her. The "seemingly ceaseless violent wind and rain" that beat against the window bring her "to hallucinate repeatedly and without end the vision of torture; she nearly lost consciousness countless times" (82). Not long after, her younger stepbrother breaks in her window and rapes her; we learn that her elder stepbrother has been raping her only from the line that he "spread her legs even more roughly" than the elder brother.

Soon she is pregnant. On several occasions, she had come home with an employee of her stepfather's after running into him on her way home from school, and her mother assumes that this man is the culprit. As she pleads with her daughter to tell her who impregnated her, the narration notes that the daughter realizes that her mother hopes it is this employee because then the problem could be resolved simply by having them marry, and then "the purple ring and the diamond ring ingrown in the flesh of her middle and ring fingers blurred in her eyes as they glistened. Her mother was probably happy now, she thought, looking at her hand" (84). At this moment, she imagines that her mother is thinking of her father, her father who went back to Saishūtō (Chejudo). The narrative then skips to a memory of the final night she saw her father, of listening to her father beating her mother from her bed, of getting up and seeing him crouched in the kitchen alone, of going outside and finding her mother in her pajamas crying "aigo, aigo" in Korean. She awoke cradled in her father's arms (84).

When the narration returns to her talk with her mother, she observes that this mother would never cry that way again. She finally tells her that it was her stepbrother. She runs to her room as her mother and stepfather confront him; there she thinks of Kyōko, who is at school: "If she had never come to this house, Kyōko might have been forced to play the part that she now played. A slightly modified version of today's commotion undoubtedly would have occurred sooner or later" (85). The reference to her mother's happiness makes it seem as if she is inheriting the role of victimized Korean woman from her mother, who is destined to never have to cry in despair (in Korean) as she once did, because she has made an almost complete transformation into Japanese woman. The narration on several occasions comments on her wearing Japanese kimono; we also see that her rings, signs of her material success and thus Japaneseness, have become "ingrown." In addition, however, the fact that the protagonist reflects on Kyōko's escape from the fate she might have been forced to bear indicates that she sees herself as a sacrificial lamb for not only Korean women, but women more generally. These painful details are relentlessly grounded in the pain of *this* world, and point us to a conclusion of a psychiatric nature: that is, that this woman's promiscuity and self-destructive behavior are the consequence of her being an incest survivor.

Keeping in mind that in Morimoto's account, her sexuality was of an almost shamanic nature, however, we can argue that her victimization here is meant to have symbolic significance as well. In Korea, undergoing countless hardships is nearly a prerequisite for becoming a shaman; nonetheless, or perhaps as a result, they have the power to dispel the misfortunes of others. This is not to say that this role brings happiness to the woman in this story; the repetition of memories of rape is represented as "torture," and in general, her inner dialogue reveals her life as causing her torment. Yet we would do well to take heed of her brief recollection of feeling tenderness and safety as she is rocked by her father, for this image gains significance at the end of the story and is essential if we are to accept the depiction of this character as coming to terms with her role as sacrificial lamb for others.

The next acquaintance of her sister's whom Kyōko is able to meet with is a woman named Kayo, much older than the protagonist, whom we learn in this segment was only twenty-three. Like Morimoto, Kayo thanks Kyōko profusely for having contacted her. Like him, she says she does not know where to begin, that she had met her at a bar where she worked. Since she disappeared six months before, she has worried about what had happened to her and has heard strange rumors. Although the suggestion is not as strong as it is in the case of Morimoto, the timing is just the same: what has the protagonist been doing for six months, we wonder, and how does this enable her to occupy, or perhaps possess, the thoughts of these former companions?

There are two particularly important details of Kayo's narrative that confirm this sense of the protagonist as shaman. Kayo reports that when she asked her why she worked at a bar rather than finding daytime employment, she replied that it was because she liked to drink. When Kayo had chastised her for drinking so much, she justified it thus: "When I drink, I feel as though I can become closer to the gods. They're usually mean and selfish, the gods, but when I drink as much as I can to pacify them, then it seems like they get in to a better mood" (87). The notion of appeasing the gods with alcohol is prevalent in shamanic practice in Korea and elsewhere. If this were not enough to suggest that this character believes that she is serving as a conduit for the gods, the rest of Kayo's interactions with her lead us even further toward this conclusion.

The following day, Kayo had asked her if she believed in god (or the gods) and received the following response: "Whether I believe in them or not, they exist, somewhere, for certain" (88).[28] Kayo, it turns out, is a member of a religious organization with a bad reputation and had invited the protagonist to a meeting with her; she was unsuccessful in persuading her to join. Kayo observes that she had nonetheless continued to speak about things of a spiritual nature; she also comments on a "certain unique look in the eyes" that the woman used to get (88).

In this passage, the protagonist's spiritual inclinations are juxtaposed with her victimization as Korean and as a woman. Once Kayo had gone to the woman's apartment because Kayo hadn't seen her for a few days. She had found her ill with a fever and tried to persuade her to go to a doctor. She refused. After Kayo took time off from work and helped nurse her to health, she had learned that the protagonist had an abortion in high school, although she did not reveal by whom she had become pregnant. On that occasion, she had developed an intense dislike for doctors, of whom she had said, "Internists, surgeons, whatever, though gynecologists are the worst. They all want to perform hysterectomies, remove the ovaries of Koreans so their numbers won't increase" (89). Kayo laughed this off, telling her it was a paranoid delusion, but she claimed that she was serious and that at age twenty, she had determined to stave off this fate by (paradoxically) choosing to have her reproductive organs removed; she could not, however, find a doctor who would agree to perform this procedure (89). At first, this episode seems disconnected from the earlier discussion of the gods, and yet next, we hear that after recognizing the ridiculousness of all this, like a "flash," she had come to recognize a "large, fantastic existence . . . that knew of all [her] terrible troubles," and in so doing, to feel as if she could simply accept things, a feeling as if she were floating in windless, colorless water. As she spoke, Kayo says, her eyes were "piercing" and "passionate," revealing "a deep, complex will with a subdued strength." They also "shone strangely" (90). We should recall here the scene of her childhood illness, in which she felt submerged in water and in which her eyes were pierced with bright light.

A final comment concludes this segment: after this conversation, the protagonist disappeared, and Kayo heard rumors that she had been engaging in "something like" prostitution; she even spoke with people who had seen her standing in the street inviting men to come with her. The narration has repeatedly suggested a spiritual power to the protagonist's sexuality, but the relationship of that quality to her seemingly self-effacing promiscuity has not been fully articulated. One might surmise that engaging in sex with multiple partners is not necessarily enjoyable for this woman in her human form, but that she believes that much like drinking in excess, it mollifies the gods. Yi might be drawing not only on shamanism here but on the idea from medieval Japanese Buddhism that the fact that courtesans have many partners and the fact that they work in inns, places where people lodge only temporarily, are manifestations of the "truth of impermanence."[29] The protagonist's countless sex partners and changes in abode take on a new significance when seen in this light.

This matter is complicated somewhat in the next section, the second to last. Here we finally see the protagonist herself contemplating her own sexual behavior, something that to this point has been only commented on by others. In her last few hours alive, as she drinks, assorted memories flood back to her. Many of them touch on sexuality. She recalls her mother dying of uterine cancer (until this point we had only learned it was cancer), then the woman doctor whom she saw in high school trying to convince her not to have an abortion, and finally the "masochistic excitement" of giving blow jobs to strangers for money. This last, she says, is a feeling reminiscent of "tearing her tongue out from the root with her three fingers as she faced the toilet so long ago" (92). She then adds, "She did not permit intercourse to herself or to these partners. She had rejected reproduction, and she had strictly forbidden herself the act of sexual intercourse and the pleasure derived from it. The only man whom she had allowed intercourse with was Morimoto Ichirō" (92). There is a sharp division in her mind, we see here, between the oral sex that she, in one possible interpretation, is engaging in for the gods and the sexual intercourse she has for her own pleasure with Morimoto. The reasoning is, intercourse has particular value because unlike other sexual acts, it enables people to reproduce, and because of this singularity, it should be shared only with a partner with whom one has a special bond. In this sense, human life and its reproduction, and the sex act itself take on a significance that far exceeds the realm of the ordinary.

Yet when she recalls that when she had long ago spoken to a doctor about having an abortion, she had spoken derisively of the fact that people speak as if they can create life, when in fact they are merely continuing it. What is the meaning of life, she asks? She recollects that on another occasion she had asked Morimoto to have a vasectomy. When he refused, saying that he is careful, she said, "No that's not it," and thought to herself, "he is deluded about something; it is the largest delusion that all human beings fall into, this delusion that all people share, this hallucination" (93). Periodically throughout the story, she speaks disparagingly of the scent of humans. If she believes that the sacredness of human life is a delusion, that reproduction is thus a futile endeavor, then it makes sense for her to reject reproduction.

But if this is the case, why does intercourse remain special in her mind? Does not this act, because she is using it to express a bond with another human (which might be termed "love") — and distinguishing it from other sex which she engages in with men to whom she has not emotional attachment — ground her firmly in the human world? Is whether or not reproduction actually takes place really the issue? Is it not her emotional ties to the human world that prevent her from entering the spiritual world that she has been destined to join? Perhaps her ultimate rejection of Morimoto and thus sexual intercourse is evidence of her desire to respond to such questions in the affirmative, to proclaim finally that all desire that ties us to the worldly must be rejected.

It is important to note that this segment ends with a peaceful image that encourages a spiritual interpretation. Just before the inebriated protagonist slides down under the water in the bath, she recalls the words she heard as the shaman performed a healing ritual on her long ago: "Go out, go out into the water." She does not struggle. Rather she hears the waves hitting the shores of Saishūtō and feels "a peace she has not felt since her birth" (92).

That she is submerged in water here is of significance, because in those scenes in which she seems to have contact with the gods (when she is sick, when she describes her moment of insight to Kayo), she mentions having had illusion of floating in water. Interestingly, this section began with her gazing at a pair of children's sneakers with flowers printed on them, reminiscent of those she owned so long ago. Looking at them, she thinks "that her whole life until this moment had been hinted at by the events of that single day of her childhood when she had mistaken water for a frog" (91). In other words, she had seen as an unwanted encumbrance that which in the end will bring her peace.

This is not all, however. It is important to note that the rendering of this island in its Japanese pronunciation and in katakana rather than in kanji or in its Korean reading — allows it to have an alternate meaning of "the final island." At the same time, the image is womblike; yet it signals also a return to the father, for we recall that the place the protagonist's father has returned to is the very island referred to here, and that the sole memory of safety the protagonist has of her youth is being held by this father. This death, then, is not merely an entrance into the world of the spirits or a return to an abstract site of spiritual comfort, but to two concretely Korean places, that is to say her parents and Chejudo.

The concluding section of the story, focused on Kyōko's perspective, is brief. As she calls a final number in her stepsister's address book, Kyōko sees an image of her stepsister's face in the bath as she found her on the day she found her body. She then notes that the sound she is listening to is the same sound she heard when trying to call her sister from the station before going to her apartment and finding her dead. At last, someone picks up, but at this moment, Kyōko hangs up the phone. One purpose of this ending, I believe, is to bring this story back into the quotidian. This is not to suggest, however, that we should infer that the protagonist is meant to still be of this world: by hanging up the phone, Kyōko is making the decision to learn no more about her sister, and in a sense, releasing not only herself from misery but her stepsister from the worldly. Closing the story with the protagonist sinking under the water, hearing waves lap against the shore, though, certainly would have been more dramatic. I believe the fact that the author chose to include this final section indicates her desire to foreground the tension between two possible interpretations of the woman's death: its significance in a spiritual context and its futility in the ordinary world.

So what are we to make of this sort of depiction of a suicide (she is conscious as her head goes under water) of a young Korean woman in Japan? The character may believe that her death grants her entrance into the spiritual world or into a place of peace, and the narration in the sections not focused on the character may support this view, suggesting that the author wishes to lead us to interpret the character's death in this way. But where do we find ourselves when we step out of the internal dynamics of the story and back into the real world? In other words, what can we make of the Yi Yang-ji's manipulation of shamanism in this story? And what of the rape? The prostitution? The rejection of childbearing?

The contrast with Chong Ch'u-wŏl and Kim Ch'ang-saeng is striking. Those authors surely disparage actual shamanism as performed by practitioners in Osaka; yet Chong adopts images from shamanism and, like Kim, a symbolism from Buddhism in their efforts to find meaning in people's participation in the continuum, or perhaps circle, of human life. In this sense — although Chong is certainly more positive about the connection to the mystery of life that women's reproductive capacity gives them than is Kim — they nonetheless share a view of the process as one of unique possibility. What they have to say is not simply about Koreanness:

I do not mean simply that they see opportunities for their children's generation that they themselves did not have. Rather, they wish to point to the way that their very closeness to the body, a result of their role as providers of food, as bearers of children, and as impoverished physical laborers puts them in proximity to the awesome fact of existence.

In contrast, within this Yi Yang-ji story, the suggestion is that shamanic power and perhaps the Buddhist ideal of impermanence are real, that connection with the gods or the eternal is what enables the protagonist to overcome her own suffering and give meaning to her existence. The narrative, however, is distinctly fictional; as I said at the beginning of my analysis, it draws attention to its constructedness as a narrative. It is not realist per se, but on the other hand, it is not fantastic. It is something more akin to magical realism. Therefore, unlike the works we saw in the last chapter, what it says bears little relation to actual Korean shamanic practice in Japan. The manipulation of shamanism as a literary theme is quite different from those earlier works because bears no relation to the continuation of a distinct Korean community or human reproduction. In fact, the only other Korean characters in this story are the protagonist's parents, one of whom is already absent and the other of whom has already denied her Koreanness when the protagonist first receives her "calling." In addition, the character's ultimate acceptance into the world of the gods (at least in her mind) seems to be dependent on the categorical rejection of reproduction.

The shamanism here, furthermore, is not even of distinctly Korean origin, and it might be said to exorcise Koreanness from Japan rather than healing and thus ensuring the continuity of a community. Indeed, it is possible to read it as a call for the Resident Korean community to self-destruct. The protagonist's masochistic impulses, her refusal to bear children, and ultimately her decision to depart from life emerge not only from a desire to serve the gods, but in a more mundane sense, from her (Resident) Koreanness. We recall that she equates Resident Korean identity with victimization, saying, "if I'm not killed, then am I Japanese?," and thus only through inflicting pain on herself is she able to feel Korean. Because the ultimate expression of her identification as Korean is death, this character could hardly be said to provide a model for Koreans in Japan.

Yet before we jump to such conclusions about this story, we need to consider the fact that symbolically, the death of an ethnic identity found only through valorizing victimization opens possibilities of other ways to live as Korean. There are several aspects in which the narrative is affirmative about holding on to Koreanness. The final place of peace the protagonist finds is the waters around Chejudo; what she ends up being (in one sense) is a "diving maid," an occupation engaged in by many women in Chejudo. On the level of fantasy, then, she ends up grasping for something beyond the national (the gods) and for the national itself (shamanism, diving, Chejudo). In addition, the narrative speaks critically of the Japanized mother, who is killed off with uterine cancer, as if to say that the desire to be assimilated deserves to be punished because it will necessarily result in the obliteration of Koreanness.

Recalling that Yi was obsessed with the *salp'uri* at the time she wrote this story, we can argue that what Yi sought here was not to postulate an equation of Koreanness and femaleness with victimization, but rather to acknowledge the fact that being Korean and female, one would face a certain amount of victimization and that one therefore would need ways to express the pain of that existence. This text, although it bears traces of the realist tradition of earlier Resident Korean writers, is not realistic per se, and if it is on any level "pleasurable," that pleasure comes from the way the text is written, from seeing a portrait of a woman gradually come into focus. If we suspend our disbelief, for a brief moment, we may find ourselves enthralled by the woman's contact with the gods and the way that it has enabled her not only to profoundly affect others but to find peace amid despair. Most readers would be aware that Yi Yang-ji herself developed an interest in shamanism as a consequence of her studying language and dance in South Korea. Although the character may provide no prototype for exploring Resident Korean identity, the author's power of imagination — fuelled by contact with Korean culture — is what is powerful here and what potentially could serve as a model for how to live as a Resident Korean. I think this is too simple a conclusion and that it goes against the sort of reading Yi herself would have hoped for this story. To appreciate "The Diving Maid" as she might have wanted us to, we need instead to sink our teeth into the contradictory, almost paradoxical, pleasure and pain of the text. We need, that is, to hold with us a nameless protagonist who is simultaneously a transcendent shaman and a suicide.

The work *Koku*, to which I now turn, was published first in 1984 but was later reprinted in a volume with "The Diving Maid." In my opinion, it not only further develops motifs that appeared in that story, but is the work that most fully explores the issues that obsessed Yi Yang-ji throughout her career: the relationship of material, physical life and its cultural or perhaps metaphysical meanings.[30] What is the relationship between women's biology and sexuality and their identity/psychology? How do history and culture (language, music, dance) express themselves in our bodies, and how do we then use our bodies to express something beyond what has been programmed into them? What sorts of meanings can we create in this process?

As I said earlier, this piece, which follows a single day in the life of the protagonist, is set in Korea. Interestingly, although its very premise would seem to be the shift in consciousness that comes from a change in location (specifically that of a diasporic woman's return to the country of her origin), the novella centers not on the experience of place, but rather on that of time, as suggested by the title, a classical Japanese term for the divisions of the day, one unit equaling approximately one hundredth of a day, depending on the season. This term was used also in premodern Korea to describe a similar unit of time, although of course the given time referred to in Korea would not have coincided with that in Japan because the "day" being divided was the time between sunrise and sunset, which would have differed according to location.

The very title, we see, harkens back to an age before territories were subsumed as equivalent (but not equal) units (nation-states) under a single system of time. The fact that the day tracked within the story is the first day of the first-person narrator's menstrual period, that one of the objects she has brought with her from Japan is a clock (140), that she uses the same words to denote the tick of her clock and the sound of her breaths (141), that on certain points throughout the day she is unable to read clocks (170, 185), and that one of the two phrases in the text that appears in Korean script is *shigye suri* ("clock repair," indicating that something needs fixing) signify that she has brought a different sense of time with her, that the natural time within her body is at odds with that of the world around her.

The majority of the narrative consists of thoughts and memories of the protagonist, Suni, so although this character moves throughout what is concretely the city of Seoul, the feeling is one of separation between her psyche and the material world. What is even more pronounced, however, is a rift between the narrator's internal self and her body. Mirrors are everywhere, and she often watches her reflection; the story begins and ends with her putting on makeup in the middle of the night, when no one else will see her. The phrase "within my breast" appears repeatedly, as do passages in which she listens to her own voice or even communicates with herself, as in "I smiled at me" (160).[31] At several points, the narrator realizes from the reactions of those around her that she has been talking about something; on one such occasion, she says, "a memory of doing that remained in my mouth" (160). That the story is filled with these sorts of remarks reinforces the sense of the narrator's being out of synch with the world around her and indeed with herself.

The author layers these different sorts of schisms on one another with considerable persistence, to the extent that any reader must feel compelled to ask what their cause might be. The simplest answer to this question is that they derive from the narrator's torment at being unable to become Korean as she had hoped. It is not simply the abstract notion that the narrator has brought a Japanese clock and sense of time with her. In addition, she has two lovers who are in their fifties, twice her age; one is Korean, the other Japanese. The Korean lover, Choi, encouraged her visit there; the other, the Japanese lover, Fujita, is her "patron." She self-consciously compares these men. At one point, she recalls a memory of a conversation with one of them — which, she cannot remember. She says to him that life is all suffering and then whispers under her breath, "the fascism of the first person." They are sitting in a car, and she wants to see whether he has heard, but she does not know which side to turn to because in Korea and Japan, cars drive on opposite sides of the street. She turns her head both ways (199).

More mundane references likewise suggest that the source of Suni's torment is the impossibility of being either Korean or Japanese. The most direct example relates to her inability speak Korean perfectly, as we witness in an outburst by Suni at school. The teacher has the students read aloud; today, like most other days, he intones in Japanese, "Your pronunciation, you should know, is the pronunciation of a Japanese." In her head, she retorts: "Your pronunciation, you should know, is the pronunciation of a Korean." When Suni is called upon to read, she says, "I'm now going to read in the pronunciation of a Japanese. Will this be acceptable?" (162). She then proceeds to lecture him about the fact that she and her fellow students have been raised in a society where they are discriminated against as non-Japanese and where the pressure to assimilate is severe; that they speak with Japanese accents is therefore natural (163).

After this act of bravery, she feels exhilarated; she ignores his lecture about the impropriety of talking back to one's superiors. Yet as in the earlier historical references, the narrative does not dwell long on the state of the teaching of history as subject, but history in a much more abstract sense, probing the question of how history — in the sense of a state of things during a certain time during which people have lived — affects the way they experience their lives. Soon, her thoughts turn to Balnibarbi, a country visited by Gulliver in his travels. In this land, there was a proposal to abolish language and to instead communicate by pointing at "things" (165–66). Could this ever be possible? she muses. She also notes that it was the women of the country who revolted against this proposal. She presumes that Swift had meant this to be a humorous reference to women's garrulousness but wonders if there might be more to it than that (166). I draw attention to this passage not only because Balnibarbi reappears later in the text, but also to show the way that the narration connects ideas about language with those about women and those about "things," which invariably appears in quotation marks in the text. These facts give me reason to believe that the splits in the narrator do not derive only from her particular position between Japan and Korea. ·

The manner in which things appear, for example, suggests that perhaps modernity and capitalism — or at the very least, a heightened aversion to them — are additional sources of the narrator's dissociative tendencies. One might assume that the text would focus on things as commodities, but in fact, outside of the Gulliver references, the only objects in the text that appear as things in quotation marks are her makeup case and clock — bought in Japan four months earlier, just before she came to Korea — and a *kayagŭm* she has owned for ten years. She refers directly to the first two things as "fulfilling the role" they had in Japan (140). The *kayagŭm*, in contrast, at different moments in the text, metamorphoses from an object to a living entity — a "naked woman" (140, 142) and back to a thing that "merely fulfills its role" (185). Clearly things are granted significance, then, for the pleasure they give the user. If there were any doubt of this fact, it disappears in the following passage:

> When I began playing the *kayagŭm*, I suddenly thought about the renowned musician, Uruk. Had Uruk really been a man, I thought, or, I began to turn over in mind, was he a man and also a woman, a woman and also a man? The *kayagŭm* of Uruk's day was made and played completely differently. Yet it was interesting to try to create a sound that approximated his art of combining male and female; wait, I thought as I played, "this sound," or again, after a bit, "no, this sound."
>
> Clearly we are blessed with the benefit of time, I sighed in my breast. The rhythm of the *kokkori*, its beat . . . precisely because people have lived, and transmitted their art, I am able to play the *kayagŭm* like this now. But the benefit of time that I've received, it's fine to have it stop with me. The meaning of "things" emerges through my stance toward those "things" (192).

Although I do not think that such a treatment of things suggests that the author wants to criticize commodity capitalism, I do think that the narrator's desire to acknowledge only the use value and not the exchange value of things is a manifestation of a romantic view of a premodern era in which things and people were not alienated.

Her invocation of Uruk, whom she elsewhere tells us is a famed musician of ancient times known for teaching the arts of "stringed instruments, dancing, and song" to three disciples (196), and presumably initiating these traditions, gives weight to such an interpretation. Investigating further, we find that in fact Uruk was supposed to have created his music in response to a certain king (although which king and which country is unclear), who, lamenting the fact that the people of different countries spoke different languages, had asked Uruk whether there was not some way that a single system of "voice sound" could not be formulated.[32] These arts, then, were intended to serve as a form of communication that could overcome linguistic barriers, not unlike that proposed by the scholars of Balnibarbi. I need to revise what I said a moment ago, for it now seems that the unalienated state to which she gestures is not one of an actual precapitalist age, but of a mythical time when gods came into people allowing them to animate things (instruments, their bodies) and to communicate with one another without language.

Also noteworthy is that when Suni dances, as she does when she plays the *kayagŭm*, she muses about Uruk's gender, concluding that the gods "surely would prefer to descend dizzily into the body of one possessing a lascivious and alluring double sexuality" (197). That Suni herself wishes to return to a state in which such things are possible is suggested at one point when, after wondering whether it might not behoove her to wear a lipstick of a studentlike color, something with an orange tone rather than the red she is wearing, she thinks, "but the gods should like mouths shining a bewitching bright red" (159). What does it mean that Suni insists that this mythical character who has the ability to connect to both gods and other people through art must necessarily have been not only highly sexual but both male and female at the same time?[33] It seems as if she sees biological sex itself as a form of alienation that has not always existed, something that hinders human communication.

Indeed, being female seems to be another source of Suni's feelings of fragmentation. Although the majority of the text is in the first person, in five or six instances, the narration shifts to *onna* (the woman). The word *onna* is not the neutral third person, but rather a term with sexual nuance. In the first of these scenes, one that sets the terms for the others, she perceives her *kayagŭm*, which hangs on her wall, as the body of a naked woman. She has noticed a broken string on the instrument; she feels dizzy; she grows annoyed with the ticking of the clock. And then:

> The fifth, the eighth, the second — I haphazardly cut the strings. I could not hear my own spiraling voice or the sound of the second hand. I look intently at the two blades in my hand. I look intently at the strings. Each time I use the strength of my hands, the grain of the wood of the instrument blurs.
>
> A woman holding scissors. . . . The woman's body was hot. Each time she cut a string, she felt a brief ripple in her vagina. Her face was flushed, and she breathed quickened rough breaths over the naked body of the woman. . . . [looking in the mirror] I looked back at that woman's face. I also heard the rhythm of her breaths. Tick, tick, tick, she inhaled on a count of three, and tick, tick, tick, tick, tick, tick, she exhaled at six. I listen carefully to the woman's breaths. The woman listens carefully to my breaths. (141)

We see in this citation that it is precisely in the moment of a masochistic sexual pleasure, in the cutting the strings of what she sees as the naked body of a woman, as she herself is now also referred to as "the woman," that the splitting in the self comes to its climax. At the same time, furthermore, the ticking of the clock infiltrates her body, displacing its natural rhythms, or, if we look at it from a different perspective, putting them precisely in synch with the clock.

What are we to make of the relationship of women's specific biology to time, and what does this indicate about the divide between the earlier unalienated world and the present one? I hasten to recall that since in the mythical premodern it was implied that the ideal was dual sexuality, modern men might be experiencing the same sort of split as well. The implication here is not that women are natural and premodern and men unnatural and modern; nor is it the reverse. It was women, we recall, who rebelled against the Balnibarbi language.

The ideas being developed here are not simply about men and women, however. I want to reiterate that *onna* is a specifically sexualized term often used in a derogatory way. In contrast to the writers of the last chapter, Yi Yang-ji, here as in "The Diving Maid," rejects childbearing. As she menstruates, Suni notes happily that this signals the disabling of reproduction (165). On another occasion, when she compares her Korean and Japanese lovers, she says Choi, the Korean, is "better" because he has fewer children and got a vasectomy earlier in life. The real, remembered, and imagined sexual pleasure in the text is nonproductive: masturbation, or sex with these men.

Suni speaks disparagingly of pregnant women too. The daughter-in-law of the household in which she is boarding is pregnant, and upon hearing her yelling at a girl who serves as a maid there,[34] Suni quips that it must have been specifically pregnant women who rebelled against the abolition of language in Balnibarbi (181). What is it, though, that makes her think that pregnant women in particular would want language as it exists, national languages that divide people from each other? Elsewhere she notes that she has seen many pregnant women in her neighborhood, and that the number of children seems to be growing all the time (178). This neighborhood is one in the midst of change, many of its houses and shops to be demolished and redeveloped by a large company. It therefore seems to me that Suni sees reproduction and economic development as somehow intertwined.

The division between such women and Suni, who is an *onna*, a sexual woman, a mistress and therefore outside the family system, is stark. The women in her stories are "whores" to the "madonnas" of Ikaino. Put crudely, they receive financial support in exchange for engaging in sex with Japanese men: Fujita, not Choi, is her patron. On a simple level, it is not so surprising for a woman in 1980s Japan to criticize reproduction. Motherhood had long been seen as an imperative for all women by society and state, and Japanese women authors had been challenging this presumption, issuing works that explored nonreproductive sexuality at least since the 1960s. Yet Yi Yang-ji's success among mainstream Japanese readers was at least in part dependent on the fact that her literature addressed *ethnic* identity along with sexuality, and thus, as in the case of "The Diving Maid," many would have interpreted a repudiation of childbearing as a refusal to ensure the historical continuity of the (Resident) Korean community.[35]

Yet on the basis of both the insights gained from that earlier story, and from what she says about these matters in *Koku* itself, this is too simple a reading. She seems to be criticizing these women for accepting their role in the endless drive for progress, and at the same time, as the reference to Balnibarbi indicates, for buying into the modern world in which language and time have been made into equivalent but unequal units. This does not constitute a direct political criticism, but rather a longing for a world uncontaminated by an exponentially expansive desire for progress.

This fact becomes clearer when we examine two places where she directly refers to "history." First, she says: "[ovulation, which marks time] gives this me, this individual body, history, and marks off all of existence in this moment, in this very moment" (188). Oddly, menstruation, the disabling of reproduction, connects the individual person with history. What does she mean by history, though? One hint appears in a dream Suni has early in the narrative. In it she speaks to a man working in a clock repair shop (he appears as an actual person later, his shop in the neighborhood to be demolished for the sake of progress):

> Raising my voice, I said to the man, "A man once declared that the world lies only in the realm of thought."
> The man moved his mouth slightly.

"Before long, this world won't exist. This thinking 'I' won't exist at all."

"But what will happen to history? The only thing that is certain is the existence of time. For example. . . ."

My voice softened slightly. I blushed, and suppressing my embarrassment, I raised my voice again.

"Japanese imperialism ruled Korea for 36 years. And now, this peninsula is divided in two. 1910, 1945, 1950, 1965, and now 198X. What about it? Just try the subtraction.

The man, not moving even slightly, continued to stare at the watch.

"You're angry about something."

Like a wheedling child, I won't leave the window.

"Look at the watch in front of you. It's moving. It's still moving." (152–53)

It seems that history is time, and time is that which exists outside the realm of consciousness, something we might refer to as the "real." Clearly, obsessed as she might be with the thoughts spinning in her own head, the narrator does not believe that what is unknowable outside of language does not, or might as well not, exist. Menstruation connects her with the real because it brings into her flesh evidence that something meaningful, time, perdures beyond her own perception. It is only through her body's connection with time that she can conceive of history.

Is the implication that menstruating women experience loss (of an egg, of blood) as they mark time, whereas pregnant women misperceive time as growth, as progress? It seems pertinent that Suni asks the man to subtract to make sense of the advancement of time. Later in the same dream, Suni sits in a bathroom where there is a sign saying, "Have STD checkups regularly"; next she says aloud what seem to be exam questions about South Korea's development, including one asking for analysis of Resident Koreans' role in this process. Finally, a naked woman approaches her, saying that the signs encouraging the prevention of STDs attest to Korea's "progressiveness" (153). In this case, not only are we led to believe that Yi does indeed want to say something about not progress generally, but Korea's particular place in it. But what? Are Koreans prostituting their souls to become modern and thus in need of regular checkups? Or are Resident Koreans like Suni the promiscuous ones, caught as they are between intimacy with Japan and Korea?

In a brief analysis of this text, the author Nakagami Kenji focuses on the self-destructiveness evident in the portrayal of the *kayagŭm* as the body of a woman — "herself and Korean women." He sees her depiction of "the *kayagŭm* that cannot stop singing the tale of *han* [grief, melancholy, resentment]" as a "counteroffensive" against the more common, best-selling stories of Resident Koreans throwing off their Japaneseness and embracing their homeland.[36] He implies that her focus on the animate aspect of what seems to be a tool (the instrument) in fact reflects her refusal to be made into a tool of the nation-state. Kawamura Minato, on the other hand, focusing on the perception of time, not surprisingly describes the novella as having "made into a literary work the 'gap'" (or perhaps lag, or displacement) experienced by Resident Koreans when they go to South Korea.[37] He reads Suni as desiring to escape from menstruation, which depresses her, and likens this to a broader desire to escape from being Resident Korean. He then goes on to say that the desire to escape from being Resident Korean and from being a woman runs throughout her works.[38] It is based on this supposition that he argues (as I cited before) that Yi had determined that identity was an impossibility.

There is another interesting element of the debate between Kawamura and Nakagami that I need to mention here. Kawamura's article set off the spat; in it, he actually not only analyzes Yi's work but comments on a book issued simultaneously in Japan and Korea entitled *Monogatari Sōru* [Seoul Through Tales], a volume of photographs that also included a novella by Nakagami. I want to draw attention to only one element of Kawamura's lengthy analysis of this book: he criticizes Nakagami's focus on Korean back streets as being a representation of Korea as a feminine space. He goes on: "That is, for Nakagami Kenji, Korea is on the one hand the tale of 'victimized' [literally, attacked or raped] women — from comfort women to *kisaeng* to those who come to Japan to be prostitutes; on the other hand, it contains within it the *delusion* of the author himself being 'victimized' by Korea (or Japan) as woman."[39] He likewise complains that the photographer's perspective is that of a man viewing a woman, and then situates the volume in the context of the Japanese tendency to represent itself as male to Asia the female.[40] Nakagami's response to this is curt, even dismissive, particularly of Kawamura's implication that the camera is being used as a violent, male machine. He argues that by virtue of the fact that it contains within its body film that will give birth to photographs, it is in fact an inherently female tool. Yi Yang-ji's *Koku*, he then adds, would not have been possible without the existence of this visual technology, for its very style is "cinematic."[41] Absurd though I find these arguments, they are crucial to understanding the milieu in which Yi's work was being read. Although they do not focus on the fact that Yi Yang-ji herself is playing into, or perhaps even glorifying, the image of the Korean woman as object of sexual desire, this fact clearly had a role in the popularity of her work.

Nonetheless, I think Kawamura is simply wrong to think that Yi Yang-ji or her characters desired an "escape" from menstruation, womanhood, and Resident Koreanness. *Koku* certainly does narrate the difficulties faced by a diasporic daughter on her return to her homeland and is obsessed with women's limited choices in life. It is, on some level, a song of lamentation of that fate. That it does not propose a simple model of identity that Resident Koreans or women might take up, giving them the self-confidence and energy to challenge the discrimination and victimization they face, does not mean it is socially unaware. The story forces its readers to question the assumption that economic progress is good, and that good women become mothers. It does not suggest concrete strategies for changing the world, and it does at times seem to slip into an unrealistic utopian longing, particularly when it proposes that what appears to be self-destructive behavior is in fact a sign of communication with the gods. Yet at the same time, the story recounts the difficulties not only of being Zainichi Korean or female but of being human. The despair in Yi's work is most often tempered with joy—joy in the pursuit of real experiences, in the belief that through art, through music and dance, but perhaps even through literature, people might be able to touch what lies beyond their own, small existence. Yet art is important not only in a spiritual but in an utterly mundane sense: the arts may gain people entrance to the eternal realm of the gods, where time ticks annoyingly no more, but it also allows them to live eternally in the human world. Words, after all, continue to breathe long after their authors are gone.[42]

6

Private Traumas, Public Therapies

In the 1990s, Japan sank into a deep malaise. The economy, which had seemed indefatigable, began to slump. Unimaginable crimes terrorized the public: members of a cult released deadly gas in the Tokyo subway, and a fourteen-year-old boy murdered and beheaded an even younger child. If this were not enough, people began to rediscover long-buried war atrocities, notably the sexual enslavement of women in the comfort system, in part because the fiftieth anniversary of Japan's defeat prompted reconsideration of the Pacific War, but also, more importantly, because in 1991 former comfort woman Kim Haksun had bravely stepped forward to file a lawsuit against the Japanese government.

In this era of uneasiness, the Japanese media discovered rape, incest, and child abuse. In 1993, cartoonist Uchida Shungiku's *Fazaa fakaa* [Father Fucker], about Uchida's rape by her stepfather, became a best seller. In 1996, a TV miniseries focused on the rape and subsequent psychological turmoil of a young woman played by one of the country's trendiest actresses.[1] In 2000, another TV series, *Eien no ko* [Eternal Children], based on Tendo Arata's 1999 novel about three survivors of physical abuse, became one of the year's hits. Finally, and most pertinent for us here, Yū Miri became the first Zainichi author to both win both critical acclaim and phenomenal popularity — for work focusing on sexual abuse.

Although Yū's literature was not directly inspired by the discourse of comfort women (or vice versa), I believe that consciously or unconsciously, they fed off similar arguments — or perhaps simply benefited from an audience exposed to a shared body of ideas. At any rate, we need to read Yū's work together with debates surrounding the comfort women to understand the complicated process engendering a momentous shift in the narratives of Resident Korean ethnicity in this decade.

In the previous two chapters, we saw that as early as the 1970s, and certainly in the 1980s, women authors had described their oppression as Koreans as a gendered experience. They rejected the use of the metaphor of the victimized woman's body to stand in for that of the nation. They described how living in doubly discriminated-against bodies shaped their emotional lives and their political priorities. As we also saw that Resident Korean grassroots struggles did not recognize their difference, and so women often chose not to participate. In the 1990s, at long last, this tension between literature and politics began to dissolve.

We see how they have come together when we examine the way that each draws on a single concept: trauma. In 1997, a translation of Judith Herman's landmark book *Trauma and Recovery* appeared, and a stream of Japanese books on the topic followed.[2] Even if they had not read these books, most in Japan would have become familiar with the subject they introduce, for it found its way into magazines, newspapers, and television programs like those I mentioned above.

From its inception, the psychiatric concept of trauma had both individual and social dimensions. As Herman notes in *Trauma and Recovery*, clinicians developed the term in the 1980s, when they began to observe that the symptoms suffered by rape victims bore a similarity to the syndrome found among Vietnam veterans, and the diagnosis became official when included in the manual of the American Psychiatric Association in 1980 under the diagnosis of "posttraumatic stress disorder" (PTSD).[3] Physical and psychic pain are only experienced by individual people, and psychiatric diagnoses can only be given to them as well.

When the source of trauma is a common historical event such as war, the consequence is different for its survivors. Although they may benefit from feeling that they are not alone, at the same time, their existence may have ramifications for the society as a whole. The Vietnam War clearly fits this bill. Implicitly, the war itself has been seen as a kind of trauma and the rents in American social fabric, as symptoms of PTSD. Then, in the best of cases, members of society may feel a responsibility to do what they can to help the victims heal; perhaps they may even come to see it as essential for the recuperation of community.[4] In the case of Vietnam, this might entail working for political change. Although rape clearly is not such a shared trauma, Herman takes pains to show that it is an equally social and political issue.

It is natural, therefore, that the Japanese public should come to connect these different kinds of trauma — in Herman's words, the "common atrocities" of "the experiences of domestic and sexual life, the traditional sphere of women" and "the experiences of war and political life, the traditional sphere of men."[5] And so it makes sense, too, that they should link Yū and the comfort women, although no one did so explicitly until 1997. In that year, Yū won the Akutagawa prize, the interest in trauma peaked, controversy over the inclusion of comfort women in middle school history texts raged, and finally, an odd series of events led Yū to state her position on comfort women.

Yū was already on her way to fame in the early 1990s. Although she was just in her twenties and a high school dropout, she became a stage actress and then a playwright, in 1993 winning the Kishida prize for dramatic works. By the mid-1990s, she had won several awards for her fiction and had begun to appear in mainstream magazines, and even on *News 23*, a late-night television news program run by a venerable old lefty.

After winning the Akutagawa prize in 1997, her exploits began to show up in gossip rags and her fashion-clad form in women's magazines. She even made it into the *New York Times*, with others said to have made it for being "different." She published an autobiography, telling how she had attempted suicide, shoplifted, dropped out of school. She expressed controversial views about the Kobe murders. Then, at the end of the decade and into the twenty-first century, Yū began to put her life to the page. She began with *Inochi* [Life], in which she told of bearing the son of her married lover and of joining households with a friend dying of cancer and raising the child together, and she continued by narrating the trials of single parenthood. In preparation for writing about her grandfather, who had been a marathon runner, she ran one too. The Supreme Court upheld a decision to stop publication of one of her books for "violating the pride and privacy" of the facially disfigured woman whom Yū took as a model for her main character.[6] At the very same moment, the movie version of *Life* opened at theaters across Japan. In other words, Yū became a phenomenon.

Among the factors catapulting her into stardom is her adroitness at depicting the turmoil of growing up in a dysfunctional family. Although she herself demurs when referred to as a Resident Korean author, literary figures Ri Kaisei and Takeda Seiji have wished to claim her, and they have insisted that the families she depicts are Korean. This misses precisely what is interesting in her early work: she makes the ethnicity of these families ambiguous, even though they are modeled on her own. She also gives the characters names that, unlike most Korean names but like Yū Miri, can be read as Korean or Japanese.[7] Their employment, too, gives pause. The fathers often work in pachinko parlors, as did Yū's father and as do many Resident Koreans. And yet there is no direct mention of colonialism, war, or ethnic discrimination.[8]

The point is not that she wants to deny her Koreanness: she openly acknowledges her heritage and citizenship (Republic of Korea) and uses the Korean pronunciation of her name. The ambiguity enables her to suggest that Resident Korean family is not unique, but rather shares much with other families in Japan in the late twentieth century. What they share is not dysfunctionality, broadly speaking, but a particular domestic pattern in which women face undue suffering, particularly in the form of father-daughter incest. In *Mizube no yurikago* [Cradle by the Sea], her autobiography, Yū recounts having been molested on different occasions (although not by her father). Yet critics recoil at mentioning incest, perhaps out of respect for her privacy, but at the cost of overlooking the central point of much of her work.

Interestingly, Yū even says she has lived through "trauma." What she refers to, however, is not sexual abuse, nor even discrimination faced because she is Korean (and thus implicitly related to legacies of the war). Rather, she identifies as traumatic being raised by an aunt for the first three years of her life. She says, "I read in a psychology book that children who have a distant relationship with their mothers before the age of three often develop psychological problems."[9] Yū too seems to want to keep some small bit of her life private. Or perhaps she merely thinks that such things are better conveyed in literary form.

Indeed, in the first work I will examine, *Green Bench*, issued in print form in 1994 and performed in 1992 and 1995, the focus at first appears to be not sexual trauma but mother-daughter conflict. The mother is controlling. In particular, she has encouraged, even coerced, her children to study hard to gain admission to certain schools, to wear certain clothes, to play certain sports, and so on, because she believes these will enable them to make their way into Japan's (upper) middle class. In other words, she is a perfect *kyōiku mama*, or education mom, and as such, a paragon of contemporary Japanese motherhood. However, Yū takes the stereotype to a parodic extreme. If this mother is a tangible, visible source of her daughter's woes, the father, although he never appears on stage, casts as dark a shadow over all that happens. As in so many of Yū's works, the daughter has been raped by her father.

The coexistence in the play of incest and an extreme version of the perfect Japanese family is no coincidence. In order for us to appreciate why and how she makes this connection, we should take a closer look at Japanese discourse on trauma. To begin with, it has been paired with a notion that has everything to do with family, that of "adult children," or, in common parlance, the "AC." Although in the United States PTSD is probably better known, in Japan it was "AC" that caught on. Soon after President Clinton referred to himself as an adult child in an interview in an American women's magazine in 1995, a flood of books on the topic appeared, selling upward of 100,000 copies.[10] Numerous prominent public figures, from former prime minister Hashimoto Ryūtarō to the wildly popular singer Misora Hibari and the bestselling author Murakami Haruki, were identified as AC. So was Yū Miri.

The term is less precise than that of PTSD, and less stigmatizing. In the United States, the term refers to adult children of alcoholics and occasionally of "dysfunctional families." A wide range of characteristics are associated with this condition, but some of the more common include perfectionism, excessive seriousness, a strong desire for affirmation from others, and an intense belief in one's "difference" from others that leads to difficulty in developing intimate relationships.[11]

Important for understanding Yū's work, though, is not just that she is singled out as an adult child, but that in this respect she is seen as representative of a whole generation of Japanese. Indeed prominent psychologist Saitō Satoru and others have identified a "Japanese-type AC." They grew up not with alcoholism, but with a workaholic father and a mother who compensated for the father's absence by becoming a *kyōiku mama*. As another leading authority on AC, Nobuta Sayoko, points out, this is the model family that supported Japan's economic miracle.[12]

Although Yū Miri's background far from fits this profile, as we shall soon see, in *Green Bench* she clearly connects this pervasive ideology of family with women's sexual victimization. The setting for the entire play is on and around a tennis court of a fancy girls' school. Only four characters appear: Taiko, age fifty, her daughter Yōko, twenty-one, her son Akira, seventeen, and her lover, Taniguchi, twenty-five. The father is notably absent. As in many of Yū's works, these factors reproduce for the audience the characters' sense of being hemmed in by circumstance. They also compel us to attach greater significance to the setting and to the emotional tangles of these characters' lives. Of these tangles there are a lot: over the course of the play's three acts, we discover Taiko has left Yōko and Akira's father many years earlier and moved in with another man. Her lover, however, left her recently, and she has been plotting to reunite the family. Her plan is to build a house on some land that their father had bought, again many years in the past. This isn't all: she is dating a man her daughter's age, and Yōko, a man her mother's age.

At the opening of the first act, the siblings play tennis in blistering heat while the mother narrates their game as if they were the crown prince and Princess Michiko (who, at the time the play was written, were emperor and empress) and serves them a lunch that is beginning to rot in the bright sun. From here on, we witness Taiko getting stranger and stranger. In the middle act, she tries to set up Yōko, whom she has made up to look like herself, with her lover Taniguchi; by the end, Taiko and Yōko beat Taniguchi to death with a tennis racket.

From the moment the play opens, it is clear that Taiko, the mother, is at the very least eccentric: her hair is curly like a "French doll," she wears a yellowed white dress from her younger days, and she swings her feet like a child as she sits on a green bench watching her children on the tennis court (6). As mentioned, she narrates this game as if the players are Princess Michiko and the crown prince. This is significant because Michiko was the first commoner to enter the imperial family, and her romance with the emperor-to-be was publicized widely in the 1950s, as were the births of her children, and imperial family life more generally. Thus they were touted in the media as the model Japanese family, and their home, filled with (Japan-made) appliances, became the exemplar of what a home should be.[13] And where should Michiko and the crown prince have met but on a tennis court. Thus Taiko's obsession reveals her class aspirations — and, whether or not we read her character as Resident Korean, aspirations toward a particular kind of Japaneseness as well. We witness her desire for the material goods of middle-class home life; she says that when they build the house, she wants a dishwasher, central floor heating, a bath that can be set by telephone, and so on (30). She is also overly concerned with educational status: she derides Yōko when learning that her lover has only graduated from high school, saying, "men should go to Gakushūin [which has traditionally been the school of the imperial family], women to Sacred Heart" (40).

Taiko of course perfectly fits the profile of the family said to produce the Japan-type AC, but she is not just that. She is also aware of or even abettor to her daughter's abuse.

Here is the first we hear of Yōko 's childhood victimization:

TAIKO: *(smiling)* Do you remember Rika, who lived next door?

YŌKO: Hmmm? Next door? (Pause.) You mean Rika, the girl I was friends with in kindergarten, the landlord's daughter?

TAIKO: Yes. That Rika. Well, her father hugged you a lot, didn't he? It was a strange sort of hug, wasn't it?

Yōko is overcome with nausea, as if sucked into a deep whirl-pool, . . . everything spinning.

TAIKO: He touched your body all over . . . (with a kind laugh). Maybe I'll bring a suit against him.

YŌKO: Forget it . . . it's ancient history.

TAIKO: *(smiling)* I used to give you medicine when you went over to Rika's to play, do you remember? Do you know what that medicine was?

YŌKO: . . . I have no idea.

TAIKO: *(giggling)* It was the pill!

     Yōko suddenly feels like vomiting.

TAIKO: *(her expression stiffening)* Yōko, you can't be . . .

     Taiko glares at Yōko's abdomen.

YŌKO: *(blurting it out)* Mom! Stop thinking such strange things. If I were pregnant, I wouldn't be playing tennis, would I? (60–61)

If the abuse is in itself alarming, the revelation of Taiko's complicity is more so, and Yōko's nausea intensifies when she learns of it. How, we wonder, could a mother be so callous as to collude in her child's abuse rather than attempting to prevent it, or to suggest that she (and not that daughter) might take such a case to court at this late date? But she seems not vindictive, but entirely lacking in social or moral standards: not only did she feed birth-control pills to a five-year-old, but she smiles and laughs throughout.

Bit by bit, the dialogue brings us to see the reason that Taiko has treated her daughter this way. At the end of the first act, just before Taniguchi arrives, as Taiko begins making her daughter up to look like herself, drawing on wrinkles, she says, "When you were born you absorbed all my color [*iro*, which also means "sexual appeal"]. That's how I became ashen like this. (*Giggling ruefully*) I broke in two. Yōko, you grew and grew, stealing my nutrients like a parasite, stealing away the woman in me" (90–91). Taiko blames her daughter for her own loss of youthful sexuality. We see now why she gave Yōko the pill: she insisted on seeing her as an adult.

Specifically, she has seen her from childhood not as a girl but as a woman competing for the same men: it is implied that Yōko and her father had a sexual relationship, and that Taiko, rather than being angry at her husband, was jealous of her daughter. The clearest suggestion of this incest comes straight from Yōko, when she is speaking with her brother:

YŌKO: *(As if delirious with fever)* Every night, when I closed my eyes, a horse's neigh stuck in my head like a cloud of yellow smoke, and I couldn't sleep.

     That night, I was wearing a white nightie; Dad, Dad, what color pajamas could he have been wearing? Oh, I can't remember. I always slept next to Dad, but Mom? Mom was asleep. But later she woke up. Then she was still sleeping . . .

(Akira stares intently at Yōko's mouth as he listens to her tale of a horse continuing like a dark tide.)

YŌKO: I was naked, and freezing, and terribly embarrassed.

Somewhere, far away — when I think of it — I heard the neigh of a yellow horse, giving me pain in my chest.

The horse, in order to escape from me, ran away in the rain, and then was swallowed up by the darkness and rain.

(Breathing hard as if in pain) I . . . I . . . (135–36)

Note that the mother is again present and passive: she is asleep at the very moment she could have protected her daughter. This reads like a harrowing narration of abuse, but the stage directions (or commentary?) tell us that Akira has discovered that Yōko "only truly loves their father," and that this fills him with sadness (136–37).

But how could that be? The above passage has delirium, fever, cold, embarrassment, and pain, but no joy. Are we really supposed to believe that "love" is what Yōko feels for her father? Is their mutual love what Taiko envies? Here I cannot help recalling the following passage from Yū's autobiographical *Cradle by the Sea*:

"This girl, she's such a Daddy's girl," my mother said grumpily.

My mother never peeked at my diary. I despised my father so much and yet . . . I had thought that my mother read my diary every time I went out. I suppose you could say I was sorely disappointed that she hadn't. If she'd had any interest in me, she would have. I had thought that my Mom had read what I was hiding in my heart and was carefully guarding it in her own breast. But she didn't have the slightest care for the raw-smelling pain in my heart.[14]

Of courses this play is fiction, and its details need not match Yū's narrative of her own life. Still, the stage directions indicate that Yōko feels revulsion, while at the same time Akira senses how much she loves her father.

Perhaps these are not mutually exclusive feelings: Yōko's conscious mind may love even as her body responds with disgust. Tracking horse imagery in the play, we find further evidence of contradictions in Yōko's emotions. Horses first appear to have little meaning. When Yōko tells of her plans to marry her lover, Akira says, "I'm sure dad will be disappointed," and she retorts that they would get along, because they both like to bet on the horses (71). The next mention of horses comes only a few pages later: Yōko recalls a dream she had the night her mother left her father, taking Yōko and Akira with her. In this dream, a large black horse walks slowly, and although it is sunny, it is drenched with rain. She then says in a shaky voice, "I threw my arms around the horse and clung to it even though I did not know whether I should love this horse or hate it" (77). Alone, this too is opaque. However, by the time the audience hears Yōko using the metaphor of a horse to confess of her father's abuse, she has already associated them with her father and her lover and a confused jumble of love and hate.

Significantly, the horses extend even into Taiko's lines, when she says that she saw when Yōko's father "mounted [Yōko] like a horse." Taiko follows this observation with an assertion that she is not jealous of Yōko (148). No longer can anyone hold on to the illusion that Yōko had imagined her abuse.

If Taiko is still defensive at this point, how is it that the play ends with Yōko and Taiko joining together to beat Taiko's young lover to death with a tennis racket? To understand, we need to identify what is parallel between the relationships of Yōko and her lover and Taniguchi and Taiko. We have seen that Yōko suffers from "repetition compulsion," reproducing certain behaviors with her much older lover, a replacement father, in "an attempt to relive and master the overwhelming feelings of the traumatic moment."[15] We soon learn that Taniguchi similarly uses the much older Taiko to try to create a more comfortable ending with a mother figure. Accused of taking advantage of Taiko, he denies it, saying he is "nursing her back to health." She so resembles his mother just before her death, he says. His father died when he was a child, and he and his mother were like lovers: he called her by her name and complimented her on her looks. Before she died, however, she was left disfigured by illness, and he made the mistake of answering her honestly when she asked how she looked, saying, "you look ugly." He now wishes he had simply said, "you look quite pale" (139–44).

Finally, we witness a scene in which Yōko and Taiko simultaneously realize that they are stuck in such similar relationships. A strange stream of speech issues from Taiko's mouth just after she admits that she saw Yōko's father "mounting her like a horse." She says she is like Princess Michiko, that Michiko plays tennis well, that her dress is like Yōko's white nightie, that Yōko's father will not be able to tell them apart, and so on (149). Her disturbing and seemingly endless prattle is finally interrupted when Taniguchi tells Yōko that when Taiko recently met with her father, he reported that he was planning to get married to someone else. Yōko, we are told, pales (152). Taiko's speech has deteriorated to unconnected words; Taniguchi approaches her, strokes her hair, and says, "You look quite pale," just the phrase, we recall, that he wished he had said to his mother before she died (153). As a result, both Yōko and Taiko become aware of being trapped in the dynamic of repetition compulsion.

It is not long before Yōko and her mother beat Taniguchi to death with a tennis racket (154–55). In the final very brief act (approximately two pages long), Yōko "feels as if she is soaking in the warm blood of her mother's womb," and both she and her mother smile as they bury Taniguchi "with identical motions" while Akira calls the police (160). Yōko and Taiko begin to play tennis, each exactly mirroring the other's expression. The curtain falls (161). In contrast to the glaring sun and unbearable heat of most of the play, the stage is lit with soft moonlight; there is an image, bleached bluish in the moonlight, of Taiko's fantasy of a garden at the family house, filled with flowers of every color (159). Thus the murder seems to have brought them contentment.

It is not at all obvious, however, how we are to read this sudden reconciliation or why they choose Taniguchi as their victim. Although at one point in the play Taniguchi does force an unwanted kiss on Yōko, he is not really a double of the father, and we cannot see them both as abstract men, or even abstract abusers, as we can in the next work of Yū's I examine. The sexual abuse of girls may make them angry, but what makes them livid is recognizing that they are thoughtlessly participating in the reproduction of incestuous desires and fantasies. Yōko pales when she learns that her father will be remarrying; Taiko's face "contorts with fear" when she learns that Taniguchi is attracted to her because she resembles his mother in her illness (140). In this sense, it seems that it is the pervasive influence of incestual sexuality — in which women are objects of desire only as nubile youths or maternal figures — that they wish to destroy.

It is pertinent, however, that the narrative ends not only with this killing but with the fantasy of reconciliation between mother and daughter. Yū speaks of her writing as a form of healing and the trauma she identifies in her own life is her mother's neglect, and in particular, being sent, when she was a toddler, to live with an aunt. In this play, the neglect takes the form of collaboration in abuse through passivity. At the end of the play, both women have the appearance of aged women, because Taiko has drawn wrinkles on Yōko's face. This detail makes me want to add to my interpretation of the ending. What ultimately brings these women to beat Taniguchi and allows them to come to a reconciliation is their recognition not only of their victimization within cycles of incest, but of something much broader: their victimization as women in a society in which women get access to power only through physical attractiveness to men — or as mothers.

By examining the mother's responsibility for her daughter's victimization, this play acknowledges that women have a role in the reproduction of their oppression within the family structure. The recovery from incestual trauma thus depends on the reconciliation of mother and daughter and their recognition of this fact. As a consequence, it proposes that not only men but women must change if the cycles of maltreatment are to cease. They have to stop playing the roles they are cast in.

The family structure she satirizes here is the very one that is said to have produced Japanese-style adult children. The daughter, however, is also a trauma survivor. Interestingly, such distinctions would likely be overlooked, in part because of Saitō Satoru, who has been the most ardent introducer of adult children to Japan. Although he acknowledges that AC began as a notion from a "supermarket rack book," he argues that when severe, adult children's symptoms overlap significantly with complex PTSD (a diagnosis proposed by Herman and others to refer to the condition seen in those who have suffered ongoing trauma, such as child abuse).[16] He prefers to use the term AC, however, because it a vague layman's term and thus does not scare people away; if they do not see AC as stigmatizing, they will be more likely to identify as such and to seek help.

In Japan there has been great reluctance, Saitō and two colleagues observe, to address abuse, despite the fact that "there is not a single child in the average Japanese family who has never been abused."[17] They argue that this is because the group has taken precedence over the individual person. If they seem to be lapsing into essentialism, they then go on to try to historicize: they see the origins of this tendency in the ideology of the emperor system, and in the failure, at the end of the war, to hold the emperor responsible.

In this sense, they find the legacy of war responsible for the current situation: As a consequence of these failures, Saito's colleague suggests, "Japan is dragging along PTSD from a war that happened more than fifty years ago." After the war, Japan may have adopted a "modern" constitution (respecting the rights of individual citizens, and particularly women and children, he implies), but the people did not change so quickly.[18]

Interestingly, similar notions found their way into the mainstream press. A prominent news magazine, for example, called the following statement by author Murakami Haruki an "AC declaration": My father's experience in China "must be a trauma for him. So it's a trauma for me as well. We don't get on well. Perhaps that is why I can't have children."[19] And whose picture should appear beside his but Yū Miri's. The caption reads: "Murakami Haruki and Yū Miri. The two have different literary styles, but each bears the effects of 'trauma.' It might even be said that they have made the 'emotional scar' the theme of all of their fiction."[20] There is no mention of the source of Yū's trauma, but the elision suggests to the reader that the war is the cause of her troubles as well.

In a separate article, another authority on AC, Nobuta Sayoko, finds fault not only in lack of resolution of war responsibility, but the whole of Japanese modernity. Since the Meiji period, she notes, the family has "conformed to the values of the state, and functioned as its tentacles [literally, fingers]. I call this a structure of concentric circles."[21] This social system has perdured because Japan's citizens continue to believe that they are protected by the state. They saw it as proper to subordinate their own needs as individual people for those of Japan as a whole, and in so doing, provided "the very energy for capitalist development."[22] The family that sustained such development was of a piece. It may have seemed kind but the needs of its members were subordinated to those of the father (much like the state). Although this family was oppressive, and although the father's power was reinforced by the threat of violence, few rose to challenge it. With the bursting of the economic bubble, however, the system began to crumble. People have begun to call everything into question, thus the much-touted collapse of the family and the interest in such concepts as the adult child.[23]

Reading the play through this lens encourages us to understand Taiko's collusion in her daughter's sexual abuse as the result of blind adherence to a certain model of family, just as is her more commonplace obsession with her children's achievement. It also enables us to see the mother's fixation on keeping up with the royals with greater clarity, as a jab at the way the imperial family has been used to instill a national ideology of a (consuming, striving) domestic unit in the postwar era.[24]

My convictions about what Yū Miri wants to say about the royals are buttressed by other such references elsewhere. In an entry in *Shigo jiten* [My Personal Dictionary] entitled "the crown prince," she cites a friend saying, "the imperial family plays the role of the phantom family that has perished, that no longer can be found anywhere in Japan."[25] Her own snideness about the matter, however, comes through in the definition for this entry: "a mega-famous guy, a mega-idol, a superstar Japan can be proud of in front of the whole world, a hero in the trendy drama of real society."[26] We also find this satirical perspective (the crown prince, in fact, is usually thought of as lacking charm) in a dream she recounts in this same essay. She gets on a bus, and as she is deciding where to sit, a gray-haired gentleman in front of her turns in her direction. It is the emperor. He grins and nods in her direction, indicating that she should sit behind him. She sees Empress Michiko seated next to him. And then: "As I sat down, at once but in slow motion, all of the people on the bus turned to look at me. They were all members of the imperial family. The bus slowly began to move. I looked at the man beside me. It was the crown prince. He (oh, what the heck, I might as well write it) seemed to have fallen for me at first sight."[27] As Yū herself says in closing, this sort of essay "in the olden days . . . would have been a crime of lèse majesté."[28] Yū nowhere says that the issue of emperor's war responsibility needs to be confronted before Japanese society can come to terms with its war experience, yet the presence of the imperial family in her work in a mocking tone forces her readers to consider the place of the imperial institution in postwar ideologies of Japaneseness.

The accounts of postwar Japanese society provided by theorists of the adult child enable us to make sense of Yū Miri's work — indeed, to read it as a scathing critique of the interlocking ideologies of nation, family, and gender that bolstered Japan's economic rise in the postwar era. Yet I am skeptical of these psychologists' generalizations about the Japanese family. They make it seem as if everyone is exactly the same; they also ignore social movements that have challenged state power directly or state-supported ideologies of gender and the family. Although certain aspects of the imperial prewar system have persisted into the postwar era, it is overly simplistic to posit either that postwar democracy has had only marginal effect on people's values systems or that people did not have a sense of individual rights' in the prewar period.

Nobuta, and to some degree Saitō and his colleagues, are raising the question — debated vehemently in both the pre- and postwar eras — of whether Japan has achieved modernity. Indeed, Nobuta seems to be arguing that only now is Japan beginning to throw off the shackles of a premodern organic, corporatist system.[29] The model of Japanese society propounded here comes perilously close to the *Nihonjinron* (theories of Japaneseness) prevalent in postwar sociology.

In this case, however, the view is critical rather than affirmative. This is an important distinction, as is the fact that Saitō, Nobuta, et al. make an attempt to historicize. They suggest that the "concentric circles" and the sense of Japan as a kind society are ideologies, that this is not the way things have to be.[30] Even if they oversimplify, it is heartening to find mainstream journalists and popular psychologists questioning the enduring impacts of the war, a task until recently left to a few intellectuals and activists.

The elision of gender in the accounts of practitioners so devoted to healing the traumatized, however, is puzzling. Of course, despite efforts to distinguish kinds of trauma, the very notion can be said to minimize gender, acknowledging as it does correspondences between the horror of war and that of rape. In Japan, the collapsing of trauma into the "AC" and linking its causes to a distant war allowed for continued obscuring of the particular abuse of women and girls.

And yet there was a media buzz around Yū — perhaps because she embedded her depictions of sexual abuse in other themes critics could focus on. Nonetheless, this attractive woman speaking so plainly was nonetheless a source of anxiety for some. A prime example is comic book author turned revisionist historian Kobayashi Yoshinori, who associated Yū Miri's name with the comfort women movement.

The story is an odd one, but it demonstrates how passionate people were at this moment about who was expressing what in the media — particularly when those people were Korean women and their subject sexual violence. In 1997, not long after she won the Akutagawa prize, several shops where Yū had scheduled book signings canceled them in response to threats of violence in phone calls from people claiming to be members of rightist organizations. The only objection the callers made was that Yū was an upstart Korean.

At about the same time, a journalist named Sakurai Yoshiko was shocked to find her speaking engagements canceled in response to protests by human rights organizations. These groups had demanded that she retract a statement she had made at a previous lecture that no proof existed of the Japanese military's recruitment of comfort women. Some argued that the Yū incident involved a threat of physical harm (for no other reason than the author's ethnicity) and should be distinguished from the Sakurai affair, which demanded an apology for perceived misstatements at a publicly sponsored event; others contended that both women had been deprived of their freedom of speech.

This is where Kobayashi Yoshinori weighed in. Although originally known as an author of boys' comics, by this time, Kobayashi was also famous for his alliance with a revisionist history group.[31] Since Kim Haksun's emergence in 1991, the former comfort women and their supporters had met resistance from certain camps. This opposition heightened after the 1994 decision to include the history of these women in middle school textbooks, when a group of conservative academics and public figures expressed their indignance by forming the Jiyūshugi shikan kenkyūkai (the Research Society on the Liberalist View of History) and the Atarashii rekishi kyōkasho o tsukuru kai (the Society to Create New School Textbooks). Kobayashi joined the latter.

He has been one of their most effective publicists, outlining their activities in a comic serial in *SAPIO*, a right-of-center news magazine. It was in this forum too, that he attacked Yū. First he lambasted the *Asahi shinbun* [Asahi Newspaper] for defending Yū and ignoring Sakurai, and he subsequently mocked Yū herself for treating the cancellations as a restriction of her freedom of expression, arguing that she was only "an author of stories" and that book signings are only "performances for the purpose of increasing sales."[32]

Yū was so angered by Kobayashi's portrayal of her — and his claim that the *Asahi* had only paid attention to her because she was Resident Korean — that although she had until then refrained from commenting on political matters (particularly those involving Koreans), she began doing so in a column in another weekly news magazine, *Shinchō 45*. Yū not only defended herself against Kobayashi, but stated her position on comfort women's inclusion in textbooks, Japan-U.S. relations, child abuse, and the infamous child murder.[33]

By speaking out against Kobayashi and his colleagues in the revisionist historical groups, Yū was stepping into a battle that had been raging for some time. Many activists, lawyers, and scholars had already denounced them for, among other things, their stalwart nationalism. These groups took issue with the textbooks' overall perspective of the war, which would make children ashamed of being Japanese in its replication of the "Tokyo War Crimes Trial view of history." They issued an alternate series of history books that would instead introduce children to the great men and occasional great woman of Japan (notably, not the women usually included in feminist volumes). These sold astonishingly well.[34]

They provided additional justification for excluding the history of comfort women from textbooks. First, they took a decidedly positivist approach to history. They claimed that no official written documents proved that the comfort station system was instituted by the military or that the state had forcibly recruited women for that purpose. They all but ignored the testimony of former comfort women, disparaging their accounts as unreliable not only because of their advanced age, but because they stood to profit from claiming victimhood.

In addition, they suggested that violent sexuality and/or prostitution were inappropriate subjects for middle school students. They maintained that the comfort stations were an extension of the public (not state sponsored, but state sanctioned and licensed) prostitution system existing in Japan (and, I would add, colonial Korea) at the time. Evidently, in their view, students did not need to learn about this sordid history either.

Among the many scholars and activists to take these groups to task was Yoshimi Yoshiaki, who in 1992 discovered a document in the Defense Department Library indicating that the Japanese military had been in charge of managing the "comfort stations." He therefore challenged these revisionists on their own terms. Rather than questioning what constitutes "proof" or appropriate educational material, he methodically pointed to the documents that did exist and that had been recognized by the Japanese government.

Feminist scholar Ueno Chizuko, who took up this issue far later than he had, lambasted Yoshimi for being as much of a positivist as his foes.[35] She maintained that it was necessary to problematize the notion of fact, complicate historical methodology, value testimony, and acknowledge the existence of plural realities and thus plural histories. She went so far as to refute the existence of complete or objective history.[36] Ōgoshi Aiko, a philosopher and prominent feminist, defended Yoshimi and others Ueno had attacked, noting that he had heeded the voices of the former comfort women from the very beginning. She then disparaged Ueno for "playing with theory."[37]

One might assume that Yū's frustration with Kobayashi would have led her to join hands with either Yoshimi, Ōgoshi, and countless members of nongovernmental organizations supporting the comfort women or even with Ueno. In "Kamen no kuni" [The Country of Masks], the first essay she wrote in response, however, she did nothing of the sort. This column, interestingly, incited many angry attacks on Yū Miri by men with conservative leanings, but brought out scarcely a comment, either scathing or laudatory, from anyone on the left.

In the essay, she denounces both extremes, disparaging the all too common tendency to subscribe to the views of polarized camps. In this controversy, leftists should stop taking advantage of anti-Japanese sentiment in Asia, she cries, and the revisionist historians "would do well to be more considerate about the trauma suffered by Koreans under colonial rule."[38] She forges ahead: Koreans' feelings about colonialism are not to blame, however, but rather resentment that festered in the postwar as they watched Japan soar economically as their own people and land were torn apart, drenched in blood, and stifled under dictatorship. Furthermore, "the clumsiness of the Japanese government in its diplomatic relations" did nothing to help.[39]

Her own position, following Katō Tenyō, a prominent if controversial intellectual, is that facts of course exist, but history itself is a *monogatari*, a narrative we've constructed to understand those facts; each of the positions on comfort women is such a story, and unfortunately we don't have facts that enable us to judge which is right.[40] There can be, she says, again citing Katō (who is citing Takeda Seiji citing Husserl), no such thing as sure knowledge.

Interestingly, this leads her to commend the stance of Sakurai Yoshiko. Sakurai, she says, thinks for herself rather than producing documents to fit her point of view. The textbook controversy should be put to an end by including both perspectives on the history; then the combatants could spend their time on the more valuable tasks of gathering further documentation and helping these aging women. Although Yū's avowed standpoint is that there is no such thing as "absolute knowability," I would note that here she insists that documents will aid in resolving this issue, indicating that she does not actually believe the past to be beyond our comprehension.[41] Her real point seems to be that we must sensitively accept the contradictions in what we know of history and use our knowledge responsibly.

Furu hausu [Full House], to which I will turn momentarily, she further explores this subject. Although Yū claimed that she had responded to Kobayashi in a critical essay because unlike stories, this form has "real effect," in her fiction, she accomplishes something she could not through abstract argumentation, both because she navigates these waters more skillfully and because the waters themselves allow different things to be said. In addition, through it she reaches an audience who might not otherwise be inclined to think about such issues.

In *Full House*, a gradual escalation of psychological tension propels the narrative forward. The two main passages that make up most of the novella are set in a house and in its immediate surroundings and cover a period of just a few days. Only a brief interlude outside the house separates them — and we are told an entire month has passed. This telescoping of time and space produces an anxiety in readers, especially when coupled with the tense dialogue and odd events that punctuate the narrative.

In the first section, the narrator Sumi and her younger sister Yōko visit this house, which their father has built with a massive loan, roughly half a million dollars at the exchange rate in 1995. They are shocked because they know that their father, who works in a *pachinko* parlor, is not well off.[42] The house is not only immense but also replete with the trappings of middle-class life: Ainu wooden dolls, every kitchen appliance imaginable, numerous bottles of expensive liquor, many brands of shower gel. It soon becomes clear that he hopes to entice his family — the two girls and their mother, who left sixteen years earlier — to live together again under this roof.

During this first visit, Yōko makes it clear that she has no intention of doing so, but Sumi hedges, saying she'll stay "some of the time" (13). This sets the tone for the story: Sumi, we already see, is powerless to express or do what she actually wishes. Yōko leaves the next morning when their father goes to work, but Sumi hangs on, unable to say no to her father as he stares at her and says, "you're staying, right?" (20). The entire day, which she spends looking through the house and wandering in the neighborhood, is uncomfortable. She notices an odd silence. Although it is July and there are several parks and empty lots, she does not hear the familiar hum of cicadas. Twice she ventures outside, and twice strange men grab her by the shoulder. We learn only minimal details of her ordinary life outside this house.

That evening, after her father returns, the discomfort intensifies. While they are eating together, her father abruptly asserts that he has never abused her, and later that same evening, we learn that although she is staying, her father is going back to his apartment. She is left alone in the house. We witness a dreamlike sequence in which she recalls her own rape by a man, apparently a stranger. When she awakens, she is overcome by the feeling that she must leave the house, and does so.

In the second main section of the story, Sumi has come to the house again after an urgent call from her father. She arrives only to find not her father, but a man and a woman and two children she does not know. They have made themselves at home, even taken over. At first she assumes they must be distant relatives, but before long, she discovers that they are strangers, a family made homeless when their business failed as a result of the recession. Her father, it seems, took pity on them and welcomed them into his home.

Even after she learns the names of family members, she refers to them as *otoko, onna, shōnen, shōjo* (man, woman, boy, girl). If the depiction of the man, woman, and boy is flat, that of the girl is laced with eroticism. When Sumi first sees her, for example, she notices her "lips red like sucking candy" (53). The narrative development of the story from this point forward revolves around Sumi's relationship with the girl over just a few days.

The girl, we learn, never talks, and the narrative provides intimations that she is a victim of abuse; it notes, for example, the presence of bruises on her inner thighs. The abused Sumi then becomes abuser: before long, Sumi acts on her erotic pull toward the girl. At the end of this scene, Sumi observes that the "oxygen returned to her brain," as if to suggest she had not been fully conscious as she acted. She says she does not know why she stays, that she feels a visceral hatred for the family. A part of her, however, has been ensnared by the girl, and she is seeking some sort of resolution, although what kind she claims not to know. The narrative portrays Sumi's father, too, as unable to do what he wishes: that is, to eject the family or even to refuse outlandish demands, such as to build a pond in the garden. The apparent powerlessness of the characters over their own actions, their seeming inability to extract themselves from subtly or blatantly abusive relationships, is finally broken in two episodes involving the young girl, one of which is the culminating scene of the story. In these scenes Yū Miri is showing us a way out of the abusive dynamic.

First, we need to examine how Yū's narrative initially brings the issue of trauma to the reader's attention. The second night Sumi stays in the house, her father, as they are eating together, says abruptly, "I suppose you think it's my fault that that woman, your mother, left. But at the very least I never was violent. . . . I never abused you. The only time I ever got violent was with that woman's mother, and then only twice" (32–33). This awkward assertion of innocence makes readers doubt the father's truthfulness. His actions magnify our suspicions: he chucks a plastic cigarette out in favor of the real thing.

The narrator then thinks, "As I brought each bite of fried rice to my mouth, I went back over my memories, and counted the number of times my mother had been hit. One time for each spoonful" (33). Then, the father says, "I also never sexually abused you. Do you have any memories of my doing that?," which the narrator follows with: "Putting my spoon down after three bites, I quietly put the lid on my memories, and shook my head. 'No, I don't have any memories of that either'" (33). The voices may be at odds, but the characters' uncontrollable actions and unspeakable thoughts are more powerful than their words.

This scene is immediately followed by one the same evening, in which, as I mentioned above, Sumi has a memory of her own abuse. At age six or seven, she is alone at home. She is dozing but wakes to a sound. She hides. Just as she thinks she was just imagining things, her mouth is covered, and she is held down. Here I quote:

> I could hear the man's rough breaths and my heartbeat. The man put his hands in my underpants, and roughly pushed a finger like the tip of a tree inside me. The pain spread through my legs but my throat only gave off a sound like a balloon with a hole in it. Just then the man shivered. He clung to me like a drowning person to a piece of driftwood.
>
> At that moment there was the sound of a key turning in the door. My mother and sister came home. The man hurriedly separated his body from mine, pulled up his zipper, and ran off. I heard the man escaping from the kitchen window and running down the street, and then all of this was put to an end with my mother's voice saying "We're home." I hurriedly put on my underpants, which were around my ankles, went into the bathroom, and locked the door. I gently stroked my sore hollow with my fingers. (40–41)

At this crucial juncture there is a break in the text. Then comes the line *Yume datta no ka mo shirenai* ("Perhaps it was a dream"). Although it is tantalizingly placed so that it might refer to what comes before, this statement appears to refer to what comes after — a dreamlike sequence mostly in present tense.

The apparent dream begins with a girl gazing at a girls' school on a hill. And then:

> The girl crawls through the gap below the iron gate and takes the sweaty lighter out of her pocket. A pleasant feeling like cool water radiates from her spine and wells up in her. Flicking the lighter with her thumb, she lights the wilting grasses along the iron fence on fire. The fire crackles and begins to blaze softly, coming toward the girl. The girl ducks out under the gate and hides in the woods, waiting to see what happens. With the fluttering flames, the welcoming breeze,

the shrubs and grass burn. Already her heart is not beating so strongly; she grows sleepy with the ticks of her watch, far away, faintly. . . . The girl slowly begins the walk home. Behind her, flames like the tongue of a snake begin licking the walls of the caretaker's shack.

In the field the sun had set and the girl, standing on her tiptoes, gazed at the girls' school. All the people and the fire truck had already vanished. The tears on her cheeks had dried. (41–42)

We shall see at the end of the story, however, that this passage may not be a dream at all. Nonetheless, at this point, the effect is destabilizing, for we no longer know whether to trust the narration.

That is, in the conversation between Sumi and her father, his actions and her thoughts, supplied by the narration, intimated that a different "truth" lay beneath their words. In this case, by contrast, reality is unstable. Yet here, too, we see memories triggering bodily reactions. Sumi wakes (though from which dream it's not clear) and is overcome by a feeling that she needs to leave the house.

I want to pause for a moment here to consider how this fiction might affect the way readers perceive the debates about comfort women and history. Whether or not it is Yū's intent, this story forces us to listen to the claims of perpetrators and the "testimony" of victims with heightened sensitivity. It also prevails on us to see history as an "imagination" of the past (as Yū says elsewhere), because in certain cases, only memories remain, and evidence, strictly speaking, may no longer exist.

As I mentioned earlier, however, Yū's narrative deemphasizes the act of maligning perpetrators and vindicating victims in favor of pointing to structures that encourage the abusive dynamic. In fact, in this text, she does not portray characters as fixed in the role of perpetrator or victim, but rather caught in cycles of abuse. She even shows how these cycles reach beyond individual families and out into the world to become social patterns. In the second main section of the novella, we see the father (the abuser) turn passive and Sumi (the abused) turn dominant.

In this portion of the text, Sumi ends up taking a bath with the girl. The scene is dreamlike, not unlike the earlier scene of Sumi's own victimization. I quote: "Finding pale purple bruises on her sides and hips, I say foolishly, as if laughing or speaking in my sleep 'You bumped into something, didn't you, Kaoru? You're a tomboy, aren't you!,' and try pressing on the bruises with my fingertips" (67). The girl does not resist when Sumi washes her nipples, her belly button; nor does she resist when her hand moves downward. "She just left her body to me like a plant" (67–68). She smells the girl, who does not even resist when she washes "the most recessed place in the girl's body with her finger" (68). The scene ends with the line "when her body was hidden by her towel, at last the oxygen returned to my brain" (68).

When I first read Yū's work, my impulse was to interpret it as showing readers who had similar experiences how they could speak out against victimization. Confronted with a scene like this one, though, I began to wonder why her readers want to read not only about being abused but about abusing. The controversial argument that survivors of abuse exhibit a tendency to engage in similar acts themselves is well known (in a kind of reversal of repetition compulsion). Yet does the fact that Yū points to the compliance of victims in their own abuse rob her of the opportunity to blame specific real abusers? Could this be what her readers want to hear? If we then apply these insights to the comfort women issue, would it make the same true in that case?

This is too simplistic a conclusion, I think. Yū's point is more complex. It is not that people are not responsible for their own actions, but that they necessarily act within the structures in which they live, and that those structures need to be changed in order for people to change. In an interview, Yū says, "the family is influenced by the social circumstances and nation-state of its time, and on occasion, cracks; I think writing thoroughly about the family enables me to write about the warp of the nation-state itself."[43]

Now, before I go any further with this line of thought, I have to point out that the story does not end with Sumi's act of violence, but rather with two startling acts on the part of the young girl. Although it might be simplest to see them as acts of rebellion against her abuser, I don't think this is what they actually are. At this juncture, I want to suggest an alternative reading, one dependent on an understanding that the girl, consistently referred to as "the girl" in the narration despite the fact that we know her name, is an alter ego of Sumi's. At several points in the text, these characters are superimposed on one another. Not only is the girl living in her room, but their characters are similar: even Sumi's sister comments on how like Sumi the girl is, and, as Sumi tells us, she, like the girl, is unable to rebuff unwanted advances (73 and elsewhere).

In addition, the vocabulary used in the depiction of their abuse is strikingly similar. Although the man who raped Sumi was referred to only as *otoko* ("the man"), the scene in which her father says, "you don't have any memory of my sexually abusing you, do you," implies that either she was raped both by a stranger and her father or that *otoko* was indeed her father.

The girl, too, we soon learn, has been raped not only by Sumi but by *otoko*. One day Sumi follows the girl on bicycle. Out of the blue, the girl takes Sumi's wrist and bites. Then at last she speaks, albeit in cryptic syllables: "chichi, kite, kite, teki, chichi, chichi, kite, iku, ku, ku, ku, ku" (80). This line at first seems mere gibberish, but it is actually laden with meaning: "father," she begins, then *kite*, or "come!" (which has no sexual connotations in Japanese), and in a reversal of syllables, *teki*, or "enemy," followed again by "father" twice, and then *kite*, followed by a word reversed in meaning, *iku*, literally, "I go," but in Japanese the equivalent of saying "I'm coming" (to orgasm), and then the last syllable of "I go," or *ku*, meaning pain, resounding four times. Thus it could be translated "father, come!, enemy, father, father, come, come, I'm coming, pain, pain, pain, pain." Given that the father is called *otoko* throughout the text, the layering here is blatant.

We thus may read the bath scene as Sumi's reenactment of her own abuse from the perspective of the abuser. The ending of the story lends further credence to my alternative interpretation. The girl calls the fire department; when they come, there is no fire. The father begins beating his son, whom he assumes has made the prank call. As soon as the firemen leave, the girl sets the curtains ablaze, then the trash can, then the newspaper sitting atop the desk. Sumi's father chuckles and says simply, "insurance" as he watches the man and woman frantically putting the fire out. They succeed; the man yells at the girl and raises his hand to strike her. She covers her face to protect herself, and, in the first line we hear from her, screams, "That's why this is all a lie!" (91). The narrator says her voice has a "familiar ring, one with fond memories." Here we need to recall that after Sumi remembers her rape as a child, she dreams of a girl setting a school yard afire and gazing at it after the fire engines have left.

The girl runs out, and Sumi follows her on bicycle. She begins to tire but keeps going, her "hands stuck to the handlebars as if nailed to a cross," suggesting the urgency she feels about confronting the girl (92). In the culminating passage, the distinction between Sumi's voice and the girl's is blurred. What might be dialogue or a monologue between two parts of the self comes in rapid succession, undivided by spacing or quotation marks: "The girl's bicycle sped off in the darkness emitting light as if ablaze. I can't keep up with you, I can't pedal, forgive me, about my setting the fire, that was a lie, I'll never be as strong as you, it was probably a lie, please, wait, no one's going to hit you, when you're an adult you won't be hit, you'll see" (92). The story ends with Sumi collapsing, "bicycle and all," seeing only "the night swirling like a fingerprint" when she summons the strength to open her eyes (93).

If I follow through with the analysis of the girl representing a part of Sumi, or her alter ego, what we are witnessing here is one part of Sumi, ostensibly the adult, caught in the swirling, vicious cycle of the repetition of abuse as the child manages to ride off boldly into the distance of adulthood. To take this one step further, the ending seems to argue that trauma can never simply be overturned. Even if memories of trauma present themselves in ways that seem unreliable, their traces, not merely bruises but psychological scars, manifest themselves nonetheless. Yū Miri has often spoken of her writing as her own form of "healing." In this story, crucially, it is the coming to voice, the confession of having been raped (which we see in the girl's odd syllables and her statement that it is "all a lie") that enables the survivor of abuse to grasp some modicum of freedom.

Although I used the word *confession* just now to speak of this action, I think now that I want to be more specific. Confession in its religious sense implies a release from pain, from the past, from guilt. Instead I want to emphasize the act of narrativization of the traumatic memory as a way to transform it into a comprehensible entity that can be integrated into self-understanding. I also want to emphasize the way in which this act of self-revelation is an effort to share with others with similar experiences in hopes that they too will be able to achieve such understanding. My notions come out of contemporary psychotherapeutic theories of trauma and traumatic memory, which describe the narrativization of what have been frozen as inassimilable memories as a key step in the healing process.[44]

These theories build on the work of the nineteenth-century psychologist Pierre Janet and suggest that there are differences between "traumatic memory" and ordinary memory, which is identified as taking narrative form. Unlike ordinary memories, traumatic memories are described as frozen in an unnarrated state, as smells and sounds and feelings, unintegrated into the person's self-understanding through language; they return repeatedly as nightmares or flashbacks in exactly the same form.[45] Furthermore, clinicians Bessel van der Kolk and Onno van der Hart argue, because it is not put into language, "traumatic memory has no social component; it is not addressed to anybody," whereas ordinary memory "fundamentally serves a social function . . . [for example] as an appeal for help and reconnection."[46]

One element of the healing process is the transformation of the frozen, somatic memory into narrative; van der Kolk and van der Hart admit that some might be disinclined to integrate a terrible experience that they wish had never happened to them into their everyday existence, but propose that people might be able to alter their recollections of a terrible event when they return to it. They give the example of one therapist working with a survivor of the Holocaust who "had the patient imagine a flower growing in the assignment place in Auschwitz — an image that gave him tremendous comfort."[47] They then pose the question of whether it might not be a "sacrilege" to play with the past in this manner. As clinicians, however, their main objective is to assuage the pain of their patients, and they conclude that such strategies may help people but say nothing more of the matter of the ethics of this approach. Finally, often group therapy — in which one comes to see that others have undergone similar trials — is a major part of the recovery process.

In the story Sumi/the girl frees a part of herself by voicing her (albeit seemingly unreliable) memories. Yet it is significant that in no instance in this story is a victim of abuse capable of saying, "I was raped," or indeed "I was raped by my father." In fact, the character has to recreate language itself, from syllabic sounds, to even make it possible for her to state such a thing. If we think about this in the terms proposed above, we see that although a memory might be perfectly clear in one's own mind, it might nonetheless take time and practice before one could express it in language.

The multiple references to somaticized signs of abuse make perfect sense in this context. Another point: when the girl, Sumi's alter ego, tells, in however coded form, that she has been raped, then we must acknowledge that this simple act will in no way free her from her pain. It is only the start of a long process — a hopeful beginning, perhaps, but still only a beginning. If the girl is able to ride off, Sumi, who exists in the ordinary world, is still confused, after all. We might read this ending as Yū's explanation of why she again and again confesses that she is an incest survivor, but does so indirectly. At any rate, *Full House* places a value on narrativizing memories, no matter how unreliable they might seem.

Interestingly, Yū's insights in this story correspond greatly with points made by the supporters of the comfort women. Many comfort women were unable to speak or write of the horror and injustice of their victimization. Their emphasis was on survival. They were mostly illiterate and uneducated, and they were unaware of courts of law prosecuting such crimes. The society they were raised in saw them as ruined. And so on. However, when they did come out and speak, they were accused of not remembering accurately, but those defending them point to their bodily and emotional scars as evidence of the genuineness of their recollections. There is another subtle insight that also has significance for the debate over the treatment of comfort women in historical discourse. That point is related to Yū Miri's insistence on looking at the structures that enable violence. The structures her story uncovers include not only ideologies of gender and family useful to the state, but also to the economic system itself.

Why, we need to ask, is the title of this novella "Full House," a term for a hand in poker? The suggestion is not only that Sumi's father is gambling on the fact that he will be able to gather all the necessary cards (members) to make this "home," but that money is part of what is at stake here. This is a posteconomic bubble tale of the Japanese dream of *mai hōmu* ("my home," that is, home ownership) gone awry, showing that buying a house and filling it are not sufficient to bring happiness. The frustrated class aspirations of the men in the story contribute to their sense of powerlessness and as a consequence to their violence against those over whom they do have power, usually women and children. Yet

Yū Miri would be unlikely to suggest that there is more violence among the poor. Perhaps the point here is rather that Japan's economic downturn has facilitated an exposure of violence that was there all along.

As I have tried to imply, although I do not believe Yū to be directly commenting on the comfort women issue in her story, the Japanese capitalist system was a major factor in determining who was made a comfort woman. Those engaged in political movements to aid the comfort women have often used them as an example for the general exploitation of Koreans under colonial rule. Those now fighting for the inclusion of comfort women in textbooks, though, do often highlight the fact that these women's oppression also depended on certain conceptions of sexuality, such as the tacit acceptance of rape and prostitution. Most often, however, they downplay the extent to which poverty was a necessary condition for becoming a comfort woman. That is to say, poor Japanese women became comfort women too, whereas rich Korean women did not. It was poverty and not simply ethnicity that made it possible to force countless Korean women into comfort houses, for poverty was also what made men desperate enough to sell their wives and daughters. Pairing *Full House* with the textbook debate is ultimately fruitful because it exposes the dangerous but prevalent tendency to overlook the way that the economic structure underscores the particular ideologies of sexuality, family, and ethnicity in Japan's history and its present.

I want to emphasize that my point here is not to suggest that ethnicity is or was unimportant. Between 80 and 90 percent of comfort women were Korean, and it would be preposterous to argue that the fact that class was also important somehow negates the racist component of their oppression. Some observers both in and outside Japan have likened what they term the sexual enslavement of Korean women through this system to the recent rapes of women in Bosnia-Herzegovena, calling the comfort women system genocidal or at least destructive of Korean identity. They point to the rapes of these women as part of a strategy against the colonized, although others, such as Yoshimi Yoshiaki, do not see this as part of a planned strategy. What is certain, however, is that this practice demoralized men by taking "their" women away and kept many of these women from reproducing themselves because they were made infertile.[48] Although state policy was not in my eyes genocidal, it was explicitly racist: fees charged soldiers differed according to the woman's ethnicity.[49] Korean comfort women's testimonies also reveal that individual soldiers treated them as if they were expendable.

These factors reveal that what we think of as racial or ethnic prejudice cannot in this case be separated from class or gender discrimination. If we want both to understand how it was possible for such a thing to have happened and to truly respect its victims, we need to look at all of these variables. It is sometimes mentioned that the Japanese women who became comfort women were professionals — that is to say, they had been prostitutes before. It is also said that they received preferential treatment. It would not surprise me if this were indeed the case, yet it does not make me feel any less sorry for those Japanese women, or feel that their history should be buried. Did they want to be prostitutes to begin with? What economic system, what gender ideology was it, that brought them to sell sex to begin with? Even if their quality of life was better than Korean women's, could their living conditions be said to have been humane? Do they not suffer from the after-effects of traumatic experiences?

I do not want to conflate these different instances of trauma, or that of comfort women with other kinds of war trauma. At the same time, however, I do not see much point in quibbling over whose pain is worse. In addition, I think it is useful to bring together these different cases of sexual abuse because they are borne of the similar sexist ideologies of gender and sexuality in Japan and Korea, ideologies manipulated by the Japanese colonial empire.

In fact, many of the Resident Korean women involved in the movement to support former comfort women — although they have rejected the term *feminism*, which they see as an academic field engaged in and largely defined by elite Japanese women — argue that the true resolution of the comfort women issue would require not only compensation and apologies for these women, but also a major change in ideologies of gender and sexuality in Japan and Korea. They also have argued that the oppression they have faced in their own lives has been caused by the same Confucian ideologies of gender and sexuality that allowed comfort women to meet the tragic fate they did.

Looking at a particular example from the pages of a newsletter put out by Uri yoson nettowaaku (Uri yŏsŏng net'ŭwŏk'ŭ, or Korean Women's

Network), a group formed in November 1991 by Resident Korean women concerned with the comfort women issue, it is evident that women have used the movement as a vehicle for discussing their place as women within the Zainichi family as well as in Japanese society more generally.[50] For example, in October 1995, Chŏng Yŏng-hae penned an essay given the title "Watashi ga 'ianfu' mondai o shinai riyu" (Why I Don't Do the "Comfort Women" Issue). In this piece, Chŏng, probably the best-known Resident Korean woman academic in Japan today, argues that fighting sexism broadly is more important than focusing narrowly on the comfort women issue.

She begins by observing that even those Korean women who did not become comfort women often led terrible lives (she gives an anecdote about one such woman). Therefore, she suggests, it is not only Japanese imperialism or the comfort woman policy that was the problem, but Confucianism, a patriarchal system in which a high value is placed on women's chastity and sexual fidelity to their husbands (because these ensure continuation of the male line) and does not recognize women as people with subjectivity. Living in a world imbued with this sort of gender ideology, women forgot that their bodies were their own, and thus they were unable to object to what happened to them.

She then goes on to claim that "we" (by which she seems to mean Zainichi women) are still caught within a patriarchal system in which marriage is seen as obligatory. We are "jūbu ianfu" (comfort women to husbands), just as comfort women were to the military (the Japanese term for comfort women is *jūgun ianfu*, the term *gun* meaning "military"), even if we are economically comfortable. This is all the more true, she says, when we are beaten by our husbands. She argues that women like herself, who have chosen to bear children without getting married, are equally held back by this ideological system, because they do not live in the "safety zone" of marriage and thus may be ostracized as whores. Because the source of comfort women's oppression and that of Resident Korean women today can be found within the patriarchal ideology of marriage, a genuine resolution of the comfort women issue would require not only supporting those women but "the overcoming of our own everyday circumstances, of the control and humiliation we suffer because we are women."[51]

Finally, Chŏng blames the length of time that this issue took to surface on the fact that Korean society had shunned these women. She points out that Korean men would have been as likely to engage in such behavior as Japanese men: during the Vietnam War, the Korean military even considered setting up comfort stations. She criticizes Zainichi men who argue that talking about sexism among Koreans is divisive of the community, which should rather be uniting to fight ethnic discrimination. Many of these men are tyrants in their own homes, she observes, and then asks, "Should we overlook their oppressiveness and violence?" She also points to the way that women have participated in the reproduction of their own oppression by reinforcing the ideology of marriage by being prejudiced against homosexuals or by continuing to call women *ŏmŏni* (mother). Ultimately, she concludes that what is most needed for the resolution of these related problems (that of the comfort women and that of the marriage system making Zainichi women "comfort wives") is a place for (Resident) Korean women to freely exchange views and support one another in their efforts to challenge both ethnic discrimination and sexism.

Chŏng's pieces elicited a number of responses, several of which took her to task for implying that her choice to be a single mother somehow makes her more radical than women who are married. Several women reported that the movement has forced them to reevaluate their personal lives and to push their husbands to change. The main point of these pieces, however, was that precisely through participating in the comfort women movement, these women found a site in which to engage in the sorts of discussion that Chŏng saw as necessary. One letter in particular, by Kim Yŏng, describes her objective in participating in this movement as being not simply to fight for reparations or against the sexism that makes women "comfort wives" but to "find [her] own feminist language," one that will be comprehensible to the woman closest to her who most suffers from sexism, her own mother.

In a final response to these letters, Chŏng reveals that the title to her first article was assigned by the editors, and that she in no way wished to imply that the comfort women movement is unimportant. Rather, she says, she only has a given amount of time, and has therefore made a priority of the more expansive goal of fighting sexism. She comments on the fact that she held back from using the term *feminism* to describe her objectives because those Japanese who have identified as such have tended to overlook other forms of discrimination. She concludes by slightly revising Kim Yŏng's statement: what she wants to do is not to find but to *create* a new feminist language, one that will help liberate their mothers.

Although as far as I know neither has acknowledged it, the correspondence of Yū Miri's views (and indeed her actions) with those of Ch'ŏng Yŏng-hae is remarkable. Both have insisted on the need for forging new language to change the world in which they live, both have named the problem as ideologies of family and gender, both have defied social norms by becoming single mothers, and both have contended that sometimes Koreanness is not the most powerful force shaping who they are and how they act.

Thirty years before, these sorts of women scarcely could have been imagined. In the late 1960s and early 1970s, we recall, the dominant image of Resident Korean women in both literature and in courtrooms was that of the silent mother, beautiful in her forbearance amidst the violence of colonialism, discrimination, and domestic life. Now, as Japan enters the twenty-first century, financially solvent single women who speak their minds are at the fore. In Yū Miri's case, her life and work even provokes responses — whether good or bad — from not only other Zainichi, but from all Japanese.

The presence of Resident Koreans in Japan's cultural and political life can no longer be disputed. For many of these people, their residence in Japan is as important as their Koreanness. Does this herald the completion of assimilation, the end of Zainichi ethnicity as we know it? No, at least as long as the Japanese state denies Resident Koreans citizenship as their birthright — and as long as vocal members of the community reject the very notion. And no, as long as the government and people refuse to come to terms with the history that brought Koreans to Japan in the first place. And no, finally, as long as most people in Japan continue to think of ethnicity as a matter of blood. In the concluding chapter, we shall see that for these reasons, the primary forums for identity formation (that is, legal and literary narratives) continue to be intertwined in complex ways that resonate with and yet differ from that of minorities elsewhere in the world.

7
Afterword

As I researched this book, a number of new writers and several new social movements found their way into the limelight. In the literary world, just as Yū Miri had become a familiar face in the Japanese mass media, her contemporary Kaneshiro Kazuki made a splash with *GO* (2000), for which he won the most coveted prize for popular fiction, the Naoki, and which was made into a highly commercially and critically successful movie (2001). Some identified this work as heralding a new generation of Zainichi literature, not only because of its stance toward citizenship, ethnicity, and being in and belonging to Japan, but also because of its hip romanticism: it's a love story. In the political arena, some activists continued to demand postwar reparations, but more and more of them devoted their energy to legal struggles by noncitizens to work for the government, to vote, and to stand in local elections.[1]

Citizenship, in other words, became *the* issue on everyone's mind. As I take a quick peek into the turn-of-the-century discourse surrounding this topic, I will reflect on how it reinforces the main points I have been putting forward in this book: that if we do not wish to oversimplify the emergence and evolution of Resident Korean identity between the mid-1960s and the turn of the century, we need to (1) closely track politics and literature and their parallel development and frequent productive cross-fertilization, (2) take life narratives as being central to identity formation, and (3) examine the degree to which this process is gendered and sexualized.

I will start with the political realm. In the mid-1980s, certain municipalities began to allow foreigners to hold certain government positions. For example, they became postal employees and nurses and in 1991 were accorded the right to become full-time educators. A number of cases, however, set a legal precedent of excluding aliens from any employment that put them in a position of "exercising the authority of the nation" or "participating in decision-making for the state," or, in the case of municipalities, of "contributing to decision-making for the local community."[2] In practice, this meant that foreigners were barred from certain jobs, particularly any with managerial responsibility. In 1996, the Home Affairs Ministry decided that decisions about these matters should be left to the municipalities but reinforced the aforementioned restrictions.[3]

In a landmark case in 1997, Japan's Supreme Court, although it upheld the above conditions, decided that certain managerial positions in municipalities did not bear any direct relation to state power. The city of Tokyo had denied Chŏng Hyang-gyun, a nurse who made home visits, the right to take the exam to enter a management-level position. When her case made it to the Supreme Court, it ruled that this action was unconstitutional because it denied the guarantee of legal equality under the law and of the freedom of occupational choice. It demanded that the city pay damages and permit her to take the exam.[4] Although in one sense this was a victory, the decision upheld the limit on the sort of employment available to permanent resident aliens.

In the arena of electoral rights, progress was much slower. After Mintōren made local voting rights an objective in 1988, many cases worked their way through the courts, all unsuccessfully. Beginning in 1993, various municipalities began to demand that permanent residents be given the right to vote in local elections, and in 1995, the Supreme Court ruled that it was not unconstitutional for resident foreigners to vote. This ruling did not, however, result in any concrete changes, because at the same time, the court deemed that neither was it unconstitutional for localities to deny aliens suffrage. Indeed, it added that further laws would need to be passed before noncitizens could actually vote.[5] The government began to seriously consider enacting such legislation after South Korean President Kim Dae Jung specifically asked Japanese Prime Minister Obuchi Keizō to consider the matter when he visited Japan in October 1998. In a visit to South Korea in March 1999, Obuchi responded that he would make a decision on the matter pending studies being conducted by the Liberal Democratic Party and by a Diet panel.[6] Other political parties have already adopted recommendations calling for local voting rights for foreigners. For his own part, then President Kim Dae Jung vowed to have similar laws implemented in South Korea.[7] In 2002, a town in Shiga prefecture was the first to allow permanent foreign residents to vote in a referendum.[8] Since then, other municipalities have followed suit. In addition, by 2003, a Mindan survey found that roughly 45 percent of local governments had adopted resolutions requesting that the national government grant voting rights to permanent residents.[9]

Such testing of the boundaries of citizenship is not unique to Japan but is rather a worldwide phenomenon. A number of European countries have begun granting resident foreigners local suffrage, and in 1999, Germany, which like Japan has historically been known as a country closed to immigration, changed its nationality laws to allow long-term resident aliens the ability to become German citizens. Concepts of nationality, citizenship, and ethnicity as well as the words we use to designate them of course differ from country to country and language to language. At least since the inception of the modern era, however, these notions and terms have been molded within global political, economic, and cultural networks. This is all the more true today with the increase in speed of the dissemination of information. Lawsuits challenging the meaning of national citizenship, such as those I have cited above, have been influenced not only by the direct relationship between South Korea and Japan, but also by the rest of the world. Activists in Japan learn from activists elsewhere — if not by meeting in person, then from reading about their efforts. Those working within the Japanese state and its localities also worry about how they will appear before the other countries of the world.[10] It is not insignificant that many of the details I have cited above are noted in reports issued by the U.S. Department of State.[11] We need to take note of the fact, however, that many of the changes have been initiated and effected locally, particularly in certain areas, such as the city of Kawasaki.[12]

Another example of the resistance to taking on Japanese citizenship can be seen in the case of Chŏng Yang-yi, an activist and schoolteacher who became a citizen as a child, after his father filed an application for the whole family. He so strongly objects to being a citizen that he refuses to inflict the same on his children and thus has not legally registered their births. The procedure of naturalization is what angers him the most: when becoming a citizen of Japan, people have been forced (or coaxed) to take on Japanese names. Chŏng, in fact, was of the first of several naturalized Japanese citizens to file lawsuits demanding to be allowed to legally adopt Korean names. In 1982, he and several others began to hold study meetings and, in 1985, banded together in a group called Minzokumei o torimodosu kai (Association to Regain Ethnic Names). In 1987, one member of the organization won his suit, and others, including Chŏng, followed in his path. Even after its core members achieved their objective, the group continued to work to help others do the same.[13]

Although the law now enables people with Japanese citizenship to have non-Japanese-sounding names, few have opted to take the same route as Chŏng and the members of his group. Chŏng understands this fact, noting that among the roughly ten thousand Resident Koreans naturalized each year, few go against the government's entreaty to them to take on Japanese names. Indeed, many Koreans — even those with South Korean citizenship or Chōsen status — use a Japanese name in some aspect of their lives. A newspaper article from 1998 observes that more than 90 percent of Korean students use Japanese names.[14] But it is not just children: I recall my shock (early in my research) when I stopped by an apartment building housing employees of Sōren and saw that most of the mailboxes had both Japanese and Korean names.

As a consequence of this state of affairs, Chŏng argues, the emphasis should be not on pointing out to such people that they have "betrayed" their people, but rather to propose ways that they might nonetheless preserve a sense of their ethnic background. Pak Il, a university professor whom I heard speak on a panel with Chŏng in 1995, argues that even if Zainichi Koreans no longer ate Korean food or observed Korean customs, they should at the very least make certain that either first or last name is Korean.[15] Only thus can they assure that the presence of people of Korean heritage not become invisible.

Although the Chŏngs and the Paks of the Zainichi community insist on the importance of acknowledging the increasing numbers of people naturalizing each year, they do not advocate taking on Japanese citizenship. They rather stress that it is possible to become legally Japanese and yet to resist assimilating; but even this is not their ideal. Rather, they advocate preserving both Korean cultural attributes and some form of Korean citizenship (either South Korean or Chōsen). In this they are of a like mind with other circles of people who strongly identify as Korean, for whom naturalizing is still taboo. The Japanese edition of *Newsweek* in 2004, in an article in the issue with a cover reading "Korian Japaniizu: Shizentai de ikiru 'nyū Zainichi' ga Nihon o motto hippu ni suru" [Korean Japanese: The "New Zainichi," Living Naturally, Make Japan More Hip], not only notes the continued pressure by officials to take on a Japanese name when naturalizing, but also acknowledges the continued shame for Koreans who do decide to become Japanese.[16] According to one person it quotes, "They say that in America people celebrate when they naturalize; most Zainichi do so secretly. There's nothing to celebrate."[17]

At one point in my stay in Japan, as I was beginning to figure out the degree to which those I met were averse to taking on Japanese citizenship, I asked an activist friend whether she would consider becoming a Japanese citizen on any condition. She replied that if Japan both changed the naturalization system to make the procedure automatic for those who, like Resident Koreans, have permanent resident status as a result of being descendants of people who came to Japan when their place of origin was a colony, and if it adequately educated its people about its history, she would cease to have objections to becoming a Japanese citizen. Japan is a long way from actually doing so, however, she observed ruefully.

In fact, she and her whole family did undertake a change in citizenship while I knew them. The shift, however, was not from Korean to Japanese, but from Chōsen status to South Korean citizenship. Indeed, in addition to the 10,000 or so Koreans becoming naturalized Japanese each year, thousands of people are making this switch.[18] No doubt this trend is in part the result of the changing economic and political situations of South and North Korea, which in turn we must see as tied to global transformations. People have begun to recognize that North Korea's political system is oppressive and its people are starving, and that the "Little Tiger" South is no longer the military dictatorship it was for decades. In addition, surely many have grown weary as they have become aware of the unlikelihood of Korean reunification and the inconvenience of holding Chōsen status.

Interestingly, Ri Kaisei also recently become a citizen of the South, something the Ri we learned about in Chapter 2 would never have done. Clearly, Ri has changed with the times. He now openly calls Resident Koreans a "minority" and likens their position to that of minorities elsewhere.[19] When he gave up his Chōsen status in 1998, he published a lengthy explanation in *Shinchō* [New Tide], a literary journal that often carries his fiction.[20] The main justification he supplied for his choice was that he had decided that he wanted to contribute to the ongoing political democratization of South Korea.

Sadly, not long thereafter, he was attacked by the slightly older Zainichi author Kim Sŏk-bŏm in the left-leaning political magazine *Sekai* [The World].[21] Ri responded in the same journal a few months later, and Kim, once more after a few more months had passed.[22] The tone of these articles — particularly the first by Kim and the second by Ri, which are written as letters — is venomous. Each not merely disagrees with the other's political stance, but accuses the other of misrepresenting factual details. In fact, the exchange grew so mean-spirited that in his final piece, Kim observes that *Sekai* had received a barrage of letters from readers and he himself a number of phone calls from friends telling him that they were disappointed, that it looked bad for Zainichi Koreans to be airing their dirty laundry in this manner.

Nonetheless, there is a real argument being hashed out here, and I think it's important to note the degree to which these issues still evoke emotional responses among Resident Korean intellectuals. Kim Sŏk-bŏm accents the fact that "Chōsen" designation is not equivalent to North Korean citizenship. Although some who hold it are affiliated with Sōren, and some (but not all) of those people do support the North, for others, keeping this status enables one to identify as Korean without allying oneself with either government on the peninsula. If Japan established official diplomatic relations with the North and Resident Koreans were forced to choose between Northern and Southern citizenship, he claims that he would refuse to do so. He holds this would be the most desirable plan of action.

He expands on this a bit, imagining a scenario in which people like himself become "stateless refugees" and even eventually are able to forge some sort of new citizenship that allows them to travel freely to both North and South.[23] Ri criticizes him of being unrealistic, utopian. Although I do not wish to vilify utopianism in and of itself, I do see Kim as effectively cutting himself off from the ability to change any of the states whose laws govern the way he lives. I respect Ri Kaisei's decision to become a South Korean citizen; I now wonder when politically inclined Zainichi Koreans will take the even more practical step of fighting for the right to choose Japanese citizenship.

But what do the "new" Zainichi authors, such as Yū Miri or Kaneshiro Kazuki, have to say about this? The work of Yū Miri not only explores deep-seated problems of Japanese society that have nothing to do with Koreans per se but also challenges the state to develop policies to eradicate them. In so doing, I would argue, she makes clear to readers the degree to which Resident Koreans are already involved in Japan's politics, whether or not they have the right to vote. I therefore take the success of her work to be a positive sign. It compels readers to ask whether it is really fair to see permanent resident aliens as "foreigners" in any true sense, and whether it is therefore fair to exclude them from the political process.

Yet although Yū clearly sees herself as committed to Japan, she has not naturalized herself. Is this perhaps because of the taboo against naturalization that persists in the Zainichi community? We remember that Yū has called herself "neither Korean nor Japanese," but in a conversation with Ri Kaisei in April 1997, not long after she won the Akutagawa prize, she said that she was "grateful that [her] father didn't naturalize." She continued, "Being caught between Japan and South Korea, that is, being in a situation that I had to consider, has been useful for me as a writer, I think. I'm not thinking of naturalizing. There may be various burdens I have to bear as a result, but I want to bear those. I really don't want to run away."[24] Although her justification for choosing to remain a South Korean citizen has a somewhat different nuance from historically more common assessments of naturalization as assimilation and thus betrayal, I do sense a hint of that form of reasoning. She also associates Resident Koreanness with hardship, a view prevalent thirty years ago that has since receded into the background. Becoming Japanese, she implies, would make life too simple and would make her inclined to forget the tumultuous history of Koreans' presence in Japan.

However, Yū's story gets more complicated when we follow her to into 1999, the year she gave birth, out of wedlock, quite publicly, to a son. In her phenomenally popular work *Inochi* [Life, 2000], in which she tells of her experience of becoming a mother, Yū recounts her decision to acquire Japanese citizenship for her son, whose father (a married man with whom Yū had an affair) is Japanese.[25] She tells of the hassles she goes through to have the man officially declare paternity before the child's birth, because if he waited until after the birth, the child would have to take on his father's last name (95–104). She expresses her anger at the fact that it is up to the man to decide the citizenship of a child born between a Korean woman and a Japanese man (104). "I think it's more severe discrimination than local voting rights," she adds, "so why aren't Mindan or other Zainichi political groups bringing it up? It's got to be because it's a culture that is ashamed of the very women who face this sort of problem" (104). She then notes that she decided not to respond to any of the requests to speak to the Korean press, because she knew that it was likely she would be labeled a traitor to her country.

It's not entirely clear in the book, but it seems that Yū justifies taking on Japanese citizenship for her child only because he is half Japanese by "blood." In 2001, in an interview about the third book in her autobiographical series, she discusses the uproar caused when she decided to wear a kimono to her son's first visit to a Shintō shrine, in and of itself an action some Zainichi Koreans might find traitorous, whatever her attire. She is up front about her increasing ambivalence about her citizenship:

> Giving my son Japanese citizenship forced me, as his mother, to consider whether there was a basis for me to refuse to give up my own Korean citizenship. It's strange to hold on to your citizenship if you have no intent at all to learn the language, so — even though I don't know how long it will take — I decided to try to learn Korean. I'm also reading South Korean history textbooks and general Korean histories.

> In my own family . . . Japanese culture held a much more prominent place so for us kids nothing that you could call Korean culture really stayed with us.
>
> [Now] I'm making a conscious effort to learn the [Korean] language, and I'm going to decide whether to keep Korean citizenship or to change to Japanese citizenship.[26]

This is a groundbreaking stance to take. I find it fascinating that motherhood was the experience that pushed her to come to it.

Kaneshiro Kazuki's *GO*, too, despite the author's ROK passport, has a view of citizenship and belonging that puts its author in the category of the hip "new Zainichi." The author describes himself on the cover of the first edition of the book as, in Japanese phonetic writing, "Korean Japanese." The cover also bears a line from the book: "No soy coreano, ni soy japonés, yo soy desarraigado." The phrase actually comes from the protagonist's father, but it applies to the thoughts of the son as well.

Although the book never advocates naturalization, from its very opening, we see that it has something to say about citizenship. It begins with Sugihara, the protagonist narrator, telling us about how his parents changed their citizenship from Chōsen (the "Korea" designation) to the ROK in order to more easily take a trip to Hawaii over their winter vacation. The narration is sarcastic: "I guess I need to explain a bit more. Why did my father, who was born in Chejudo, part of South Korea, have Chōsen citizenship? And why did he need to change his citizenship to South Korean to go to Hawaii? The story's boring, so I'll try not to go on too long. I'd like to mix in a bit of humor, but it might be kind of hard" (7).

As I said before, however, the serious stuff is made palatable with romance. The cover advertises *GO* not only as about ethnic identity, but also as a tale of love: "Me: I fell totally, completely, in love. The girl: Super cute, and Japanese," and by the second chapter, we see this to be true. All the while, we learn of Sugihara's adjustment to his switch from a Korean (Sōren) school to a Japanese one (he literally fights his way into acceptance), and his battle of will and of fists with his old-fashioned *pachinko* parlor–employed and former boxer father.

Even so, at the novel's center is the hero's burgeoning relationship with the very middle-class beauty whom he meets in Chapter 2. We (and he) know only by her last name, Sakurai. The climax of this plotline comes when, about two-thirds of the way through the novel, the hero and his girl are about to have sex for the first time. It is only at this time that he confesses his Korean identity, claiming that he had not brought it up because he did not think it mattered. She responds: "Why didn't you say anything till now? If you didn't really think it was a big deal, then you should have said something" (181). She shrinks back from him, having been told by her father never to date a Korean or a Chinese because of their tainted blood. He leaves. So no climax after all. When they meet again after a long separation, he asks what he is, and she says she has learned that he is a Zainichi Kankokujin (South Korean resident in Japan). He angrily retorts:

> Sometimes I want to kill every one of you, you Japanese. How can you so call me a "Zainichi" without thinking twice? I was born and raised here, dammit. How dare you use the same language you use for people who've come from other places, like the "Zainichi" American Army or "Zainichi Iranians"! It's like you're saying I'm some foreigner who's going to leave some day. Do you get it? Had the thought ever even crossed you mind?. . . .
>
> But if you want to call me "Zainichi," go right ahead. You guys, you're afraid of me, right? If you don't analyze me and give me a name, you won't rest easy, right? But I don't' have to accept it. It's just like "lion." Lions don't think of themselves as "lions." You just decided yourselves to give that name and act as if you know what a "lion" is. Just try coming close and calling me that name, I'll spring right at you and sink my teeth in your carotid and kill you. Do you get it? As long as you guys continue to call me "Zainichi," you'll be the ones being eaten up. Doesn't that bother you? I'll tell you. I'm not "Zainichi," I'm not South Korean, I'm not North Korean, and I'm not Mongoloid. Stop trying to put me into some neat little box. I'm ME. No, even that's no good. I want to be free even from having to be me. I'm going to look for something that lets me forget even that I'm me. I'll go wherever I have to. If I can't find it in this country, I'll leave, the way you all wish I would. You guys can't do that. You guys are trapped by the state, or land, or position, or convention, or tradition, or culture, or something. You'll die that way. Take a good look. I don't have any of that, so I can go anywhere I please. I can go whenever I want to. Doesn't that bother you? Doesn't it bug you at all? Shit. Why am saying this? Shit, shit, shit. (233–34)

But not to worry: by the end, all is well. She then says "those eyes" and goes on to tell him the story of how she first fell for him. He had thought that they met by chance, but she confesses that she engineered their meeting after seeing him getting in a fight at a high school basketball game, jump kicking the boys around him. Seeing the spirit in his eyes as he fought, she became sexually aroused. "Even now," she tells him, "I'm wet. Do you want to feel for yourself?" (239). Then she adds: "I don't care more what race you are. If you'll just do that jump for me and give me that intense look once in a while, I wouldn't even care if you couldn't speak Japanese. Nobody can jump the way you do, and no one can give me that intense look the way you do" (239). Thus we see that the skill Sugihara not only gains acceptance in the Japanese school through violence, but that it is his hypermasculinity and fighting ability that get him the Japanese girl as well. It is through male heterosexual sexuality, indeed, that this book proposes a minority define his relationship to his identity. The Spanish quote on the cover comes through the voice of the father, responding to the son's saying he's going to run off to Norway, marry a pretty Norwegian girl, and have a half-Norwegian child. When he was young, he says, he wanted to become Spanish. Why? Because he heard that there were "lots of beauties" in Spain (97). Finally, when talking to an acquaintance who's organizing a group of young Resident Koreans (regardless of affiliation) to discuss and work on Zainichi issues, he explains his desire not to join them by saying, "The reason I'm not going to change my citizenship is that I can't stand the idea of being newly integrated into or swallowed up or strangled by the likes of a country. No more living dominated by the feeling that I belong to some big thing" (220). What's interesting here, though is that he goes on to say, "But if Kim Basinger came up to me right now and said, 'Change your citizenship. Please, for me,' I'd file the application in a second" (221). He muses about the seeming contradiction of his stance but makes no attempt to resolve it. This, it seems, is what it means to be a new Resident Korean.

What is disturbing to me in all this is how little has changed. Why the obsession with using relationships with women to make a point about the level on which citizenship is and is not important? Why the gender- and class-stereotyped narrative (working-class fighting boy woos middle-class pretty girl) to tell the tale of boy's finding his place as Korean in Japan?

As gratified as I am that *GO* may have brought many who might not otherwise have thought about these issues to do so, I continue to be bothered by the basic point of the narrative, that if a man, whatever his origin, is tough enough, he can be accepted into Japanese culture. This leaves homosexual men and women out of the loop. Romantic relations, particularly heterosexual ones, are powerful as fictional metaphors for integration into Japanese society. Obviously, in reality, they are powerful as well: a good many of the Resident Koreans who become Japanese citizens do so through marriage. Yet recalling Yū Miri's fate as described in *Life*, we must remember that women are put at a legal disadvantage. Her other work, with its attention to gender norms and sexual abuse, implies that they are at a social disadvantage as well. My point here is not to decry the writings of men like Kaneshiro or praise the Yū Miris of the world. Rather, I want to argue that we cannot understand ethnicity without examining it in its interaction with gender and sexuality.

I want to believe that someday the stories told by Resident Koreans will have the power to transform the way that all Japan's residents see their place in society. I hope that they will come to believe full citizenship should be granted to all Resident Koreans as a matter of course. But this will not suffice, because liberation and dignity depend equally on an honest and emotional engagement with history. To this end, schools must begin to teach children about Japan's past, including the dark era of colonialism. Yet even this would not be sufficient. A true commitment to history — that is to say, to the future — is surely evoked not only through an abstract and logical understanding of the world, but also through one that is complex, sometimes contradictory, and decidedly emotional. Culture generally and literature specifically play a crucial role in shaping the way we perceive our own place and the place of others in the world. For this reason, I believe that we must begin to understand and teach Resident Korean literature as an integrated part of Japanese literature. Indeed, many have already begun this task.[27] It is my fervent hope that my own efforts will contribute to this ongoing transformation of Japan and Japanese studies.

Reference Matter

Notes

1. I use two main terms to speak of people of Korean descent residing in Japan: Resident Korean and Zainichi Korean. The former I have borrowed from Norma Field. See her "Beyond Envy, Boredom, and Suffering: Toward an Emancipatory Politics for Resident Koreans and Other Japanese," *positions* 1, no. 3 (Winter 1993): 640–70. Until quite recently, *Zainichi Chōsenjin* was the most common appellation. *Chōsen*, a term used before the Korean war, had referred to the entire Korean peninsula, but thereafter it came to point to North Korea and *Kankoku*, to South Korea. During the late 1970s and early 1980s, when the consciousness of South Korean economic development and of the fact that the majority of Resident Koreans were of South Korean not North Korean citizenship, the cumbersome *Zainichi Kankoku-Chōsenjin* emerged to replace the earlier term. Today the most common terms are *Zainichi Kankoku-Chōsenjin* and, more informally, *Zainichi*. In the 1990s the term *Zainichi Korian* also came into use. I have chosen to use Resident Korean and Zainichi Korean because they do not divide the community on the basis of their citizenship and/or politics. I will also occasionally use "Zainichi" as an adjective. See Yun Kŏn-a, " 'Zainichi Kankoku-Chōsenjin' to iu kotoba," in *Horumon bunka I: Issatsu marugoto Zainichi Chōsenjin* ["Tripe Culture" I: The Complete Book on Resident Koreans], ed. Horumon bunka henshū iinkai [Tripe Culture Editorial Committee] (Tokyo: Shinkansha, 1990), 56–73.

2. Because the two countries do not have formal diplomatic relations, Japan does not recognize North Korean citizenship, and thus the designation under nationality remains simply *Chōsen*, a term referring to the Korean peninsula rather than to either state that exists there. According to Ministry of Justice data for 1995, there were 666,376 Koreans living in Japan. Cited in Harajiri Hideki, *"Zainichi" to shite no Korian* [Koreans as "Zainichi"] (Tokyo: Kōdansha Gendai Shinsho, 1998), 56–57.

3. Yang Tae-ho notes that by 1994, roughly 190,000 Koreans had taken on Japanese citizenship. Of course, some of this number are no longer living. On the other hand, many of these people have no doubt since had children. Yang, who also includes recent immigrants from South Korea, estimates that there may be as many as one million Resident Koreans. Yang Tae-ho, *Zainichi Kankoku Chōsenjin dokuhon: Rerakkusu shita kankei o motomete* [Reader on Resident Koreans: Toward a More Relaxed Relationship] (Tokyo: Rokufū Shuppan, 1996), 13–14.

4. Political scientist Erin Aeran Chung has written an illuminating dissertation about the place of citizenship in Zainichi Korean political identity. She argues that

given their small numbers, activists actually have a more powerful voice as noncitizens than they would as a voting block. Erin Aeran Chung, *Exercising Citizenship: Korean Identity and the Politics of Nationality in Japan* (Evanston, IL: Northwestern University, 2003).

5. Until recently, Germany, like Japan, bestowed citizenship on the basis of *jus sanguinis*, and the Turkish there faced a similar predicament to that of Resident Koreans. In 2000, however, it changed its citizenship laws, granting German nationality to all born there, and reducing residency requirements for naturalization.

6. For a meticulously documented account of the migration of Koreans to Japan, see Michael Weiner, *The Origin of the Korean Community in Japan, 1910–1923* (Manchester: Manchester University Press, 1989).

7. Those who remained did so for a range of reasons, including the fact that after SCAP (Supreme Command for the Allied Powers, the U.S.-controlled occupation government in Japan) took control of the repatriation program in 1946, it imposed many restrictions, such as on the amount of luggage and money people were allowed to take with them when they left. In addition, apparently many had heard that there were riots, disease, and famine in Korea itself. As a consequence, a good many who had hoped to return decided that they would not, or left once and then returned. Many had spent a good portion of their adult life in Japan and did not wish to return to a land where they had no assurance of employment: the majority came from impoverished farming areas such as Kyŏngsang-do or Cheju-do, and they had no guarantee of having land to farm. Put bluntly, returning to Korea was not a simple matter for those Koreans in Japan at the time of liberation. See *The Korean Minority in Japan: 1904–1950* (New York: Institute of Pacific Relations, 1951), by Edward Wagner, who served in the United States occupation forces; this text provides one of the most detailed accounts of such matters in any language.

8. Research/Action Institute for Koreans in Japan (RAIK), *Japan's Subtle Apartheid: The Korean Minority Now* (Tokyo: RAIK, 1990), 13–14. One of many books in Japanese delineating legal details is Yang's *Zainichi Kankoku Chōsenjin dokuhon.*

9. RAIK, *Japan's Subtle Apartheid*, 16–17. Also Yang, *Zainichi Kankoku Chōsenjin dokuhon*, 15–16.

10. Yang, *Zainichi Kankoku Chōsenjin dokuhon*, 140–41; RAIK, *Japan's Subtle Apartheid*, 18. This also applied to Resident Taiwanese in the same predicament.

11. Yang, *Zainichi Kankoku Chōsenjin dokuhon*, 20–21. 1990 data from the Ministry of Justice indicated that there were 323,197 who had "permanent resident" status by virtue of the 1965 treaty and 268,178 people with "special permanent resident" status. Quoted in Sonia Ryang, *North Koreans in Japan: Language, Ideology, and Identity* (Boulder, CO: Westview Press, 1997).

12. Here again, see Chung, *Exercising Citizenship.*

13. Holding nonmanagement level jobs, such as that of mail carrier, is already permitted.

14. I use the contemporary names for these organizations, which have changed

their names over the years. For the English translations, I follow RAIK, *Japan's Subtle Apartheid*, 26. Hereafter I will refer to these groups as they are best known in Japan, Sōren and Mindan.

15. Ryang, *North Koreans in Japan*, 90.

16. Ibid., 113.

17. For more on Sōren and its ideology, see Ryang, *North Koreans in Japan*.

18. United Nations Population Division Executive Summary, "Replacement Migration: Is It a Solution to Declining and Ageing Population?," http://www.un.org/esa/population/publications/migration/execsu . . . , accessed April 26, 2004.

19. Stephen Murphy-Shigematsu, "Emerging Paradigms of Minority Citizenship in Japan," presented at the Conference on Citizenship, Immigration and Minority Politics in Contemporary Japan, Reischauer Institute, Harvard University, March 13, 2004.

20. There are too many books to list them all, but some notable volumes include the following. On Okinawa: Laura Hein and Mark Selden, eds., *Islands of Discontent: Okinawan Responses to Japanese and American Power* (Oxford: Rowman and Littlefield, 2003), and the fiction collection *Southern Exposure: Modern Japanese Literature from Okinawa*, ed. Michael Molasky and Steve Rabson (Honolulu: University of Hawai'i Press, 2001); on Ainu: Richard Siddle, *Race, Resistance, and the Ainu of Japan* (London: Routledge, 1996), and the translation of a memoir, Kayano Shigeru, *Our Land Was a Forest: An Ainu Memoir*, trans. Kyoko Selden and Lili Selden (Boulder, CO: Westview Press, 1994); on Burakumin: Ian Neary, *Political Protest and Social Control in Pre-War Japan: The Origins of Buraku Liberation* (Atlantic Highlands, NJ: Humanities Press International, 1989), and a translation of some of the most prominent works by author Nakagami Kenji, *The Cape and Other Stories from the Japanese Ghetto*, trans. Eve Zimmerman (Berkeley: Stone Bridge Press, 1999); on Resident Koreans: Michael Weiner, *Origin of the Korean Community in Japan*; and Sonia Ryang, ed., *Koreans in Japan: Critical Voices from the Margin* (London: Routledge, 2000); on Nikkei returnees: Daniel Touro Linger, *No One Home: Brazilian Selves Remade in Japan* (Stanford: Stanford University Press, 2001); and, finally, an edited volume on minorities more generally: Michael Weiner, ed., *Japan's Minorities: The Illusion of Homogeneity* (London: Routledge, 1997).

21. I am indebted to Patricia Chu for her concise description of the "ethnic relations cycle" developed by Robert E. Park and the Chicago school of sociology. See Chu, *Assimilating Asians: Gendered Strategies of Authorship in Asian America* (Durham, NC: Duke University Press, 2000), 7.

22. Michael Omi and Howard Winant, *Racial Formation in the United States: From the 1960s to the 1990s*, 2nd ed. (London: Routledge, 1994), 21.

23. Ibid., 22.

24. Ibid., 22–23.

25. Ri Takanori, "Posutocorinaru no seiji to 'Zainichi' bungaku" [Postcolonial Politics and "Zainichi" Literature], *Gendai shisō* 29 (July 2001): 154–69.

26. Kōichi Iwabuchi, *Recentering Globalization: Popular Culture and Japanese Transnationalism* (Durham, NC: Duke University Press, 2002), 3.

27. Herbert Marcuse, *The Aesthetic Dimension: Toward A Critique of Marxist Aesthetics* (Boston: Beacon Press, 1988), 13.

28. Raymond Williams, *Marxism and Literature* (Oxford: Oxford University Press, 1977), 129.

29. Ibid., 130.

30. Ibid., 151.

31. See, for example, Peter Brooks and Paul Gerwitz, eds., *Law's Stories: Narrative and Rhetoric in the Law* (New Haven: Yale University Press, 1996) and Guyora Binder and Robert Weisberg, *Literary Criticisms of Law* (Princeton: Princeton University Press, 2000).

32. Peter Brooks, "The Law as Narrative and Rhetoric," in Brooks and Gerwitz, *Law's Stories*.

CHAPTER 2

1. For further on the student movement, see George Katsificas, in *The Imagination of the New Left: A Global Analysis of 1968* (Boston: South End Press, 1987). A detailed history of the anti-Narita movement can be found in David E. Apter and Nagayo Sawa, *Against the State: Politics and Social Protest in Japan* (Cambridge: Harvard University Press, 1984).

2. In a presentation at the 1997 meeting of the Association for Asian Studies in Chicago, "From Public Phones to Community Newsletters: The Localization of the Public Sphere in the 1960s," Wesley Sasaki-Uemura made this precise argument. See also Frank Upham, *Law and Social Change in Postwar Japan* (Cambridge: Harvard University Press, 1987), 54–56; and Beverley Smith, "Democracy Derailed: Citizens Movements in Historical Perspective," in *Democracy in Contemporary Japan*, ed. Gavan McCormack and Yoshio Sugimoto (Armonk, NY: M. E. Sharpe, 1986).

3. Utsumi Aiko, a prominent scholar and activist, has recounted that this was her own experience.

4. Mun Kyŏng-su, "Zainichi Chōsenjin," in *Sekai minzoku mondai jiten* [Encyclopedia of Nations and Ethnic Relations (English title included)] (Tokyo: Heibonsha, 1995), 457.

5. Takeda Taijun and Ri Kaisei, "Chōsen no kokoro Nihon no kotoba" [Korean Heart, Japanese Language], *Bungei shunjū* 50, no. 6 (June 1972): 133.

6. The term *identity* (with a Japanized pronunciation) is usually defined in terms of its meaning in psychology; often Erik Erikson's seminal work is cited. The term is often glossed with Chinese characters meaning "subjectivity" or indicating "self-sameness." Its use in the Resident Korean community (to refer to a sense of ethnic consciousness) can be dated, I believe, to the period I am covering here. The con-

servative literary critic Etō Jun relied heavily on Erikson's thought in a prominent book on modern Japanese literature, *Seijuku to soshitsu* [Maturity and Loss], published in 1966. I will return to a discussion of this matter in the next chapter.

7. For an English account, see Changsoo and George De Vos, *Koreans in Japan: Ethnic Conflict and Accommodation*, ed. Changsoo Lee (Berkeley: University of California Press, 1985), 253–79. A concise Japanese account appears in Kabushikigaisha Kōdansha [Kodansha, Inc.], ed., *Shōwa nimannichi no zenkiroku dai 14 maki: yureru Shōwa Genroku, Shōwa 43nen-46nen* [Twenty Thousand Days of Shōwa, Volume 14: The Wavering Genroku of Shōwa, 1968–1971] (Tokyo: Kodansha, 1990), 44–45.

8. In a discussion held not long after the event, the author Kō Shi-mei observed that the transcripts were the most extensive discussion of Korean issues from a Japanese perspective that he had seen. In Iinuma Jirō, ed., *Hikokumin no susume: Zainichi Chōsenjin o kataru III* [A Traitor's Advice: Discussing Resident Koreans III], ed. Iinuma Jirō (Tokyo: Bakushūsha, 1985), 113. This discussion was originally published in 1973.

9. Cornel West, "A Matter of Life and Death," in *The Identity in Question*, ed. John Rajchman (New York: Routledge, 1995), 16.

10. Kim Shi-jŏng, "Nihongo no obie — tozasareta Kim Hŭi-ro no kotoba o otte" [Fear of Japanese — Searching for the Closed-in Language of Kim Hŭi-ro], in *"Hikokumin" no susume: Zainichi Chōsenjin o kataru III* [Recommendations of a "Traitor": Tales of Resident Koreans III], ed. Iinuma Jirō (Tokyo: Bakushūsha, 1984).

11. Yi Byŏng-su, December 17, 1971, in Kim Hŭi-ro Kōhan Taisaku Iinkai [Committee for the Trial of Kim Hŭi-ro], ed., *Kim Hŭi-ro mondai shishū VII: Shōgenshū 3* [Materials of the Kim Hŭi-ro Incident VII: Testimonies 3] (Tokyo: Kim Hŭi-ro Kōhan Taisaku Iinkai, 1972), 23.

12. Ibid., 25.

13. Ibid., 26.

14. Kim Hŭi-ro Kōhan Taisaku Iinkai [Committee for the Trial of Kim Hŭi-ro], ed., *Kim Hŭi-ro mondai shishū III Bengodan no bōtō chinjutsu* [Materials of the Kim Hŭi-ro Incident III: Opening Statement of the Defense] (Tokyo: Kim Hŭi-ro Kōhan Taisaku Iinkai, 1972), 6.

15. Ibid., 7.

16. Suzuki Michihiko, January 18, 1972, in Kim Hŭi-ro Kōhan Taisaku Iinkai [Committee for the Trial of Kim Hŭi-ro], *Kim Hŭi-ro mondai shishū VII* [Materials of the Kim Hŭi-ro Incident VII], 99–107.

17. Ibid., 99–100.

18. Ibid., 100–101.

19. Ibid., 101.

20. Ibid., 102.

21. Ibid., 99.

22. Ibid., 103–4.

23. Ibid., 105.

24. Mihashi Osamu, "Kin Kirō jiken — sore kara sannen" [The Kim Hŭi-ro Incident — 3 Years Later], *Chōsen kenkyū* [Korea Research] 103 (March 1973): 34–35.

25. Kim Shi-jŏng, December 17, 1971, Kim Hŭi-ro Kōhan Taisaku Iinkai [Committee for the Trial of Kim Hŭi-ro], *Kim Hŭi-ro mondai shishū VII* [Materials of the Kim Hŭi-ro Incident VII], 59–67.

26. Ri Kaisei, December 17, 1971, in ibid., 29–40. Also reprinted in edited form in Ri Kaisei, *Kita de are minami de are waga sokoku* [North or South, Our Homeland] (Tokyo: Kawade Shobo Shinsha, 1974), 173–84.

27. Kim Hŭi-ro Kōhan Taisaku Iinkai [Committee for the Trial of Kim Hŭi-ro], *Kim Hŭi-ro mondai shishū VII* [Materials of the Kim Hŭi-ro Incident VII], 38.

28. Kim Shi-jŏng, in ibid., 64.

29. Ibid., 65.

30. Ibid.

31. Yang Sŏk-il, *Ajiateki shintai* [The Asian Body] (Tokyo: Seibōsha, 1990).

32. Ōe Kenzaburō, Kim Sŏk-bŏm, and Ri Kaisei, "Nihongo de kaku koto ni tsuite" [On Writing in Japanese], *Bungaku* 38, no. 11 (1970): 1–27.

33. George De Vos and Daekyun Chung, "Community Life in a Korean Ghetto," in *Koreans in Japan: Ethnic Conflict and Accommodation*, ed. Changsoo Lee (Berkeley: University of California Press, 1985), 225–51. The authors report that 3,576 of the 7,450 marriages that year were between Koreans and Japanese (226).

34. Pak Shil, "Zainichi Kankoku Chōsenjin o meguru tōkei no hanashi" [The Story of Statistics About Resident Koreans], in *Horumon Bunka I: Issatsu Marugoto Zainichi Chōsenjin* ["Tripe Culture" I: The Complete Book on Resident Koreans], ed. Horumon Bunka Henshū iinkai [Tripe Culture Editorial Committee] (Tokyo: Shinkan-sha, 1990), 85–88.

35. Kajii Noboru, "Zainichi Chōsenjin Bungaku no Sakuhin Nenpyō" [A Calendar of Literary Works by Resident Koreans], *Kikan Sanzenri* 20 (1979): 55.

36. Ōe Kenzaburō et al., "Nihongo de kaku koto ni tsuite" [On Writing in Japanese] 3–4.

37. Ibid., 9.

38. Ibid., 6.

39. Ibid., 25.

40. "Nihongo to no kakawari" [My Relationship to Japanese], originally printed in the *Tokyo shinbun*, April 14, 1972, evening edition, reprinted in Ri Kaisei, *Kita de are minami de are waga sokoku* [North or South, Our Homeland], 206.

41. *Shutaisei* is a term of unparalleled inportance for post–World War II Japanese thought. See J. Victor Koschmann, *Revolution and Subjectivity in Postwar Japan* (Chicago: University of Chicago Press, 1996), who outlines many of the debates that use this term as a vehicle for talking about Japan's modernity, militarism, and eventual democratization.

42. The story "Warera seishun no tojō nite" [On the Road of our Youth],

originally published in the magazine *Gunzō* in August 1969, is a prime example of such a story.

43. Ri Kaisei, "Kinuta o Utsu Onna" [The Woman Who Fulled Clothes], *Bungei Shunjū*, March 1972, 318–39. All translations are my own. Future references will refer to this edition and will appear in parentheses in the body of the text. I have also referred to Ri Kai-sei, "The Woman Who Fulled Clothes," trans. Beverly Nelson, in *Flowers of Fire: Twentieth-Century Korean Stories*, rev. ed., ed. Peter Lee (Honolulu: University of Hawai'i Press, 1986), 344–72.

44. That an older way of life would be evoked by such an implement is perhaps obvious. Norma Field pointed out to me the fact of the fulling board being a common motif in premodern literature, most notably *Ise monogatari* [The Tale of Ise].

45. Karatani Kōjin, *Origins of Modern Japanese Literature*, trans., ed. Brett deBary (Durham, NC: Duke University Press, 1993), 73.

46. Louis Althusser, "Ideology and Ideological State Apparatuses (Notes Toward an Investigation), in *Lenin and Philosophy and Other Essays*, trans. Ben Brewster (New York: Monthly Review, 1971), 127–86.

47. Ibid., 176.

48. Beverly Nelson, "Korean Literature in Japan, A Case Study: Ri Kai Sei," in *Studies on Korea in Transition*, ed. David R. McCann, John Middleton, and Edward J. Shultz (Honolulu: Center for Korean Studies, University of Hawai'i, 1977), 145.

49. Chong-Sik Lee, *Japan and Korea: The Political Dimension* (Stanford, CA: Hoover Institution Press, Stanford University, 1985), 9.

50. Oda Makoto and Ri Kaisei, "Bungakusha to sokoku" [The Author and His Fatherland], *Gunzō* 27, no. 5 (May 1972): 195.

51. Nelson, "Korean Literature in Japan," 134.

52. In "My Relationship to Japanese," Ri speaks extensively about the fact that sometimes he chooses Chinese characters that are less common because he wants to emphasize something different from what people usually indicate by that word. I have noticed that in other pieces of fiction, Ri also writes "she" in this manner. More often the word is written with the character for "he" followed by the character for woman, instead of with the phonetic "kano" (over there) followed by "woman." Still, I think it would be reading too much into this to see it is another indication of Ri's "othering" of women in general.

53. Kobayashi Hideo is perhaps the most prominent critic to have done so. See his "Watakushi shōsetsu ron" [Theory of the I-novel], in *Shōwa Bungaku zenshū 9: Kobayashi Hideo, Kawakami Tetsutarō, Nakamura Mitsuo, Yamamoto Takekichi* [Anthology of Shōwa literature 9: Kobayashi Hideo, Kawakami Tetsutarō, Nakamura Mitsuo, Yamamoto Takekichi] (Tokyo: Shogakkan, 1987), 53–67. In his *Origins of Modern Japanese Literature*, Karatani Kōjin goes even further to locate the emergence of this form at the time of the "creation" of a modern sense of interiority.

54. *T'aryŏng* refers to common lament as well as to one part of the Korean shamanistic ritual, or *kut*.

55. Nelson, "Korean Literature in Japan," 139.

56. Kitada Sachie, "Kinuta o utsu onna," *Nihon bungei kanshō jiten: Kindai meisaku 1017–sen e no shōtai,* 20 [Dictionary of Japanese Literature: An Introduction to 1017 Modern Masterpieces] (Tokyo: Gyōsei, 1988), 190. Kitada conflates Ri Kaisei and the narrator in her commentary. I do not wish to naïvely assume that I have access to Ri's intentions; the Ri to whom I would refer is what Foucault refers to as the author-function in his essay "What Is an Author?," in *Textual Strategies: Perspectives in Post-Structuralist Criticism,* ed. Josué V. Harari (Ithaca, NY: Cornell University Press, 1979), 141–60.

57. Nelson, "Korean Literature in Japan," 142.

58. Ibid., 143.

59. *Minshū* in Japanese, usually translated from the Korean as "folk."

60. Chungmoo Choi, "Minjung Culture Movement and the Construction of Popular Culture in Korea," in *South Korea's Minjung Movement: The Culture and Politics of Dissidence,* ed. Kenneth M. Wells (Honolulu: University of Hawai'i Press, 1995), 109.

61. Ibid., 114–15.

62. Ibid., 115.

63. Ibid., 116.

64. Ibid., 116–17.

65. Ibid., 106–8.

66. Ri Kaisei and Kim Chi-ha, "Tokubetsu taidan: Minzoku to kojin" [A Special Discussion: The Nation and the Individual], *Shinchō,* February 1996, 234–58.

67. This information is included in "Ri Kaisei nenpu" [Ri Kaisei — Biographical/Publication Data], *Akutagawa shō zenshū* 9 [The Complete Collection of Akutagawa Prize–Winning Stories, 9] (Tokyo: Bungei Shunjū, 1982), 381–87.

68. In a 1988 roundtable discussion with Korean scholar Paik Nak-chung [Paek Nak-ch'ŏng], Ri states that *madangguk* were not introduced in Japan until the early 1980s. Paek Nak-ch'ŏng, Ri Kaisei, and Yang Min-gi, "Minzoku bungaku to Zainichi bungaku o megutte" [On National Literature and Resident Korean Literature], *Kikan Zainichi bungei mintō* 3 (May 1988): 15.

69. Suh Kyung-sik (Sŏ Kyŏng-shik), "Kim Chi-ha e no tegami: jikō bunretsu no itami" [A Letter to Kim Chi-ha: The Pain of Self-Disintegration], *Gendai shisō* [Modern Thought], October 1995, 30–44. Suh reports that Kim admitted in the Korean press that he did not write all the works credited to him. See also the English translation, "A Letter to Mr. Kim Chi-ha; or, The Pain of the Split Self," trans. Norma Field, *positions* 5, no. 1 (Spring 1997): 316–20.

70. Suh Kyung-sik (Sŏ Kyŏng-shik), "Kim Chi-ha e no tegami: jikō bunretsu no itami" [A Letter to Kim Chi-ha: The Pain of Self-Disintegration], 39.

71. My assessment of Kim's turn to nativism relies on Suh's article and the conversation between Kim and Ri Kaisei.

72. Chungmoo Choi, "Minjung Culture Movement," 107.

73. See Henry Louis Gates Jr., "Critical Fanonism," *Critical Inquiry* 17, no. 3 (Spring 1991): 457–70, for a criticism of Bhabha's and other critics' appropriations of Fanon. Bhabha has penned numerous essays on Fanon, including the second chapter of his *The Location of Culture* (London: Routledge, 1994).

74. Ibid., 458.

75. Here I echo Gates on Albert Memmi's reading of Fanon. Ibid., 468–69.

76. Nelson, "Korean Literature in Japan," 133–35.

77. Of course I have the benefit of hindsight, which Nelson, writing shortly after the publication of "Kinuta," did not.

78. Ibid., 135.

79. The narrator refers to his grandmother's *shinse t'aryŏng* as possessing *in*, indicating its poetic character, i.e., its rhythm or meter (332). Beverly Nelson's attention to the meter of certain sentences was extremely helpful to me in my development of this point, although I differ with her on the conclusions I draw from it.

80. Ibid., 150.

81. Ri Kaisei, "'Kinuta o utsu onna' no koto" [About "The Woman Who Fulled Clothes"], in *Kita de are minami de are waga sokoku* [North or South, Our Homeland], 237.

82. Fredric Jameson, *Marxism and Form: Twentieth-century Dialectical Theories of Literature* (Princeton: Princeton University Press, 1971), 219.

83. Ibid., 221–28.

84. Ibid., 228.

85. Fredric Jameson, "Third-World Literature in the Era of Multinational Capitalism," *Social Text* 15 (Fall 1986): 69.

86. Gilles Deleuze and Félix Guattari, "What is a Minor Literature?," in *Out There: Marginalization and Contemporary Cultures*, ed. Russel Ferguson, Martha Gever, Trinh T. Minh-ha, and Cornel West (New York: New Museum of Contemporary Art, and Cambridge, MA: MIT Press, 1990), 59.

87. Aijaz Ahmad, "Jameson's Rhetoric of Otherness and the 'National Allegory,'" *Social Text* 17 (Fall 1987): 3–25.

88. Laura Mulvey, "Visual Pleasure and Narrative Cinema," in *Feminisms: An Anthology of Literary Theory and Criticism*, ed. Robyn R. Warhoal and Diane Price Herndl (New Brunswick, NJ: Rutgers University Press, 1991), 432–42. The essay, a much-debated classic of feminist film theory, was originally published in 1975.

89. Ri Kaisei, "'Kinuta o utsu onna' no koto" [About "The Woman Who Fulled Clothes"], 236–37.

90. See Takeda's chapter on Ri, in Takeda Seiji, *"Zainichi" to iu konkyo* ["Zainichi" as Foundation] (Tokyo: Chikuma Shobo, 1995), 11–98, esp. 71–98.

91. Ibid., 98.

92. I do not think Takeda would disagree with my assessment, but his emphasis differs.

93. One might argue that earlier Zainichi writers had done so already, but

because those writers mostly saw their Korean identity as arising from their "blood," I would contend that it is not until Ri's spectacular success that the notion of creation of identity spread in the Zainichi community.

CHAPTER 3

1. Takeda Seiji, *"Zainichi" to iu konkyo* ["Zainichi" as Foundation] (Tokyo: Chikuma Shobo, 1995), 237. This paperback edition is an expansion of the original hardcover book, which appeared in 1983.

2. Chŏng Yŏng-hae, "Aidentitii o koete" [Getting Beyond Identity], in *Iwanami kōza, Gendai shakaigaku 15: Sabetsu to kyōsei no shakaigaku* [Iwanami Lectures, Modern Sociology 15: The Sociology of Discrimination and Coexistence], pub. Yasue Yōsuke (Tokyo: Iwanami Shoten, 1996), 10.

3. Kimura Hisashi (chair), Ozawa Nobuo, Kijima Hajime, and Kobayashi Masaru, "Kyōkaisen no bungaku — Zainichi Chōsenjin sakka no imi" [Literature on the Borderline — The Meaning of Resident Korean Writers], *Shin Nihon bungaku* [New Japanese Literature] 278 (September 1970): 46–77.

4. Matsuzaki Haruo, in "70-nendai no Yi Hoe-sŏng to *Mihatenu yume*" [Yi Hoe-sŏng in the '70s and *The Unfinished Dream*], *Minshu bungaku* [Democratic Literature] 168 (November 1979): 90–112, tracks correspondences between characters in the novel and "real" historical figures. He also observes that in the afterword to the paperback edition of the book, Ri thanks a group organized in support of the Suh brothers for supplying him with information (104). Itō Naruhiko also mentions the correlation between Ri's fictional characters and well-known historical figures. Itō, *Jihyō to shite no bungaku 1984–1995* [Literature as Timeline, 1984–1995] (Tokyo: Ochanomizu Shobo, 1995), 476–77.

5. Kin Kakuei, *Kogoeru kuchi* [The Benumbed Mouth], in *Kin Kakuei shū* [Collected Works by Kin Kakuei] (Tokyo: Sakuhinsha, 1986), 9–97. Subsequent page references are cited parenthetically in the text.

6. Unless otherwise noted, all citations are from the King James version of the Bible, which is closest in tone to the passages included in *The Benumbed Mouth*.

7. Takeda Seiji, *"Zainichi" to iu konkyo* ["Zainichi" as Foundation], 240.

8. I have not been able to find a reference to his having a stutter, although he is described in the earlier citation as a poor speaker. One commentary argues "to plead 'uncircumcised lips' may mean that his lips are not adequate. Or it may mean that he is an outsider to Pharaoh, who will never take him seriously." *New Interpreter's Bible Volume 1* (Nashville: Abingdon Press, 1994), 735.

9. Takeda Seiji, *"Zainichi" to iu konkyo* ["Zainichi" as Foundation], 150–51. For more on the *shishōsetsu* genre and Japanese modern literature, see Kobayashi Hideo, "Watakushi shōsetsu ron" [Theory of the I-novel], in *Shōwa bungaku zenshū 9: Kobayashi Hideo, Kawakami Tetsutarō, Nakamura Mitsuo, Yamamoto Takekichi*

Shōwa Bungaku zenshū 9: Kobayashi Hideo, Kawakami Tetsutarō, Nakamura Mitsuo, Yamamoto Takekichi [Anthology of Shōwa Literature 9: Kobayashi Hideo, Kawakami Tetsutarō, Nakamura Mitsuo, Yamamoto Takekichi] (Tokyo: Shogakkan, 1987); Karatani Kōjin, *Origins of Modern Japanese Literature*, trans., ed. Brett deBary (Durham, NC: Duke University Press, 1993); Edward Fowler, *The Rhetoric of Confession: Shishōsetsu in Early Twentieth-Century Japanese Fiction* (Berkeley: University of California Press, 1988); James A. Fujii, *Complicit Fictions: The Subject in the Modern Japanese Prose Narrative* (Berkeley: University of California Press, 1993); Tomi Suzuki, *Narrating the Self: Fictions of Japanese Modernity* (Stanford: Stanford University Press, 1996).

10. Takeda Seiji, *"Zainichi" to iu konkyo* ["Zainichi" as Foundation], 171.

11. Takeda Seiji, "Zainichi to taikōshugi" [Resident Koreans and Oppositionalism], in *Iwanami Gendai Shakaigaku 24: Minzoku•Kokka•Esunishiti* [Iwanami Modern Sociology 24: Nation/State/Ethnicity] (Tokyo: Iwanami Shoten, 1996), 103.

12. Takeda Seiji, *"Zainichi" to iu konkyo* ["Zainichi" as Foundation], 207. He does not use either "post" term, although the influence of such philosophies on his interpretations of Kin is evident.

13. Kitada Sachie, " 'Zainichi' suru 'ba' no imi: Kin Kakuei ron" [The Meaning of the "Site" of "Zainichi": An Analysis of Kin Kakuei], *Kikan Zainichi bungei mintō* 1 (November 1987): 108.

14. In this book, he uses the ideas of Erik Erikson, something of a fad in Japanese literary studies beginning with Etō Jun's *Seijuku to soshitsu* [Maturity and Loss], a study of early postwar Japanese writers that was published in 1966. As Ann Sherif points out in "The Politics of Loss: On Etō Jun," a paper presented at the Association for Asian Studies Conference held in Chicago on March 16, 1997, although the subtitle to Etō's book is "The Decline of the Mother," the work in fact deals almost exclusively with the loss of authority of the father in postwar Japan.

15. Kitada Sachie, " 'Zainichi' suru 'ba' no imi: Kin Kakuei ron" [The Meaning of the "Site" of "Zainichi"], 113.

16. Ibid., 108.

17. Martin Jay, *Downcast Eyes: The Denigration of Vision in Twentieth-Century French Thought* (Berkeley: University of California Press, 1993), 410. My discussion of Foucault relies heavily on Jay's analysis in the chapter entitled "From the Empire of the Gaze to the Society of the Spectacle: Foucault and Debord," 381–434.

18. Quoted in ibid., 406. The citation is from Foucault's *The Order of Things*, 312.

19. Georg Lukács, *History of Class Consciousness*, quoted in Fredric Jameson, *Marxism and Form: Twentieth-century Dialectical Theories of Literature* (Princeton: Princeton University Press, 1971), 186–87.

20. See, for example, Harry Braverman, *Labor and Monopoly Capital: The Degradation of Work in the Twentieth Century* (New York: Monthly View Press,

1974), whose work is pointed to by Stanley Aronowitz in "The Production of Scientific Knowledge: Science, Ideology, and Marxism," in *Marxism and the Interpretation of Culture*, introduced and ed. Cary Nelson and Lawrence Grossberg (Urbana: University of Illinois Press, 1988), 519–41.

21. Ch'ŏi Sŏng-gu, Pak Chŏng-sŏk, Satō Katsumi, Yi Yin-ha, Kōra Tetsuo, and Wada Jun, "Hitachi kyūdan e no ayumi" [The Path to the Denunciation of Hitachi], in *Minzoku sabetsu — Hitachi shūshoku sabetsu kyūdan* [Ethnic Discrimination — The Denunciation of Hitachi's Employment Discrimination], ed. Paku-kun o kakomu kai [The Committee for Pak] (hereafter cited as *Minzoku sabetsu*) (Tokyo: Aki Shobo, 1974), 11. The statement is by Ch'ŏi.

22. Ibid., 4.

23. The church in fact is a member of the Korean Christian Church in Japan (KCCJ), in which Yi has held a variety of posts.

24. Ibid., 12.

25. Ibid., 12–14.

26. Pak Chŏng-sŏk, "Pak Chŏng-sŏk no shuki" [A Note from Pak Chŏng-sŏk], in *Paku-kun o kakomu kai kaihō* [The Committee for Pak Newsletter] 1 (no date): 7.

27. Ch'ŏi Sŏng-gu et al., "Hitachi kyūdan e no ayumi" [The Path to the Denunciation of Hitachi], 15.

28. Pak Chŏng-sŏk, "Pak Chŏng-sŏk no shuki" [A Note from Pak Chŏng-sŏk], 7.

29. Ch'ŏi Sŏng-gu et al., "Hitachi kyūdan e no ayumi" [The Path to the Denunciation of Hitachi], 15.

30. Kōra Tetsuo, "Paku-kun o kakomu kai no san nen" [The Three Years of the Committee for Pak], in *Minzoku sabetsu*, 71–72.

31. Ch'ŏi Sŏng-gu et al., "Hitachi kyūdan e no ayumi" [The Path to the Denunciation of Hitachi], 15–16.

32. Ibid., 16.

33. Wada Jun, "Saiban no keika to hanketsu no imi" [The Progress of the Trial and the Meaning of the Decision], in *Minzoku sabetsu*, 135.

34. Ibid., 138–39.

35. Ibid., 140–41.

36. Paku-kun o kakomu kai [The Committee for Pak], "Sabetsu to yokuatsu no soko kara — Shūshoku sabetsu saiban saishū junbi shomen" [From the Depths of Discrimination and Oppression: Final Notes for the Closing of an Employment Discrimination Suit], in *Minzoku sabetsu*, 179.

37. Ibid., 181–91.

38. Wada Jun, "Saiban no keika to hanketsu no imi" [The Progress of the Trial and the Meaning of the Decision], 142.

39. Ibid., 143.

40. Ibid., 193–96.

41. Paku-kun o kakomu kai [The Committee for Pak], "Sabetsu naki shakai e

no tegakari — Shūshoku sabetsu saiban hanketsu (riyū bubun)" [Hints for a Society Without Discrimination — The Decision of an Employment Discrimination Trial (Portion Providing Justification)], in *Minzoku sabetsu*, 279.

42. Quoted in Ishizuka Hisashi, "Bengoshi da kara — de wa naku" [Not Because I'm His Lawyer], in *Minzoku sabetsu*, 161.

43. See, for example, John W. Dower, "Peace and Democracy in Two Systems: External Policy and Internal Conflict," in *Postwar Japan as History*, ed. Andrew Gordon (Berkeley: University of California Press, 1993), 28.

44. Dal-Joong Chang, *Economic Control and Political Authoritarianism: The Role of Japanese Corporations in Korean Politics 1965–1979* (Seoul: Sogang University Press, 1985), 50–51.

45. This was true of both Japanese and non-Japanese scholars. See Dal-Joong Chang, *Economic Control*.

46. Ch'ŏi Sŏng-gu et al., "Hitachi kyūdan e no ayumi" [The Path to the Denunciation of Hitachi], 20–21.

47. I found this nugget of information in Shigeto Tsuru, *Japan's Capitalism: Creative Defeat and Beyond* (Cambridge: Cambridge University Press, 1993), 129. The pun is my own.

48. Pak Chŏng-sŏk, "Minzokuteki jikaku e no michi — Shūshoku sabetsu saiban jōshinsho" [My Path to Ethnic Consciousness — A Report Submitted for This Employment Discrimination Trial], in *Minzoku sabetsu*, 237–60.

49. Takeda Seiji, *"Zainichi" to iu konkyo* ["Zainichi" as Foundation], 15–19, 176–207.

50. Ibid., 178.

51. Ibid., 178–79.

52. Ibid., 180–81.

53. Ibid., 189–96.

54. Kin Kakuei, "Ishi no michi" [The Stone Path], in *Kin Kakuei shū* [Collected Works by Kin Kakuei] (Tokyo: Sakuhinsha, 1986), 278–315. Subsequent page references are cited parenthetically in the text.

55. Song Mi-ja, "Zainichi nisei sakka ron — (1) — Kin Kakuei no bungaku (shimo)" [An Analysis of Second-generation Resident Korean Authors (1): On Kin Kakuei's Literature (2)], *Chōsen Kenkyū* [Korea Research] 216 (December 1981): 8.

56. Ibid.

57. Ibid., 13.

58. Ibid.

CHAPTER 4

1. David Harvey, *The Condition of Postmodernity* (Cambridge, MA: Blackwell, 1990).

2. Masao Miyoshi and Harry Harootunian, eds., *Postmodernism and Japan* (Durham, NC: Duke University Press, 1989).

3. I have given a simplified description of postmodernism for reasons of space. Two indispensable texts arguing the connection between changes in capitalism and shifts in cultural expression are David Harvey, *Condition of Postmodernity*; and Fredric Jameson, *Postmodernism: Or, the Cultural Logic of Late Capitalism* (Durham, NC: Duke University Press, 1995). The quote is from Jameson, *Postmodernism*, 26. One more essential piece: Doreen Massey has criticized Jameson and Harvey as well as Edward Soja (his *Postmodern Geographies: The Reassertion of Space in Critical Social Theory* [London: Verso, 1989]) in an essay entitled "Flexible Sexism," in her *Space, Place, and Gender* (Minneapolis: University of Minnesota Press, 1994), 212–48.

4. I find Caren Kaplan's account of this trend particularly helpful. Caren Kaplan, *Discourses of Travel: Postmodern Discourses of Displacement* (Durham, NC: Duke University Press, 1996), 143–87.

5. Massey, *Space, Place*, 168–69.

6. Kim Shi-jŏng, "Ikaino shishū" [Ikaino Poems], in *Kikan sanzenri* (1975): 184. This and all translations to appear in this chapter are my own. A slightly longer selection from this poem is included in David Suzuki and Keibo Oiwa, *The Japan We Never Knew: A Journey of Discovery* (Toronto: Stoddart, 1996), 182–83.

7. Kim Ch'ang-saeng, "Zainichi Chōsenjin no kurashi/seikatsu" [Resident Korean's Daily Life], in *Zainichi Kankoku Chōsenjin: Wakamono kara mita iken to omoi to kangae* [Resident Koreans: The Opinions, Feelings, and Thoughts of Young People], ed. Kim Yŏng-kwŏn and Yi Chŏng-yang (Tokyo: San'ichi Shobo, 1985), 16.

8. Song Yŏn-ok, "Osaka ni okeru Zainichi Chōsenjin no seikatsu—1945 izen" [The Lives of Resident Koreans in Osaka Before 1945], in *Zainichi Chōsenjin no rekishi: Hirakata de no horiokoshi no tame ni* [The History of Koreans in Japan: For Digging Up Their History in Hirakata], ed. Hirakata-shi Kyōiku Iinkai [Hirakata City Council on Education] (Hirakata: Hirakata City Council on Education, Social Education Department, 1991), 58–63.

9. Song Yŏn-ok, "Osaka ni okeru Zainichi Chōsenjin no seikatsu—1945 izen" [The Lives of Resident Koreans in Osaka Before 1945], 55–56.

10. Kim Ch'ang-saeng, "Zainichi Chōsenjin no kurashi/seikatsu" [Resident Korean's Daily Life], 13–14.

11. Yang Yŏng-fu, *Sengo Osaka no Chōsenjin Undō: 1945–1965* [The Postwar Korean Movement in Osaka: 1945–1965] (Tokyo: Miraisha, 1994), 178.

12. Song Yŏn-ok, "Osaka ni okeru Zainichi Chōsenjin no seikatsu—1945 izen" [The Lives of Resident Koreans in Osaka Before 1945], 80.

13. Yun Kŏn-a, *"Zainichi" o ikiru to wa* [To Live as "Zainichi"] (Tokyo: Iwanami Shoten, 1992), 238.

14. Kang Sang-jung, "Hōhō to shite no 'Zainichi'—Yang Tae-ho shi ni kotaeru" ["Zainichi" as Method—In Response to Yang Tae-ho], in *Zainichi Kankoku Chōsenjin—sono Nihon ni okeru sonzai kachi* [Resident Koreans: The Value of their

Existence in Japanese Society], ed. Iinuma Jirō (Tokyo: Kaifūsha, 1988), 275–87. This piece was originally published in 1985 in the magazine *Kikan sanzenri* [3000 Ri]. These debates are also outlined in English by Norma Field, in "Beyond Envy, Boredom, and Suffering: Toward an Emancipatory Politics for Resident Koreans and Other Japanese," *positions* 1, no. 3 (Winter 1993): 640–70.

15. Yang Tae-ho, "Kyōson/Kyōsei/Kyōkan — Kang Sang-jung shi e no gimon (II)" [Shared Existence/Shared Lives/Shared Feelings — Questions for Kang Sang-jung (2)], in *Zainichi Kankoku Chōsenjin — Sono Nihon ni okeru sonzai kachi* [Resident Koreans: The Value of their Existence in Japanese Society], ed. Iinuma Jirō (Tokyo: Kaifūsha, 1988), 289–301. This essay was originally published in 1985 in *Sanzenri*.

16. Mun Kyŏng-su, "Zainichi Chōsenjin." In *Sekai minzoku mondai jiten* [Encyclopedia of Nations and Ethnic Relations (English title included)] (Tokyo: Heibonsha, 1995), 456–57.

17. I think here of recent anthropological work in a conversational style, and particularly that by feminists, such as those included in Ruth Behar and Deborah A. Gordon, *Women Writing Culture* (Berkeley: University of California), 1995.

18. Reprinted from her 1971 collection in Chong Ch'u-wŏl, *Ikaino•Onna•Ai•Uta* [Ikaino/Woman/Love/Poems] (Osaka: Bureen Sentaa, 1984), 86–87, and in *Saran he/aishite imasu* [*Sarang hae*/I Love You] (Tokyo: Kage Shobo, 1987), 113–14. I have not been able to locate this first collection, but the fifth section of *Ikaino•Onna•Ai•Uta* [Ikaino/Woman/Love/Poems], 86–164, is composed of selections from that book.

19. M. M. Bakhtin, *The Dialogic Imagination*, trans. Caryl Emerson and Michael Holquist, ed., Michael Holquist (Austin: University of Texas Press, 1981).

20. Chong Ch'u-wŏl, *Ikaino taryon* [Ikaino Lament] (Tokyo: Shisō no Kagakusha, 1986), 174. Kim Shi-jŏng, the male poet whom I quoted earlier, similarly characterizes women of Ikaino. He observes that because they have the responsibility of appeasing the hunger of their families, and the stomach is an "incredible thing." "The women are strong, oh yes. Exceptionally so" ("Ikaino shishū" [Ikaino Poems], 184–85).

21. Ibid., 119–20.
22. Ibid., 179.
23. Ibid., 9.
24. Ibid., 10.
25. Ibid., 20.
26. Ibid., 23.
27. Ibid., 24.
28. Ibid., 24–25.
29. Ibid., 25.
30. Ibid., 117.
31. Ibid., 195.
32. Linda Alcoff, "Cultural Feminism Versus Post-structuralism: The Identity

Crisis in Feminist Theory," *Signs: Journal of Women in Culture and Society* 13, no. 3 (1988): 414.

33. A translation of this poem appears in Leza Lowitz and Miyuki Aoyama, trans. and ed., *Other Side River: Free Verse* (Berkeley, Stone Bridge Press, 1995), 40–43, under the title "Two Names."

34. Chong Ch'u-wŏl, *Saran he/aishite imasu* [*Sarang hae/*I Love You], 185–88.

35. Chong Ch'u-wŏl, "Mun Kon-bun *omoni* no *ningo*" [Mun Kon-bun Ŏmŏni's Apple], *Shin Nihon bungaku* [New Japanese Literature] 450 (1985), 14–30. This story also appears in *Ikaino taryon* [Ikaino Lament], 212–24; however, I have used the pagination of the journal, because it is more readily available in libraries outside of Japan. Subsequent page references are cited parenthetically in the text.

36. Ri told me that he prefers to be referred to by the Japanese pronunciation of his name, Ri Kaisei, which he calls his pen name.

37. Julia Kristeva's "Women's Time," in *The Kristeva Reader*, ed. Toril Moi (New York: Columbia University Press, 1986), 187–213, and Mikhail Bakhtin's "Forms of Time and of the Chronotope in the Novel" *Dialogic Imagination*, 84–258, were helpful to me in making this distinction.

38. "Ŏmŏni," which means "mother," is a term used in Korean to speak of any woman who has had children.

39. Bakhtin, *Dialogic Imagination*.

40. Takeuchi Yasuhiro, "Hirakareta gengo o kakutoku suru tame ni — Chong Ch'u-wŏl 'Mun Kon-bun *omoni* no *ningo*' ga shisa suru mono" [In Order to Attain More Open Language: The Implications of Chong Ch'u-wŏl's "Mun Kon-bun {hac}Ŏmŏni's Apple"], *Shin Nihon bungaku* [New Japanese Literature] 456 (1985): 19.

41. Ibid., 19–20.

42. Ibid., 21. The English translation of the work cited here, *Marxism and the Philosophy of Language*, is actually credited to V. N. Volosinov, although it has been widely assumed to be Bakhtin's work. The Japanese translation of the work lists the author as Bakhtin.

43. Bakhtin, *Dialogic Imagination*, 293.

44. Ibid., 294.

45. Karatani Kōjin's *Origins of Modern Japanese Literature*, first published in book form in 1980, is a preeminent example of literary criticism with strong post-structuralist/postmodernist influences (particularly Foucauldian).

46. Massey, *Space, Place*, 167.

47. Hitosashiyubi no jiyū henshū iinkai [Editorial Committee for Freedom of the Index Finger], *Hitosashiyubi no jiyū* [Freedom of the Index Finger] (Tokyo: Shakai Hyōronsha, 1984), 232.

48. Ibid., 93.

49. Ibid., 93–95.

50. Ibid., 96.

51. Ibid., 69–71.

52. Ibid., 72.

53. Ibid., 73.

54. Kim Dŏk-hwan shi no gaitōhō saiban o shien suru kai [Committee to Support Kim Dŏk-hwan's Alien Registration Law Trial], ed., *Igyora! (Ganbare!): Tokkan-san no shimon saiban* [Igyŏra! (Win!): Tokkan-san's Fingerprinting Trial] (Tokyo: Shinkansha, 1990), 184–85.

55. Ibid., 203–7.

56. Ibid., 250.

57. Ibid., 38.

58. Ibid., 40.

59. Ibid., 41–43.

60. Ibid., 43.

61. Ibid., 44. The scholars Tani Tomio and Harajiri Hideki, both of whom have done fieldwork in Ikaino, report that there is relatively little contact between local Japanese and Korean groups. They also note the presence of somewhat exclusionary associations of members of Japanese families who have lived in the area since before the influx of both Koreans and Japanese from other parts of the country in the early modern era.

62. Ibid., 277.

63. Pae Chŏng-jin (chair), Kim Ch'ang-saeng, Cho Pak, Ch'ae Hyo, Kang Na-mi, Chŏng Yun-hǔi, and Chŏng Tae-sŏng, "Zainichi bungaku wa kore de ii no ka" [Resident Korean Literature: Is This Good Enough?], *Kikan Zainichi bungei mintō* 1 (November 1987): 77.

64. Kim Ch'ang-saeng, *Watashi no Ikaino: Zainichi ni totte no sokoku to ikoku* [My Ikaino: Homeland and Foreign Country as Seen by Zainichi] (Nagoya: Fūbosha, 1982), 35–36. Subsequent page references are cited parenthetically in the text.

65. Kim Ch'ang-saeng, "Zainichi Chōsenjin no kurashi/seikatsu" [Resident Korean's Daily Life], 23

66. Pae Chŏng-jin et al., "Zainichi bungaku wa kore de ii no ka" [Resident Korean Literature: Is This Good Enough?], 61.

67. Ibid., 77.

68. Ibid.

69. Kim Ch'ang-saeng, *Watashi no Ikaino: Zainichi ni totte no sokoku to ikoku* [My Ikaino: Homeland and Foreign Country as Seen by Zainichi], 76–77.

70. Ibid., 82–83.

71. Kim Ch'ang-saeng, "Akai mi" [The Red Fruit], *Kikan Zainichi bungei mintō* 3 (Summer 1988): 276.

72. "Resident Korean Literature: Is This Good Enough?," 78.

73. Ōta Jun'ichi, *Onnatachi no Ikaino* [Women's Ikaino] (Tokyo: Shobunsha, 1987), 131.

74. Chong Ch'u-wŏl, *Saran he/aishite imasu* [*Sarang hae*/I Love You], 246.

75. Joan W. Scott, "Multiculturalism and the Politics of Identity," in *The Identity in Question*, ed. John Rajchman (New York: Routledge, 1995), 11.

CHAPTER 5

1. According to data from 1996, the collection that included her Akutagawa prize–winning novella, *Yuhi*, sold more than 130,000 copies and was ranked nineteenth in sales of works that have won that prize. Hayami Yukiko, "Akutagawashō ga tsumaranai" [The Akutagawa Prize is Dull], *Aera* 9, no. 1 (January 1996): 47.

2. Kawamura Minato notes that *Koku* [Koku], one of the stories I will read in this chapter, appeared in book form in Korean a week before it came out in Japan. "Sai no mukōgawa — Yi Yang-ji *Koku*" [On the Other Side of the Gap: Yi Yang-ji's *Koku*], *Gunzō* 40, no. 5 (May 1985): 332.

3. In English, see Masao Miyoshi, *Off Center: Power and Culture Relations Between Japan and the United States* (Cambridge: Harvard University Press, 1991), 234–36.

4. Kuroko Kazuo, "Zainichi Chōsenjin bungaku no genzai — 'Zainichi' suru koto no imi" [Resident Korean Literature Today: The Meaning of "Residing in Japan"], *Kikan Zainichi bungei mintō* 1 (November 1987): 89.

5. This is particularly evident in the discussion of Resident Korean literature I cited in the previous chapter. Pae Chŏng-jin (chair), Kim Ch'ang-saeng, Cho Pak, Ch'ae Hyo, Kang Na-mi, Chŏng Yun-hŭi, and Chŏng Tae-sŏng, "Zainichi bungaku wa kore de ii no ka" [Resident Korean Literature: Is This Good Enough?], *Kikan Zainichi bungei mintō* 1 (November 1987): 56–85.

6. Kawamura Minato, "Kankoku to iu kagami — Gendai bungaku fuiirudo nōto" [Korea the Mirror: Field Notes on Contemporary Literature], *Bungei* 24, no. 4 (April 1985): 170.

7. Takeda Seiji, "Yobiyoserareta 'Zainichi' no mochiifu — Yi Yang-ji *Koku*" [Motifs Recently Called Forth by "Zainichi": Yi Yang-ji's *Koku*], in *"Zainichi" to iu konkyo* ["Zainichi" as Foundation] (Tokyo: Chikuma Shobo, 1995), 296.

8. Yi Yang-ji, "Watashi ni totte no bokoku to Nihon" [What the Motherland and Japan Mean to Me], in *Yi Yang-ji zenshū* [The Complete Works of Yi Yang-ji] (Tokyo: Kōdansha, 1993), 654.

9. Kim Yŏng-hŭi, "Yi Yang-ji no koto" [On Yi Yang-ji], *Seikyū* 19 (Spring 1994): 64.

10. Ibid., 656.

11. Ibid., 655–56.

12. Ibid., 267.

13. Kawamura Minato, "Intabyū taidan — 'Zainichi bungaku' o koete: Yi Yang-ji" [An Interview — Getting Past "Zainichi Literature": Yi Yang-ji], *Bungakkai* 43 (March 1989): 268.

14. Ibid.

15. Ibid., 279.

16. Ibid.

17. Frederic Jameson, "Third-World Literature in the Era of Multinational Capitalism," *Social Text* 15 (Fall 1986). See discussion in Chapter 2.

18. "Nenpu" [Biographical data], in *Yi Yang-ji zenshū* [The Complete Works of Yi Yang-ji], 685.

19. "Kazukime" [The Diving Maiden], in *Yi Yang-ji zenshū* [The Complete Works of Yi Yang-ji], 63–95. Subsequent page references are cited parenthetically in the text.

20. Further information on the foreign protests against textbook screening can be found in Caroline Rose, "The Textbook Issue: Domestic Sources of Japan's Foreign Policy," *Japan Forum* 11, no. 2 (1999): 205–16.

21. In Korea, this is known as *shinbyŏng*.

22. Hyun-key Kim Hogarth, "Pursuit of Happiness Through Reciprocity: The Korean Shamanistic Ritual," *Shaman* 5, no. 1 (Spring 1997): 57–58, is one of many sources that tells of this process.

23. Mircea Eliade, *Shamanism: Archaic Techniques of Ecstasy*, trans. Willard R. Trask (London: Routledge & Kegan Paul, 1964). References to light appear on 61, 420, and elsewhere; and references to boiling on 41 and 44.

24. Hogarth, "Pursuit of Happiness Through Reciprocity," 56.

25. See Alan Carter Covell, *Folk Art and Magic Shamanism in Korea* (Seoul: Hollym Corporation, 1986), 203–4. Also see Jung Young Lee, *Korean Shamanistic Rituals* (The Hague: Mouton, 1981), 171–85.

26. Hogarth, "Pursuit of Happiness Through Reciprocity," 57. See also Richard Noll, "Shamanism and Schizophrenia: A State-specific Approach to the 'Schizophrenia Metaphor' of Shamanic States," *American Ethnologist* 10, no. 3 (1983): 443–59. In the first note of his "Role Playing Through Trance Possession in Korean Shamanism," in *Shamanism: The Spirit World of Korea* (Berkeley: Asian Humanities Press, 1988), 177, Yu Du-hyun refers to a number of Korean studies analyzing the relationship of *shinbyŏng* to mental illness.

27. See Judith Herman, *Trauma and Recovery* (New York: Basic Books, 1992, 1997).

28. I have rendered *kamisama* in the plural because of the suggestion of shamanism.

29. See the discussion by William R. LaFleur, *The Karma of Words: Buddhism and the Literary Arts in Medieval Japan* (Berkeley: University of California Press, 1983), 69–79.

30. Subsequent page references are cited parenthetically in the text. They are taken from the copy of the novella that appears in *Yi Yang-ji zenshū* [The Complete Works of Yi Yang-ji], 139–220.

31. I have chosen to translate this sentence in an awkward manner to emphasize both the awkwardness of the original and to draw attention to double self indicated by the use of the word *watashi* (I/me) twice.

32. *Hanguk minjok munhwa taebaekgwa sajŏn* [The Encyclopedia of Korean Culture], "Uruk" (Seoul: Hanguk chŏngshin munhwa yŏnguwon, 1991), 16:445.

33. Covell, in *Folk Art and Magic Shamanism*, describes the peak of the shaman's trance as a "mystical union" between the female shaman and the male god. The connection between Yi's dually sexed artistic being and the traditions of shamanism is thus evident.

34. Although she is not nice to this girl, she recalls that when the boarding house mother first told her about the girl and her origins, she had asked if Suni knew of any such unhappy — that is, poor or unfortunate — children in Japan, and Suni replied, "Yes, me." In another scene, she catches sight of the girl masturbating. She then goes to her room and, while fantasizing about the girl being raped, masturbates herself. Given the masochistic sexual proclivities of the protagonist elsewhere in the text, I read this her self-conscious superimposition of this girl's fate on to her own.

35. Sadly, they might have taken her portraits to develop a view of Korean women as promiscuous and highly sexual, as a colleague of mine, Helen Koh, has pointed out in an unpublished paper. Other critics have pointed out other ways in which her work may have been used to form or confirm certain stereotypes about Koreans. For example, in reference to *Yuhi*, in which the main character seems unable to come to terms with her Koreanness because she finds much about (South) Korean culture and society — which appear in the text in a stereotyped form — distasteful, such readers might have uncritically accepted the notion that Korean ethnicity was a source of pain or have been happy to find a confirmation of their negative views of Koreans. The former observation is from Takeda Seiji, "Rikai sareru mono no 'fukō' — Yi Yang-ji *Yuhi*" [The "Unhappiness" of Being Understood: Yi Yang-ji's *Yuhi*], in *"Zainichi" to iu konkyo* ["Zainichi" as Foundation] (Tokyo: Chikuma Shobo, 1995), 302; and the latter is from Norma Field, "Texts of Childhood in Inter-nationalizing Japan," in *Text and Nation: Cross-disciplinary Essays on Cultural and National Identities*, ed. Laura García-Moreno and Peter C. Pfeiffer (Columbia, SC: Camden House, 1996), 167.

36. Nakagami Kenji, "Yi Yang-ji *Koku*: Kankoku to Nihon no genzai" [Yi Yang-ji's *Koku*: Korea and Japan Today], *Shinchō* 62, no. 5 (May 1985): 314.

37. Kawamura Minato, "Sai no mukōgawa" [On the Other Side of the Gap], 332.

38. Kawamura Minato, "Kankoku to iu kagami" [Korea the Mirror], 169.

39. Ibid., 173.

40. Ibid., 173–75.

41. Nakagami, 312.

42. In *Yuhi*, Yi Yang-ji writes of words that breathe; *Yi Yang-ji zenshū* [The Complete Works of Yi Yang-ji], 424.

CHAPTER 6

1. This program, entitled *Mahiru no tsuki* [Midday Moon], aired between July 4, 1996, and September 19, 1996, on TBS Television.

2. Herman's book was published in the United States in 1992; in Japanese, in 1997.

3. Judith Herman, *Trauma and Recovery* (New York: Basic Books, 1992, 1997), 4.

4. "Supreme Court Upholds Ban on Book," *Japan Times* online, September 25, 2002, available at http://www.japantimes.co.jp/cgi-bin/getarticle.pl5?nn20020925a1 .htm.

5. Yū's name has the same Chinese characters as the perfectly ordinary Japanese name Yanagi Misato. Most Korean names are not written with ideograms that are also names in Japanese.

6. Herman, *Trauma and Recovery*, 27–32.

7. Yū Miri, *Mizube no yurikago* [Cradle by the Sea] (Tokyo: Kadokawa Shoten, 1997), 19.

8. Sakamoto Tetsushi, "Kakukai yūmeijin no AC do" [The AC Quotient of Famous People in Various Fields], *AERA*, August 4, 1997, 10–11.

9. In English, see, for example, Janet Woititz, *Adult Children of Alcoholics* (Deerfield Beach, FL: Health Communications, 1981); in Japanese, see chap. 3 of Saitō Satoru, *Adaruto chirudoren to kazoku* [Adult Children and the Family] (Tokyo: Gakuyō Bunko, 1998; originally published 1996).

10. Ibid., 10. See also Nobuta Sayoko, "Oya no sei ka, kodomono sei ka" [Is it the Parents' Fault? The Children's?], *Sekai*, September 1998, 228–29.

11. Amanda Seaman, "Modeling Masako: Commodities and the Construction of a Modern Princess," *Chicago Anthropology Exchange* 21 (Spring 1995): 44–45. See also Kano Mikiyo, "Remolding Tennoism for Modern Japan," *AMPO Japan-Asia Quarterly Review* 18, no. 2–3 (1986).

12. Yū Miri, *Mizube no yurikago* [Cradle by the Sea], 93–94.

13. Herman, *Trauma and Recovery*, 42. Herman refers to the work of psychoanalyst Paul Russell.

14. See Saitō Satoru, *Adaruto chirudoren to kazoku* [Adult Children and the Family], 125–32; Minagawa Kunitada, Mihashi Junko, and Saitō Satoru, "Zadankai: Torauma to kazoku" [Discussion: Trauma and the Family], *Gendai no esupuri* [Modern Esprit] May 1995: 13–18

15. Minagawa Kunitada et al., "Zadankai: Torauma to kazoku" [Discussion: Trauma and the Family], 15 (quote from Minagawa).

16. Ibid., 17 (quote from Minagawa).

17. Sakamoto Tetsushi, "Kakukai yūmeijin no AC do" [The AC Quotient of Famous People in Various Fields], 11. This statement originally appeared in the *New*

Yorker. Ian Buruma, "Profile: Becoming Japanese," *New Yorker*, December 23 and 30, 1996, 71.

18. Ibid., 11.

19. Nobuta Sayoko, "Oya no sei ka, kodomono sei ka" [Is it the Parents' Fault? The Children's?], 231.

20. Ibid., 232.

21. Ibid.

22. Seaman, in "Modeling Masako," notes that images of Princess Michiko in a home filled with Japan-made appliances encouraged consumption of these goods; the televising of her wedding to the crown prince helped the sale of (Japan-made) televisions. The "my-homeism" galvanized in these ways, she argues, thus "incorporated a nationalistic message" (45).

23. Yū Miri, *Shigo jiten* [My Personal Dictionary] (Tokyo: Asahi Shinbunsha, 1996), 44.

24. Ibid., 43.

25. Ibid., 45–46.

26. Ibid., 46.

27. Minagawa Kunitada makes this argument rather starkly, likening contemporary Japan to Europe and America during the world wars, and accepting MacArthur's determination the Japanese are all developmentally twelve years old. Minagawa Kunitada et al., "Zadankai: Torauma to kazoku" [Discussion: Trauma and the Family], 18.

28. For discussions of debates on modernity and *Nihonjinron*, see Harry D. Harootunian, "Visible Discourses/Invisible Ideologies," Naoki Sakai, "Modernity and Its Critique: The Problem of Universalism and Particularism," and J. Victor Koschmann, "Maruyama Masao and the Incomplete Project of Modernity," in *Postmodernism and Japan*, ed. Masao Miyoshi and Harry D. Harootunian (Durham, NC: Duke University Press, 1989). For a detailed examination of *Nihonjinron*, see Peter Dale, *The Myth of Japanese Uniqueness* (New York: St. Martin's Press, 1988); and Kosaku Yoshino, *Cultural Nationalism in Contemporary Japan: A Sociological Enquiry* (London: Routledge, 1992).

29. A detailed account of the textbook debates appears in Tawara Yoshifumi, *Kyōkasho kōgeki no shinsō* [The Depths of the Textbook Assault] (Tokyo: Gakuyū no Tomo Sha, 1997). The book also provides excepts from textbooks.

30. Kobayashi Yoshinori, *Shin gōmanizumu sengen daiyonkan* [The New Arrogant-ism Declaration] (Tokyo: Shōgakkan, 1998), 4:36.

31. Both Yū and Kobayashi write about this chain of events from their own perspective. See Yū Miri, *Kamen no kuni* [The Country of Masks] (Tokyo: Shinchōsha, 1998); and Kobayashi Yoshinori, *Shin gōmanizumu sengen daiyonkan* [The New Arrogant-ism Declaration].

32. The series begins with Fujioka Nobukatsu et al., *Kyōkasho ga oshienai rek-*

ishi [The History not Taught in Textbooks] (Tokyo: Sankei Shinbunsha, 1996). A number of subsequent volumes have since appeared.

33. Ueno Chizuko, "Posuto reisen to Nihonpan rekishi shūsei shugi" [The Post–Cold War Era and Japan's Version of Historical Revisionism," in *Nashonaru-izumu to "ianfu" mondai* [Nationalism and the "Comfort Women" Issue], ed. Nihon no sensō sekinin shiryō sentaa [Center for Research and Documentation on Japan's War Responsibility] (Tokyo: Aoki Shoten, 1998), 102.

34. Ibid., 102–8.

35. Ōgoshi Aiko and Takahashi Tetsuya, "Gendaa to sensō sekinin" [Gender and War Responsibility], *Gendai shisō* [Modern Thought] 25, no. 10 (September 1997), 149.

36. See Suzanne O'Brien's excellent introduction to her translation of Yoshimi's pioneering book. Yoshimi Yoshiaki, *Comfort Women: Sexual Slavery in the Japanese Military During World War II*, trans. Suzanne O'Brien (New York: Columbia University Press, 2000): 1–21.

37. Yū Miri, *Kamen no kuni* [The Country of Masks], 17, 18.

38. See Tessa Morris-Suzuki's fine discussion of Katō in "Unquiet Graves: Katō Norihiro and the Politics of Mourning," *Japanese Studies* 18, no. 1 (May 1998): 21–30.

39. Yū Miri, *Kamen no kuni* [The Country of Masks], 16.

40. Resident Koreans became involved in the *pachinko* industry from the early postwar years, when the only sorts of business opportunities available to them were such quasi-illicit endeavors. *Pachinko* parlors have the reputation of having connections with the *yakuza* (Japanese mafia). In addition, they are in essence gambling outfits: although they ostensibly provide only gift items as rewards for collecting the small metal balls that pour out of a machine when one has won the game, down the street from each shop, there is a window where one can exchange special tokens for cash. Many owners of *pachinko* parlors have become wealthy, although as Song Mi-ja, a *pachinko* parlor owner and author, writes in *Kabukichō chinjara kyōshinkyoku* [Kabuki-chō March] (Tokyo: Tokuma Shoten, 1994), it is not as easy to be successful at this business as some assume. Whether or not a given parlor is successful, employees like this father are unlikely to make much money at all.

41. Yū Miri and Ri Kaisei, "Kazoku•Minzoku•Bungaku," *Gunzō* 52, no. 4 (April 1997): 137.

42. A good introduction to current discussions of memory in psychiatry is Bessel van der Kolk and Onno van der Hart, "The Intrusive Past: The Flexibility of Memory and the Engraving of Trauma," in *Trauma: Explorations in Memory*, ed. Cathy Caruth (Baltimore: Johns Hopkins University Press, 1995), 158–82.

43. Ibid., 167–72.

44. Ibid., 163.

45. Ibid., 178.

46. In English, see Hyunah Yang, "Revisiting the Issue of Korean 'Military

Comfort Women': The Question of Truth and Positionality," *positions* 5, no. 1 (1997). She makes this particular point on 64. Hasegawa Hiroko, in "Girei to shite no sei bōryoku" [Sexual Violence as Ritual], in *Nashonaru historii o koete* [Beyond National History], ed. Komori Yōichi and Takahashi Tetsuya (Tokyo: Tokyo Daigaku Shuppankai, 1998), 287–304, makes strikingly similar points to Yang. She paints rape as a strategy in war, discussing the way that rape of women is a strategy used to demoralize the male enemy, the fact that it splits the national community because the women are seen as having done something shameful and are often forced to separate themselves from the community, the fact that it can result in the destruction of reproductive capacity, and its symbolic importance.

47. George Hicks, *The Comfort Women* (Tokyo: Yenbooks, 1995), 63.

48. Ch'in Hwang-ja, "Hakkan no goaisatsu" [Greetings on the Occasion of the Founding Issue], *Arurim* [Allim/The Notice], founding issue (February 29, 1992): 1. Many members also have been active in the group supporting Song Shin-do, the sole Zainichi former comfort woman to have come forward. Yang Chin-ja reports that she and the other members of this group first learned of Song's existence in January 1992 when she called a hotline trying to gather information about the former comfort women. Yang first visited Song at her home in northern Japan in August 1992, and in January 1993, she and others formed the Zainichi no ianfu saiban o sasaeru kai [The Association to Support Zainichi Comfort Women's Lawsuits]. Song filed suit against the government in April 1993. See Yang Chin-ja, "Song-san to Sasaeru kai no gonenkan" [Five Years with Song and the Support Association], in *Song-san to issho ni: yoku wakaru Zainichi no moto "ianfu" saiban* [With Song: A Simple Introduction to the Lawsuit of a Zainichi Former Comfort Woman], ed. Zainichi no ianfu saiban o sasaeru kai [The Support Association for the Lawsuits of Comfort Women Residing in Japan] (Tokyo: Zainichi no ianfu saiban o sasaeru kai, 1997), 4–10. The Korean Women's Network was one of the organizations sponsoring the hotline mentioned above. Pak Hwa-mi, "Ianfu hyakutōban" [Comfort Women Hotline], *Arurim* [Allim/The Notice], founding issue (February 29, 1992): 2.

49. Chŏng Yŏng-hae, "Jibun jishin to deai, katariau 'ba' o" [In Search of a "Site" to Confront and Discuss Our Selves], *Arurim* [Allim/The Notice] 16 (July 4, 1996): 4.

50. Kim Yŏng, "Jūbu 'ianfu' nareba koso" [Precisely Because We Are "Comfort Women" to Our Husbands], *Arurim* [Allim/The Notice] 14 (December 30, 1995): 5.

51. Chŏng Yŏng-hae, "Jibun jishin to deai, katariau 'ba' o" [In Search of a "Site" to Confront and Discuss Our Selves], 4.

CHAPTER 7

1. In an interview, the activist and professor Ehashi Takashi makes an interesting observation. Although the cases regarding civil service employment may be promi-

nent, "there are probably only 1,000 people or so working on the issue of the Nationality Clause, with perhaps 100 at the center. It is amazing to me that a couple of hundred people have been able to budge a society of 120 million people." "The Battle over the Nationality Clause: Finding Hope in Local Governments — An Interview with Ehashi Takashi," *AMPO: Japan Asia Quarterly Review* vol. 28, no. 2 (February 1998): 49. I agree entirely with this assessment.

2. The citations are from a Web site dedicated to the voting and employment rights of non-Japanese citizens. The URL is http://www2.interbroad.or.jp/shimada/syuuninnkenn.html. Much of the information on this page is attributed to Okazaki Katsuhiko, "Gaikokujin no kōmu shūshoku ninken" [Foreigners' Rights to Government Employment], *Jichi sōken* (August 1997).

3. U.S. Department of State, *Japan Country Report on Human Rights Practices for 1998*, Section 5, "Discrimination Based on Race, Sex, Religion, Disability, Language, or Social Status," released by the Bureau of Democracy, Human Rights, and Labor, February 26, 1999.

4. The ruling is outlined in "Jichitai no kanrishoku shōnin shiken: Gaikokuseki monzenbarai wa iken" [Exams for Promotion to Managerial Positions in Local Government: Turning Away Foreigners Declared Unconstitutional], *Asahi shinbun*, November 27, 1997, 1.

5. In English, see Sachie Tsuhata and Aya Igarashi, "Debate Simmers over Voting Rights for Foreigners," *Daily Yomiuri*, May 5, 1999, 3. A good Japanese outline of court cases surrounding foreigners' political rights can be found on the Internet at http://www2.interbroad.or.jp/shimada.vote.html. A chronology is provided at the linked URL http://www2.interbroad.or.jp/shimada.history.html.

6. See Sachie Tsuhata and Aya Igarashi, "Debate Simmers over Voting Rights for Foreigners"; and Kyodo News Service, Tokyo, "Japan: Prime Minister to Stress Efforts on Voting Rights for Koreans," in *BBC Summary of World Broadcasts, Asia-Pacific — Political*, March 17, 1999. Many other sources have of course reported these events.

7. "Kim Orders Law Revision for Foreign Residents' Suffrage," *Korea Times*, March 25, 1999. Again, many sources carried this news.

8. "Town in Shiga Prefecture First to Give Vote to Foreigners," *Kyodo News International*, March 26, 2002.

9. "Japan Poised to Give Foreigners Voting Rights," *Mainichi Daily News*, October 20, 2003, 1.

10. In *Outsiders Moving In: Identity and Institutions in Japanese Responses to International Migration* (Chicago: University of Chicago, Department of Political Science, 1998), Katherine Tegtmeyer Pak argues that localities have changed in part because they have become aware of the violence that has ensued in other countries when they have not made efforts to encorporate foreigners into the community (238).

11. See, for example, the report I cite in note 3.

12. Tegtmeyer Pak also elucidates other subtle shifts in attitudes toward immi-

gration now taking place in Japan. One of her overall arguments is that such policies have traditionally been controlled by Japan's national bureaucracy, particularly the Ministry of Justice, which has "judged the state's interest in immigration from the perspective of the *tan'itsu minzoku* [single race — M.W.] idiom," but that increasingly localities, which have "judged their communities; interest in growing foreign populations from the perspective of the *kokusaika* [internationalization — M.W.] idiom," and nongovernmental organizations have had greater influence in shaping immigration policies (*Outsiders Moving In*, 235). Tegtmeyer Pak further argues that the nongovernmental organizations have been able to have a good deal of success in part because of access to the media.

13. For more information on this movement, see Minzokumei o torimodosu kai, ed., $$Minzokumei o torimodishita Nihonseki Chōsenjin [Koreans with Japanese Citizenship Who've Regained Their Ethnic Names] (Tokyo: Akashi Shoten, 1990); and Minzokumei o torimodosu kai, *Jūnen no kiseki: Nihonseki Chōsenjin no tatakai; Kaihō "Uri irum" no shukusatsuban* [Ten Years' Worth of Tracks: The Fight of Koreans with Japanese Citizenship; A Reduced-size Reprint of the Newsletter *Uri Irum* (Our Names)] (Osaka: Minzokumei o torimodosu kai, 1994). Chŏng Yang-yi also has run a Web site on which a large amount of information on the topic can be found. In English, see Chikako Kashiwazaki, "To Be Korean Without Korean Nationality: Claim to Korean Identity by Japanese Nationality Holders," *Korean and Korean American Studies Bulletin* 11, no. 1 (2000): J48–J70.

14. Honda Masakazu, "Zainichi Chōsenjin no tomo e no tegami" [A Letter to My Korean Friend], *Asahi shinbun* (morning edition), June 10, 1998, 4.

15. A transcript of Pak's speech is available online at Chŏng Yang-yi's Web site, available at http://www.luice.or.jp/chong/pakuiru.htm.

16. "Nyū Zainichi ga Nihon o kaeru" [The New Zainichi Change Japan], in *Nyūsuwiiku Nihonban* [Newsweek Japan edition], November 26, 2003, 18–23.

17. Ibid., 21.

18. In "Zainichi Chōsenjin no tomo e no tegami" [A Letter to My Korean Friend], Honda Masakazu claims that the number is as high as 5,000. This article is cited in ibid. According to a BBC summary of a report of the South Korean news agency Yonhap, the number for the years between 1992 and 1996 was closer to 3,000. "Over 11,000 Koreans in Japan Obtain South Korean Citizenship," *BBC Summary of World Broadcasts*, Part 3, Asia-Pacific, October 6, 1997.

19. Ri Kaisei, "Kankoku kokuseki shutoku no ki" [A Record of Attaining South Korean Citizenship], *Shinchō* 95, no. 7 (July 1998): 294–317.

20. Ibid.

21. Kim Sŏk-bŏm, "Ima, 'Zainichi' ni totte 'kokuseki' to wa nani ka: Ri Kaisei-kun e no tegami" [What Does "Citizenship" Mean for "Zainichi" Today? A Letter to My Young Colleague, Ri Kaisei], *Sekai* 653 (October 1998): 131–42. It was this piece that pointed me to the *Asahi shinbun* article cited in note 3. We might recall that

Kim participated in the discussion about "writing in Japanese" that Ri and Ōe Kenzaburō engaged in in the 1970s.

22. Ri Kaisei, " 'Mukokusekisha' no yuku michi: Kim Sŏk-bŏm-shi e no hentō" [The Path of "Stateless Persons": A Reply to My Esteemed Colleague, Kim Sŏk-bŏm], *Sekai* 657 (January 1999): 257–69.

23. Kim Sŏk-bŏm, "Ima, 'Zainichi' ni totte 'kokuseki' to wa nani ka" [What Does "Citizenship" Mean for "Zainichi" Today?], 40–42.

24. Yū Miri and Ri Kaisei, "Kazoku•Minzoku•Bungaku" [The Family, Ethnicity, and Literature], *Gunzō* 52, no. 4 (April 1997): 135.

25. Yū Miri, *Inochi* [Life] (Tokyo: Shogakkan, 2000).

26. Fukuda Kazuya and Yū Miri, "*Tamashii* o megutte: 2/zen 5kai" [On *Soul*: Part 2 of 5], *Justice Library Quality Web Magazine*, April 4, 2001, available at http://justice.i-mediatv.co.jp/yuu/010402/02.html, accessed May 13, 2004.

27. Kawamura Minato's *Sengo bungaku o tou* [Questioning Postwar Literature] (Tokyo: Iwanami Shoten, 1995) contains an entire chapter on Zainichi literature.

Bibliography

ENGLISH WORKS

Ahmad, Aijaz. "Jameson's Rhetoric of Otherness and the 'National Allegory.'" *Social Text* 17 (Fall 1987): 3–25.

Alcoff, Linda. "Cultural Feminism Versus Post-structuralism: The Identity Crisis in Feminist Theory." *Signs: Journal of Women in Culture and Society* 13, no. 3 (1988): 405–36.

Althusser, Louis. "Ideology and Ideological State Apparatuses (Notes Toward an Investigation)." In *Lenin and Philosophy and Other Essays*, 127–86. Translated by Ben Brewster. New York: Monthly Review, 1971.

Amin, Samir. *Spectres of Capitalism: A Critique of Current Intellectual Fashions*. New York: Monthly Review Press, 1998.

Apter, David E., and Nagayo Sawa. *Against the State: Politics and Social Protest in Japan*. Cambridge: Harvard University Press, 1984.

Aronowitz, Stanley. "The Production of Scientific Knowledge: Science, Ideology, and Marxism." In *Marxism and the Interpretation of Culture*, introduced and edited by Cary Nelson and Lawrence Grossberg, 519–41. Urbana: University of Illinois Press, 1988.

Ashcroft, Bill, Gareth Griffiths, and Helen Tiffin, eds. *Key Concepts in Post-colonial Studies*. London: Routledge, 1998.

Bakhtin, M. M. *The Dialogic Imagination*. Translated by Caryl Emerson and Michael Holquist. Edited by Michael Holquist. Austin: University of Texas Press, 1981.

[Bakhtin, M. M.] Volosinov, V. N. *Marxism and the Philosophy of Language*. Translated by Ladislav Matejka and I. R. Titunik. Cambridge: Harvard University Press, 1986.

"The Battle over the Nationality Clause: Finding Hope in Local Governments — An Interview with Ehashi Takashi." *AMPO: Japan Asia Quarterly Review* 28, no. 2 (February 1998): 45–49.

Behar, Ruth, and Deborah A. Gordon, eds. *Women Writing Culture*. Berkeley: University of California Press, 1995.

Bhabha, Homi. *The Location of Culture*. London: Routledge, 1994.

Binder, Guyora, and Robert Weisberg. *Literary Criticisms of Law*. Princeton: Princeton University Press, 2000.

Braverman, Harry. *Labor and Monopoly Capital: The Degradation of Work in the Twentieth Century*. New York: Monthly View Press, 1974.

Brooks, Peter, and Paul Gerwitz, eds. *Law's Stories: Narrative and Rhetoric in the Law*. New Haven: Yale University Press, 1996.

Buruma, Ian. "Profile: Becoming Japanese." *New Yorker*, December 23 and 30, 1996, 60–71.

Chang, Dal-Joong. *Economic Control and Political Authoritarianism: The Role of Japanese Corporations in Korean Politics, 1965–1979*. Seoul: Sogang University Press, 1985.

———. "Minjung Culture Movement and the Construction of Popular Culture in Korea." In *South Korea's Minjung Movement: The Culture and Politics of Dissidence*, edited by Kenneth M. Wells, 105–18. Honolulu: University of Hawai'i Press, 1995.

Chu, Patricia. *Assimilating Asians: Gendered Strategies of Authorship in Asian America*. Durham, NC: Duke University Press, 2000.

Chung, Erin Aeran. *Exercising Citizenship: Korean Identity and the Politics of Nationality in Japan*. Evanston, IL: Northwestern University, 2003.

Covell, Alan Carter. *Folk Art and Magic Shamanism in Korea*. Seoul: Hollym Corporation, 1986.

Dale, Peter. *The Myth of Japanese Uniqueness*. New York: St. Martin's Press, 1988.

Deleuze, Gilles, and Félix Guattari. "What Is a Minor Literature?" In *Out There: Marginalization and Contemporary Cultures*, edited by Russell Ferguson, Martha Gever, Trinh T. Minh-ha, and Cornel West. 59–69. New York: New Museum of Contemporary Art, and Cambridge, MA: MIT Press, 1990.

De Vos, George, and Daekyun Chung. "Community Life in a Korean Ghetto." In *Koreans in Japan: Ethnic Conflict and Accommodation*, edited by Changsoo Lee, 225–25. Berkeley: University of California Press, 1985.

Dower, John W. "Peace and Democracy in Two Systems: External Policy and Internal Conflict." In *Postwar Japan as History*, edited by Andrew Gordon, 3–33. Berkeley: University of California Press, 1993.

Eliade, Mircea. *Shamanism: Archaic Techniques of Ecstasy*. Translated by Willard R. Trask. London: Routledge & Kegan Paul, 1964.

Field, Norma. "Beyond Envy, Boredom, and Suffering: Toward an Emancipatory Politics for Resident Koreans and Other Japanese." *positions* 1, no. 3 (Winter 1993): 640–70.

———. "Texts of Childhood in Inter-nationalizing Japan." In *Text and Nation: Cross-disciplinary Essays on Cultural and National Identities*, edited by Laura García-Moreno and Peter C. Pfeiffer, 143–72. Columbia, SC: Camden House, 1996.

Foucault, Michel. "What Is an Author?" In *Textual Strategies: Perspectives in Post-Structuralist Criticism*, edited by Josué V. Harari, 141–60. Ithaca, NY: Cornell University Press, 1979.

Fowler, Edward. *The Rhetoric of Confession: Shishōsetsu in Early Twentieth-Century Japanese Fiction*. Berkeley: University of California Press, 1988.

Fujii, James A. *Complicit Fictions: The Subject in the Modern Japanese Prose Narrative.* Berkeley: University of California Press, 1993.

Gates, Henry Louis, Jr. "Critical Fanonism." *Critical Inquiry* 17, no. 3 (Spring 1991): 457–70.

Graff, Gerald. *Literature Against Itself: Literary Ideas in Modern Society.* Chicago: University of Chicago Press, 1979.

Harvey, David. *The Condition of Postmodernity.* Cambridge, MA: Blackwell, 1990.

Hein, Laura, and Mark Selden, eds. *Islands of Discontent: Okinawan Responses to Japanese and American Power.* Oxford: Rowman and Littlefield, 2003.

Herman, Judith. *Trauma and Recovery.* New York: Basic Books, 1992, 1997.

Hicks, George. *The Comfort Women.* Tokyo: Yenbooks, 1995.

Hogarth, Hyun-key Kim. "Pursuit of Happiness Through Reciprocity: The Korean Shamanistic Ritual." *Shaman* 5, no. 1 (Spring 1997): 47–67.

Iwabuchi, Kōichi. *Recentering Globalization: Popular Culture and Japanese Transnationalism.* Durham, NC: Duke University Press, 2002.

Jameson, Fredric. *Marxism and Form: Twentieth-century Dialectical Theories of Literature.* Princeton: Princeton University Press, 1971.

———. *The Political Unconscious: Narrative as a Socially Symbolic Act.* Ithaca, NY: Cornell University Press, 1981.

———. *Postmodernism: Or, the Cultural Logic of Late Capitalism.* Durham, NC: Duke University Press, 1995.

———. "Third-World Literature in the Era of Multinational Capitalism." *Social Text* 15 (Fall 1986): 65–88.

"Japan Poised to Give Foreigners Voting Rights." *Mainichi Daily News*, October 20, 2003, 1.

Jay, Martin. *Downcast Eyes: The Denigration of Vision in Twentieth-Century French Thought.* Berkeley: University of California Press, 1993.

Kano Mikiyo. "Remolding Tennoism for Modern Japan." *AMPO Japan-Asia Quarterly Review* 18, no. 2–3 (1986): 24–29.

Kaplan, Caren. *Questions of Travel: Postmodern Discourses of Displacement.* Durham, NC: Duke University Press, 1996.

Karatani, Kōjin. *Origins of Modern Japanese Literature.* Translated and edited by Brett deBary. Durham, NC: Duke University Press, 1993.

Kashiwazaki, Chikako. "To Be Korean Without Korean Nationality: Claim to Korean Identity by Japanese Nationality Holders." *Korean and Korean American Studies Bulletin* 11, no. 1 (2000): J48–70.

Katsificas, George. *The Imagination of the New Left: A Global Analysis of 1968.* Boston: South End Press, 1987.

Kayano Shigeru. *Our Land Was a Forest: An Ainu Memoir.* Trans. Kyoko Selden and Lili Selden. Boulder, CO: Westview Press, 1994.

"Kim Orders Law Revision for Foreign Residents' Suffrage," *Korea Times*, March 25, 1999.

Koschmann, J. Victor. *Revolution and Subjectivity in Postwar Japan.* Chicago: University of Chicago Press, 1996.

Kristeva, Julia. *The Kristeva Reader.* Edited by Toril Moi. New York: Columbia University Press, 1986.

Kyodo News Service. "Japan: Prime Minister to Stress Efforts on Voting Rights for Koreans." In *BBC Summary of World Broadcasts, Asia-Pacific — Political,* March 17, 1999.

LaFleur, William R. *The Karma of Words: Buddhism and the Literary Arts in Medieval Japan.* Berkeley: University of California Press, 1983.

Lee, Changsoo, and George De Vos. "On Both Sides of Japanese Justice." In *Koreans in Japan: Ethnic Conflict and Accommodation,* edited by Changsoo Lee, 253–79. Berkeley: University of California Press, 1985.

Lee, Chong-Sik. *Japan and Korea: The Political Dimension.* Stanford, CA: Hoover Institution Press, Stanford University, 1985.

Lee, Jung Young. *Korean Shamanistic Rituals.* The Hague: Mouton, 1981.

Linger, Daniel Touro. *No One Home: Brazilian Selves Remade in Japan.* Stanford: Stanford University Press, 2001.

Lowitz, Leza and Miyuki Aoyama, trans. and ed. *Other Side River: Free Verse.* Berkeley: Stone Bridge Press, 1995.

Marcuse, Herbert. *The Aesthetic Dimension: Toward A Critique of Marxist Aesthetics.* Boston: Beacon Press, 1988.

Massey, Doreen. *Space, Place, and Gender.* Minneapolis: University of Minnesota Press, 1994.

Miyoshi, Masao. *Off Center: Power and Culture Relations Between Japan and the United States.* Cambridge: Harvard University Press, 1991.

Miyoshi, Masao, and Harry D. Harootunian, eds. *Postmodernism and Japan.* Durham, NC: Duke University Press, 1989.

Molasky, Michael, and Steve Rabson, eds. *Southern Exposure: Modern Japanese Literature from Okinawa.* Honolulu: University of Hawai'i Press, 2001.

Morris-Suzuki, Tessa. "Unquiet Graves: Katō Norihiro and the Politics of Mourning." *Japanese Studies* 18, no. 1 (May 1998): 21–30.

Mulvey, Laura. "Visual Pleasure and Narrative Cinema." In *Feminisms: An Anthology of Literary Theory and Criticism,* edited by Robyn R. Warhoal and Diane Price Herndl, 432–42. New Brunswick, NJ: Rutgers University Press, 1991.

Murphy-Shigematsu, Stephen. "Emerging Paradigms of Minority Citizenship in Japan." Presented at the Conference on Citizenship, Immigration and Minority Politics in Contemporary Japan. Reischauer Institute, Harvard University, March 13, 2004.

Nakagami Kenji. *The Cape and Other Stories from the Japanese Ghetto.* Translated by Eve Zimmerman. Berkeley: Stone Bridge Press, 1999.

Neary, Ian. *Political Protest and Social Control in Pre-war Japan: The Origins of Buraku Liberation.* Atlantic Highlands, NJ: Humanities Press International, 1989.

Nelson, Beverly. "Korean Literature in Japan, A Case Study: Ri Kai Sei." In *Studies on Korea in Transition*, edited by David R. McCann, John Middleton, and Edward J. Shultz, 126–59. Honolulu: Center for Korean Studies, University of Hawai'i, 1977.

New Interpreter's Bible Volume 1. Nashville: Abingdon Press, 1994.

Noll, Richard. "Shamanism and Schizophrenia: A State-specific Approach to the 'Schizophrenia Metaphor' of Shamanic States." *American Ethnologist* 10, no. 3 (1983): 443–59.

Omi, Michael, and Howard Winant. *Racial Formation in the United States: From the 1960s to the 1990s*. 2nd ed. London: Routledge, 1994.

Research/Action Institute for Koreans in Japan (RAIK). *Japan's Subtle Apartheid: The Korean Minority Now*. Tokyo: RAIK, 1990.

Ri Kai-sei. "The Woman Who Fulled Clothes." In *Flowers of Fire: Twentieth-Century Korean Stories*, rev. ed., translated by Beverly Nelson, edited by Peter Lee, 344–72. Honolulu: University of Hawai'i Press, 1986.

Rose, Caroline. "The Textbook Issue: Domestic Sources of Japan's Foreign Policy." *Japan Forum* 11, no. 2 (1999): 205–16.

Ryang, Sonia, ed. *Koreans in Japan: Critical Voices from the Margin*. London: Routledge, 2000.

———. *North Koreans in Japan: Language, Ideology, and Identity*. Boulder, CO: Westview Press, 1997.

Sasaki-Uemura, Wesley. "From Public Phones to Community Newsletters: The Localization of the Public Sphere in the 1960s." Paper presented at the Association of Asian Studies Annual Meeting, March 16, 1997.

Scott, Joan W. 1995. "Multiculturalism and the Politics of Identity. " In *The Identity in Question*, edited by John Rajchman, 3–12. New York: Routledge, 1995.

Seaman, Amanda. "Modeling Masako: Commodities and the Construction of a Modern Princess." *Chicago Anthropology Exchange* 21 (Spring 1995): 35–70.

Sherif, Ann. "The Politics of Loss: On Etō Jun." Paper presented at the Association of Asian Studies Annual Meeting, March 16, 1997.

Siddle, Richard. *Race, Resistance, and the Ainu of Japan*. London: Routledge, 1996.

Smith, Beverley. "Democracy Derailed: Citizens Movements in Historical Perspective." In *Democracy in Contemporary Japan*, edited by Gavan McCormack and Yoshio Sugimoto. Armonk, NY: M. E. Sharpe, 1986.

Soja, Edward. *Postmodern Geographies: The Reassertion of Space in Critical Social Theory*. London: Verso, 1989.

Suh Kyung-sik. "A Letter to Mr. Kim Chi-ha; or, The Pain of the Split Self." Translated by Norma Field. *positions* 5, no. 1 (Spring 1997): 316–20.

Suzuki, David, and Keibo Oiwa. *The Japan We Never Knew: A Journey of Discovery*. Toronto: Stoddart, 1996.

Suzuki, Tomi. *Narrating the Self: Fictions of Japanese Modernity*. Stanford: Stanford University Press, 1996.

Tegtmeyer Pak, Katherine. *Outsiders Moving In: Identity and Institutions in Japanese Responses to International Migration.* Chicago: University of Chicago, Department of Political Science, 1998.

"Town in Shiga Prefecture First to Give Vote to Foreigners." *Kyodo News International,* March 26, 2002.

Tsuhata, Sachie, and Aya Igarashi. "Debate Simmers over Voting Rights for Foreigners." *Daily Yomiuri,* May 5, 1999, 3.

Tsuru, Shigeto. *Japan's Capitalism: Creative Defeat and Beyond.* Cambridge: Cambridge University Press, 1993.

U.S. Department of State. *Japan Country Report on Human Rights Practices for 1998,* Section 5, "Discrimination Based on Race, Sex, Religion, Disability, Language, or Social Status." Released by the Bureau of Democracy, Human Rights, and Labor, February 26, 1999.

Upham, Frank. *Law and Social Change in Postwar Japan.* Cambridge: Harvard University Press, 1987.

van der Kolk, Bessel, and Onno van der Hart. "The Intrusive Past: The Flexibility of Memory and the Engraving of Trauma." In *Trauma: Explorations in Memory,* edited by Cathy Caruth, 158–82. Baltimore: Johns Hopkins University Press, 1995.

Volosinov, V. N. [Bakhtin, M. M.] *Marxism and the Philosophy of Language.* Translated by Ladislav Matejka and I. R. Titunik. Cambridge: Harvard University Press, 1986.

Wagner, Edward. *The Korean Minority in Japan: 1904–1950.* New York: Institute of Pacific Relations, 1951.

Weiner, Michael. *The Origin of the Korean Community in Japan, 1910–1923.* Manchester: Manchester University Press, 1989.

——, ed. *Japan's Minorities: The Illusion of Homogeneity.* London: Routledge, 1997.

West, Cornel. "A Matter of Life and Death." In *The Identity in Question,* edited by John Rajchman. New York: Routledge, 1995.

——. *Marxism and Literature.* Oxford: Oxford University Press, 1977.

Woititz, Janet. *Adult Children of Alcoholics.* Deerfield Beach, FL: Health Communications, 1981.

Yang, Hyunah. "Revisiting the Issue of Korean 'Military Comfort Women': The Question of Truth and Positionality." *positions* 5, no. 1 (Spring 1997): 51–72.

Yonhap. "Over 11,000 Koreans in Japan Obtain South Korean Citizenship." In *BBC Summary of World Broadcasts,* Part 3 Asia-Pacific, October 6, 1997.

Yoshimi Yoshiaki. *Comfort Women: Sexual Slavery in the Japanese Military During World War II.* Trans. Suzanne O'Brien. New York: Columbia University Press, 2000.

Yoshino, Kosaku. *Cultural Nationalism in Contemporary Japan: A Sociological Enquiry.* London: Routledge, 1992.

Yu Du-hyun. "Role Playing Through Trance Possession in Korean Shamanism." In

Shamanism: The Spirit World of Korea, edited by Chai-shin Yu and Richard W. Guisso, 162–78. Berkeley: Asian Humanities Press, 1988.

JAPANESE AND KOREAN WORKS

Ch'in Hwang-ja, "Hakkan no goaisatsu" [Greetings on the Occasion of the Founding Issue]. *Arurim* [Allim/The Notice], founding issue (February 29, 1992): 1.

Ch'ŏi Sŏng-gu, Pak Chŏng-sŏk, Satō Katsumi, Yi Yin-ha, Kōra Tetsuo, and Wada Jun. "Hitachi kyūdan e no ayumi" [The Path to the Denunciation of Hitachi]. In *Minzoku sabetsu — Hitachi shūshoku sabetsu kyūdan* [Ethnic Discrimination — The Denunciation of Hitachi's Employment Discrimination]. Edited by Paku-kun o kakomu kai [The Committee for Pak]. Tokyo: Aki Shobo, 1974.

Chong Ch'u-wŏl. *Ikaino•Onna•Ai•Uta* [Ikaino/Woman/Love/Poems]. Osaka: Bureen Sentaa, 1984.

———. *Ikaino taryon* [Ikaino Lament]. Tokyo: Shisō no Kagakusha, 1986.

———. "Mun Kon-bun *omoni* no *ningo*" [Mun Kon-bun *Ŏmŏni*'s Apple]. *Shin Nihon bungaku* [New Japanese Literature] 450 (1985): 14–30.

———. *Saran he/aishite imasu* [Sarang hae/I Love You]. Tokyo: Kage Shobo, 1987.

Chŏng Yŏng-hae. "Aidentitii o koete" [Getting Beyond Identity]. In *Iwanami kōza, Gendai shakaigaku 15: Sabetsu to kyōsei no shakaigaku* [Iwanami Lectures, Modern Sociology 15: The Sociology of Discrimination and Coexistence]. Published by Yasue Yōsuke. Tokyo: Iwanami Shoten, 1996.

———. "Jibun jishin to deai, katariau 'ba' o" [In Search of a "Site" to Confront and Discuss Our Selves]. *Arurim* [Allim/The Notice] 16 (July 4, 1996): 4.

Fujioka Nobukatsu et al. *Kyōkasho ga oshienai rekishi* [The History Not Taught in Textbooks]. Tokyo: Sankei Shinbunsha, 1996.

Hanguk minjok munhwa taebaekgwa sajŏn [The Encyclopedia of Korean Culture]. Seoul: Hanguk chŏngshin munhwa yŏnguwon, 1991.

Harajiri Hideki. *Nihon teijū Korian no nichijō to seikatsu: Bunkajinruigakuteki apurōchi* [The Daily Lives and Livelihood of Koreans Permanently in Japan: An Anthropological Approach]. Tokyo: Akashi Shoten, 1997.

———. *"Zainichi" to shite no Korian* [Koreans as "Zainichi"]. Tokyo: Kōdansha Gendai Shinsho, 1998.

Hasegawa Hiroko. "Girei to shite no sei bōryoku" [Sexual Violence as Ritual]. In *Nashonaru historii o koete* [Beyond National History], edited by Komori Yōichi and Takahashi Tetsuya, 287–304. Tokyo: Tokyo Daigaku Shuppankai, 1998.

Hayami Yukiko. "Akutagawashō ga tsumaranai" [The Akutagawa Prize is Dull]. *Aera* 9, no. 1 (January 1996): 47–49.

Hitosashiyubi no jiyū henshū iinkai [Editorial Committee for Freedom of the Index Finger]. *Hitosashiyubi no jiyū* [Freedom of the Index Finger]. Tokyo: Shakai Hyōronsha, 1984.

Honda Masakazu. "Zainichi Chōsenjin no tomo e no tegami" [A Letter to My Korean Friend]. *Asahi shinbun* (morning edition), June 10, 1998, 4.

Iinuma Jirō, ed., *Hikokumin no susume: Zainichi Chōsenjin o kataru III* [A Traitor's Advice: Discussing Resident Koreans III]. Tokyo: Bakushūsha, 1985.

Ishizuka Hisashi. "Bengoshi da kara — de wa naku" [Not Because I'm His Lawyer]. In *Minzoku sabetsu — Hitachi shūshoku sabetsu kyūdan* [Ethnic Discrimination — The Denunciation of Hitachi's Employment Discrimination], 149–62. Tokyo: Aki Shobo, 1974.

Itō Naruhiko. *Jihyō to shite no bungaku 1984–1995* [Literature as Timeline, 1984–1995]. Tokyo: Ochanomizu Shobo, 1995.

"Jichitai no kanrishoku shōnin shiken: Gaikokuseki monzenbarai wa iken" [Exams for Promotion to Managerial Positions in Local Government: Turning Away Foreigners Declared Unconstitutional]. *Asahi shinbun*, November 27, 1997, 1.

Kabushikigaisha Kōdansha [Kodansha, Inc.], ed. *Shōwa nimannichi no zenkiroku dai 14 maki: yureru Shōwa Genroku, Shōwa 43nen-46nen* [Twenty Thousand Days of Shōwa, Volume 14: The Wavering Genroku of Shōwa, 1968–1971]. Tokyo: Kodansha, 1990.

Kajii Noboru. "Zainichi Chōsenjin Bungaku no Sakuhin Nenpyō" [A Calendar of Literary Works by Resident Koreans]. *Kikan Sanzenri* 20 (1979): 52–67.

Kang Sang-jung. "Hōhō to shite no 'Zainichi' — Yang Tae-ho shi ni kotaeru" ["Zainichi" as Method — In Response to Yang Tae-ho]. In *Zainichi Kankoku Chōsenjin — sono Nihon ni okeru sonzai kachi* [Resident Koreans: The Value of their Existence in Japanese Society], edited by Iinuma Jirō, 275–87. Tokyo: Kaifūsha, 1988.

Kawamura Minato. "Intabyū taidan — 'Zainichi bungaku' o koete: Yi Yang-ji" [An Interview — Getting Past "Zainichi Literature": Yi Yang-ji]. *Bungakkai* 43 (March 1989): 264–84.

———. "Kankoku to iu kagami — Gendai bungaku fuiirudo nōto" [Korea the Mirror: Field Notes on Contemporary Literature]. *Bungei* 24, no. 4 (April 1985): 174–75.

———. "Sai no mukōgawa — Yi Yang-ji *Koku*" [On the Other Side of the Gap: Yi Yang-ji's *Koku*]. *Gunzō* 40, no. 5 (May 1985): 332–33.

———. *Sengo bungaku o tou* [Questioning Postwar Literature]. Tokyo: Iwanami Shoten, 1995.

Kim Ch'ang-saeng. "Akai mi" [The Red Fruit]. *Kikan Zainichi bungei mintō* 3 (Summer 1988): 256–76.

———. *Watashi no Ikaino: Zainichi ni totte no sokoku to ikoku* [My Ikaino: Homeland and Foreign Country as Seen by Zainichi]. Nagoya: Fūbosha, 1982.

———. "Zainichi Chōsenjin no kurashi/seikatsu" [Resident Korean's Daily Life]. In *Zainichi Kankoku Chōsenjin: Wakamono kara mita iken to omoi to kangae* [Resident Koreans: The Opinions, Feelings, and Thoughts of Young People], ed. Kim Yŏng-kwŏn and Yi Chŏng-yang. Tokyo: San'ichi Shobo, 1985, 1990.

Kim Dŏk-hwan, Pae Chung-do, and Mun Kyŏng-su. "Zadankai — 'Zainichi' 50–nen o kataru 3: 1970–nen kara" [Roundtable — 50 Years of "Zainichi" 3: From 1970]. In Kang Chae-on et al., *"Zainichi" wa ima* [What "Zainichi" Are Now], 204–23. Tokyo: Seikyū Bunkasha, 1996.

Kim Dŏk-hwan shi no gaitōhō saiban o shien suru kai [Committee to Support Kim Dŏk-hwan's Alien Registration Law Trial]. *Igyora! (Ganbare!): Tokkan-san no shimon saiban* [*Igyora!* (Win!): Tokkan-san's Fingerprinting Trial]. Tokyo: Shinkansha, 1990.

Kim Hŭi-ro kōhan taisaku iinkai [Committee for the Trial of Kim Hŭi-ro], ed. *Kim Hŭi-ro mondai shishū VII: Shōgenshū 3* [Materials of the Kim Hŭi-ro incident VII: Testimonies 3]. Tokyo: Kim Hŭi-ro kōhan taisaku iinkai [Committee for the Trial of Kim Hŭi-ro], 1972.

———. *Kim Hŭi-ro mondai shishū III Bengodan no bōtō chinjutsu* [Materials of the Kim Hŭi-ro incident III: Opening Statement of the Defense]. Tokyo: Kim Hŭi-ro kōhan taisaku iinkai [Committee for the Trial of Kim Hŭi-ro], 1972.

Kim Shi-jŏng. "Nihongo no obie — tozasareta Kim Hŭi-ro no kotoba o otte" [Fear of Japanese — Searching for the Closed-in Language of Kim Hŭi-ro]. In *"Hikokumin" no susume: Zainichi Chōsenjin o kataru III* [Recommendations of a "Traitor": Tales of Resident Koreans III], edited by Iinuma Jirō. Tokyo: Bakushūsha, 1984.

Kim Sŏk-bŏm. "Ima, 'Zainichi' ni totte 'kokuseki' to wa nani ka: Ri Kaisei-kun e no tegami" [What Does "Citizenship" Mean for "Zainichi" Today? A Letter to My Young Colleague, Ri Kaisei]. *Sekai* 653 (October 1998): 131–42.

Kim Yŏng. "Jūbu 'ianfu' nareba koso" [Precisely Because We Are "Comfort Women" to Our Husbands]. *Arurim* [Allim/The Notice] 14 (December 30, 1995): 4–5.

Kim Yŏng-hŭi. "Yi Yang-ji no koto" [On Yi Yang-ji]. *Seikyū* 19 (Spring 1994): 63–66.

Kimura Hisashi (chair), Ozawa Nobuo, Kijima Hajime, and Kobayashi Masaru. "Kyōkaisen no bungaku — Zainichi Chōsenjin sakka no imi" [Literature on the Borderline — The Meaning of Resident Korean Writers]. *Shin Nihon bungaku* [New Japanese Literature] 278 (September 1970): 46–77.

Kin Kakuei. "Ishi no michi" [The Stone Path]. In *Kin Kakuei shū* [Collected Works by Kin Kakuei], 278–315. Tokyo: Sakuhinsha, 1986.

———. *Kogoeru kuchi* [The Benumbed Mouth]. In *Kin Kakuei shū* [Collected Works by Kin Kakuei], 9–97. Tokyo: Sakuhinsha, 1986.

Kitada Sachie. "Kinuta o utsu onna." In *Nihon bungei kanshō jiten: Kindai meisaku 1017–sen e no shōtai, 20* [Dictionary of Japanese Literature: An Introduction to 1017 Modern Masterpieces], 187–96. Tokyo: Gyōsei, 1988.

———. "'Zainichi' suru 'ba' no imi: Kin Kakuei ron" [The Meaning of the "Site" of "Zainichi": An Analysis of Kin Kakuei]. *Kikan Zainichi bungei mintō* 1 (November 1987): 107–14.

Kobayashi Hideo. "Watakushi shōsetsu ron" [Theory of the I-novel]. In *Shōwa Bungaku zenshū 9: Kobayashi Hideo, Kawakami Tetsutarō, Nakamura Mitsuo,*

Yamamoto Takekichi [Anthology of Shōwa Literature 9: Kobayashi Hideo, Kawakami Tetsutarō, Nakamura Mitsuo, Yamamoto Takekichi], 53–67. Tokyo: Shogakkan, 1987.

Kobayashi Yoshinori. *Shin gōmanizumu sengen daiyonkan* [The New Arrogant-ism Declaration]. Vol. 4. Tokyo: Shōgakkan, 1998.

Kōra Tetsuo. "Paku-kun o kakomu kai no san nen" [The Three Years of the Committee for Pak]. In *Minzoku sabetsu — Hitachi shūshoku sabetsu kyūdan* [Ethnic Discrimination — The Denunciation of Hitachi's Employment Discrimination], edited by *Paku-kun o kakomu kai* [The Committee for Pak]. Tokyo: Aki Shobo, 1974.

Kuroko Kazuo. "Zainichi Chōsenjin bungaku no genzai — 'Zainichi' suru koto no imi" [Resident Korean Literature Today: The Meaning of "Residing in Japan"]. *Kikan Zainichi bungei mintō* 1 (November 1987): 86–97.

Matsuzaki Haruo. "70-nendai no Yi Hoe-song to *Mihatenu yume*" [Yi Hoe-song in the '70s and *The Unfinished Dream*]. *Minshu bungaku* [Democratic Literature] 168 (November 1979): 90–112.

Mihashi Osamu. "Kin Kirō jiken — sore kara sannen" [The Kim Hŭi-ro Incident — 3 Years Later]. *Chōsen kenkyū* [Korea Research] 103 (March 1973): 22–35.

Minagawa Kunitada, Mihashi Junko, and Saitō Satoru. "Zadankai: Torauma to kazoku" [Discussion: Trauma and the Family]. *Gendai no esupuri* [Modern Esprit], May 1995: 5–21.

Minzokumei o torimodosu kai. *Jūnen no kiseki: Nihonseki Chōsenjin no tatakai; Kaihō "Uri irum" no shukusatsuban* [Ten Years' Worth of Tracks: The Fight of Koreans with Japanese Citizenship; A Reduced-size Reprint of the Newsletter *Uri Irum* (Our Names)]. Osaka: Minzokumei o torimodosu kai, 1994.

———, ed. *Minzokumei o torimodishita Nihonseki Chōsenjin* [Koreans with Japanese Citizenship Who've Regained Their Ethnic Names]. Tokyo: Akashi Shoten, 1990.

Mun Kyŏng-su. "Zainichi Chōsenjin." In *Sekai minzoku mondai jiten* [Encyclopedia of Nations and Ethnic Relations (English title included)], 456–57. Tokyo: Heibonsha, 1995.

Nakagami Kenji. "Yi Yang-ji *Koku*: Kankoku to Nihon no genzai" [Yi Yang-ji's *Koku*: Korea and Japan Today]. *Shinchō* 62, no. 5 (May 1985): 312–14.

Nobuta Sayoko. "Oya no sei ka, kodomono sei ka" [Is it the Parents' Fault? The Children's?]. *Sekai*, September 1998, 226–34.

"Nyū Zainichi ga Nihon o kaeru" [The New Zainichi Change Japan]. *Nyūsuwiiku Nihonban* [Newsweek Japan edition]. November 26, 2003, 18–23.

Oda Makoto and Ri Kaisei. "Bungakusha to sokoku" [The Author and His Fatherland]. *Gunzō* 27, no. 5 (May 1972): 184–207.

Ōe Kenzaburō. "Seitōteki (ōtanteiku) na Zainichi Chōsenjin" [An Orthodox (Authentic) Resident Korean]. In "Dai jūnikai Gunzō shinjin bungakushō happyō." *Gunzō* 24, no. 6 (June 1969): 134–35.

Ōe Kenzaburō, Kim Sŏk-bŏm, and Ri Kaisei. "Nihongo de kaku koto ni tsuite" [On Writing in Japanese]. *Bungaku* 38, no. 11 (1970): 1–27.

Ōgoshi Aiko and Takahashi Tetsuya. "Gendaa to sensō sekinin" [Gender and War Responsibility]. *Gendai shisō* [Modern Thought] 25, no. 10 (September 1997): 132–54.

Okazaki Katsuhiko. "Gaikokujin no kōmu shūshoku ninken" [Foreigners' Rights to Government Employment]. Jichi sōken. August 1997.

Ōta Jun'ichi. *Onnatachi no Ikaino* [Women's Ikaino]. Tokyo: Shobunsha, 1987.

Pae Chŏng-jin (chair), Kim Ch'ang-saeng, Cho Pak, Ch'ae Hyo, Kang Na-mi, Chŏng Yun-hŭi, and Chŏng Tae-sŏng. "Zainichi bungaku wa kore de ii no ka" [Resident Korean Literature: Is This Good Enough?]. *Kikan Zainichi bungei mintō* 1 (November 1987): 56–85.

Paek Nak-ch'ŏng, Ri Kaisei, Yang Min-gi. "Minzoku bungaku to Zainichi bungaku o megutte" [On National Literature and Resident Korean Literature]. *Kikan Zainichi bungei mintō* 3 (May 1988): 8–41.

Pak Chŏng-sŏk. "Minzokuteki jikaku e no michi — Shūshoku sabetsu saiban jōshin-sho" [My Path to Ethnic Consciousness — A Report Submitted for This Employment Discrimination Trial]. In *Minzoku sabetsu — Hitachi shūshoku sabetsu kyūdan* [Ethnic Discrimination — The Denunciation of Hitachi's Employment Discrimination], 237–60. Tokyo: Aki Shobo, 1974.

———. "Pak Chŏng-sŏk no shuki" [A Note from Pak Chŏng-sŏk]. In *Paku-kun o kakomu kai kaihō* [The Committee for Pak Newsletter] 1 (no date): 6–9.

Pak Hwa-mi. "Ianfu hyakutōban" [Comfort Women Hotline]. *Arurim* [Allim/The Notice], founding issue (February 29, 1992): 2.

Paku-kun o kakomu kai [The Committee for Pak]. "Sabetsu naki shakai e no tegakari — Shūshoku sabetsu saiban hanketsu (riyū bubun)" [Hints for a Society Without Discrimination — The Decision of an Employment Discrimination Trial (Portion Providing Justification)]. In *Minzoku sabetsu — Hitachi shūshoku sabetsu kyūdan* [Ethnic Discrimination — The Denunciation of Hitachi's Employment Discrimination], edited by Paku-kun o kakomu kai [The Committee for Pak], 262–80. Tokyo: Aki Shobo, 1974.

———. "Sabetsu to yokuatsu no soko kara — Shūshoku sabetsu saiban saishū junbi shomen" [From the Depths of Discrimination and Oppression: Final Notes for the Closing of an Employment Discrimination Suit]. In *Minzoku sabetsu — Hitachi shūshoku sabetsu kyūdan* [Ethnic Discrimination — The Denunciation of Hitachi's Employment Discrimination], edited by Paku-kun o kakomu kai [The Committee for Pak], 163–236. Tokyo: Aki Shobo, 1974.

Pak Shil. "Zainichi Kankoku Chōsenjin o meguru tōkei no hanashi" [The Story of Statistics About Resident Koreans]. In *Horumon bunka I: Issatsu marugoto Zainichi Chōsenjin* ["Tripe Culture" I: The Complete Book on Resident Koreans], edited by Horumon bunka henshū iinkai [Tripe Culture Editorial Committee], 85–88. Tokyo: Shinkansha, 1990.

———. "Kankoku kokuseki shutoku no ki" [A Record of Attaining South Korean Citizenship]. *Shinchō* 95, no. 7 (July 1998): 294–317.

———. "Kinuta o utsu onna" [The Woman Who Fulled Clothes]. *Bungei Shunjū*, March 1972, 318–39.

———. *Kita de are minami de are waga sokoku* [North or South, Our Homeland]. Tokyo: Kawade Shobo Shinsha, 1974.

———. "'Mukokusekisha' no yuku michi: Kim Sŏk-bŏm-shi e no hentō" [The Path of "Stateless Persons": A Reply to My Esteemed Colleague, Kim Sŏk-bŏm]. *Sekai* 657 (January 1999): 257–69.

Ri Kaisei and Kim Chi-ha. "Tokubetsu taidan: Minzoku to kojin" [A Special Discussion: The Nation and the Individual]. *Shinchō*, February 1996, 234–58.

"Ri Kaisei nenpu" [Ri Kaisei — Biographical/Publication Data]. In *Akutagawa shō zenshū* 9 [The Complete Collection of Akutagawa Prize–Winning Stories], 381–87. Tokyo: Bungei Shunjū, 1982.

Ri Takanori. "Posutocorinaru no seiji to 'Zainichi' bungaku" [Postcolonial Politics and "Zainichi" Literature]. *Gendai shisō* [Modern Thought] 29 (July 2001): 154–69.

Sakamoto Tetsushi. "Kakukai yūmeijin no AC do" [The AC Quotient of Famous People in Various Fields]. *AERA*, August 4, 1997, 10–11.

Saitō Satoru. *Adaruto chirudoren to kazoku* [Adult Children and the Family]. Tokyo: Gakuyō bunko, 1996, 1998.

Song Mi-ja. *Kabukichō chinjara kyōshinkyoku* [Kabuki-chō March]. Tokyo: Tokuma Shoten, 1994.

———. "Zainichi nisei sakka ron — (1) — Kin Kakuei no bungaku (shimo)" [An Analysis of Second-generation Resident Korean Authors (1): On Kin Kakuei's Literature (2)]. *Chōsen kenkyū* [Korea Research] 216 (December 1981): 2–17.

Song Yŏn-ok. "Osaka ni okeru Zainichi Chōsenjin no seikatsu — 1945 izen" [The Lives of Resident Koreans in Osaka Before 1945]. In *Zainichi Chōsenjin no rekishi: Hirakata de no horiokoshi no tame ni* [The History of Koreans in Japan: For Digging Up Their History in Hirakata], edited by Hirakata-shi kyōiku iinkai [Hirakata City Council on Education], 44–84. Hirakata: Hirakata City Council on Education, Social Education Department, 1991.

Suh Kyung-sik (Sŏ Kyŏng-shik). "Kim Chi-ha e no tegami: jikō bunretsu no itami" [A Letter to Kim Chi-ha: The Pain of Self-Disintegration]. *Gendai shisō* [Modern Thought], October 1995, 30–44.

Takeda Seiji. "Rikai sareru mono no 'fukō' — Yi Yang-ji *Yuhi*" [The "Unhappiness" of Being Understood: Yi Yang-ji's *Yuhi*]. In *"Zainichi" to iu konkyo* ["Zainichi" as Foundation], 299–304. Tokyo: Chikuma Shobo, 1995.

———. "Yobiyoserareta 'Zainichi' no mochiifu — Yi Yang-ji *Koku*" [Motifs Recently Called Forth by "Zainichi": Yi Yang-ji's *Koku*]. In *"Zainichi" to iu konkyo* ["Zainichi" as Foundation], 296–98. Tokyo: Chikuma Shobo, 1995.

————. *"Zainichi" to iu konkyo* ["Zainichi" as Foundation]. Tokyo: Chikuma Shobo, 1995.

————. "Zainichi to taikōshugi" [Resident Koreans and Oppositionalism]. In *Iwanami Gendai Shakaigaku 24: Minzoku•Kokka•Esunishiti* [Iwanami Modern Sociology 24: Nation/State/Ethnicity], 103–15. Tokyo: Iwanami Shoten, 1996.

Takeda Taijun and Ri Kaisei. "Chōsen no kokoro Nihon no kotoba" [Korean Heart, Japanese Language]. *Bungei shunjū* 50, no. 6 (June 1972): 130–40.

Takeuchi Yasuhiro. "Hirakareta gengo o kakutoku suru tame ni — Chong Ch'u-wŏl 'Mun Kon-bun *omoni* no *ningo*' ga shisa suru mono" [In Order to Attain More Open Language: The Implications of Chong Ch'u-wŏl's "Mun Kon-bun Ŏmŏni's Apple"]. *Shin Nihon bungaku* [New Japanese Literature] 456 (1985): 15–25.

Tani Tomio. "Minzoku kankei no shakaigakuteki kenkyū no tame no oboegaki: Osaka-shi kyū-Ikaino/Motogi chiiki o jirei to shite" [Thoughts for Sociological Research on Ethnic Issues: The Example of the Areas Formerly Known as Ikaino/Motogi in Osaka." In *Nihon no esunikku shakai* [Japan's Ethnic Society], edited by Komai Hiroshi, 331–77. Tokyo: Akashi Shoten, 1996.

Tawara Yoshifumi. *Kyōkasho kōgeki no shinsō* [The Depths of the Textbook Assault]. Tokyo: Gakuyū no Tomo Sha, 1997.

Ueno Chizuko, "Posuto reisen to Nihonpan rekishi shūsei shugi" [The Post–Cold War Era and Japan's Version of Historical Revisionism]. In *Nashonaruizumu to "ianfu" mondai* [Nationalism and the "Comfort Women" Issue], edited by Nihon no sensō sekinin shiryō sentaa [Center for Research and Documentation on Japan's War Responsibility], 98–122. Tokyo: Aoki Shoten, 1998.

Wada Jun. "Saiban no keika to hanketsu no imi" [The Progress of the Trial and the Meaning of the Decision]. In *Minzoku sabetsu — Hitachi shūshoku sabetsu kyūdan* [Ethnic Discrimination — The Denunciation of Hitachi's Employment Discrimination], edited by Paku-kun o kakomu kai [The Committee for Pak], 129–48. Tokyo: Aki Shobo, 1974.

Yang Chin-ja. "Song-san to Sasaeru kai no gonenkan" [Five Years with Song and the Support Association]. In *Song-san to issho ni: yoku wakaru Zainichi no moto "ianfu" saiban* [With Song: A Simple Introduction to the Lawsuit of a Zainichi Former Comfort Woman], edited by Zainichi no ianfu saiban o sasaeru kai [The Support Association for the Lawsuits of Comfort Women Residing in Japan], 4–10. Tokyo: Zainichi no ianfu saiban o sasaeru kai, 1997.

Yang Sŏk-il. *Ajiateki shintai* [The Asian Body]. Tokyo: Seibōsha, 1990.

Yang Tae-ho. "Kyōson/Kyōsei/Kyōkan — Kang Sang-jung shi e no gimon (II)" [Shared Existence/Shared Lives/Shared Feelings — Questions for Kang Sang-jung (2)]. In *Zainichi Kankoku Chōsenjin — Sono Nihon ni okeru sonzai kachi* [Resident Koreans: The Value of their Existence in Japanese Society], edited by Iinuma Jirō, 289–301. Tokyo: Kaifūsha, 1988.

———. *Zainichi Kankoku Chōsenjin dokuhon: Rerakkusu shita kankei o motomete* [Reader on Resident Koreans: Toward a More Relaxed Relationship]. Tokyo: Rokufū Shuppan, 1996.

Yang Yŏng-fu. *Sengo Osaka no Chōsenjin Undō: 1945–1965* [The Postwar Korean Movement in Osaka: 1945–1965]. Tokyo: Miraisha, 1994.

Yi Yang-ji. *Yi Yang-ji zenshū* [The Complete Works of Yi Yang-ji]. Tokyo: Kōdansha, 1993.

Yū Miri. *Green Bench* [title in English]. Tokyo: Kawade Shobo Shinsha, 1994.

———. *Inochi* [Life]. Tokyo: Shogakkan, 2000.

———. *Kamen no kuni* [The Country of Masks]. Tokyo: Shinchōsha, 1998.

———. *Mizube no yurikago* [Cradle by the Sea]. Tokyo: Kadokawa Shoten, 1997.

———. *Shigo jiten* [My Personal Dictionary]. Tokyo: Asahi Shinbunsha, 1996.

Yū Miri and Ri Kaisei. "Kazoku•Minzoku•Bungaku" [The Family, Ethnicity, and Literature]. *Gunzō* 52, no. 4 (April 1997): 126–46.

Yun Kŏn-a. "'Zainichi Kankoku-Chōsenjin' to iu kotoba" [The Word "Zainichi Kankoku-Chōsenjin"]. In *Horumon Bunka I: Issatsu marugoto Zainichi Chōsenjin* ["Tripe Culture" I: The Complete Book on Resident Koreans], edited by Horumon bunka henshū iinkai [Tripe Culture Editorial Committee], 56–73. Tokyo: Shinkansha, 1990.

———. *"Zainichi" o ikiru to wa* [To Live as "Zainichi"]. Tokyo: Iwanami Shoten, 1992.

Index

"The Red Fruit" (Kim Ch'ang-saeng), *see* "Akai mi"
Reparations, war, 78, 190
Repetition compulsion, 166–67, 180
Resident Korean Christian Church, 11
Resident Koreans, *see* Zainichi Koreans
Ri Kaisei (Yi Hŏe-sŏng), 11; citizenship of, 195–96; critical evaluations of, 52, 54, 55; fathers in work of, 80–81; Kim Chi-ha and, 41, 55; at Kim Hŭiro trial, 29; "Kinuta o utsu onna" [The Woman Who Fulled Clothes], 33–53, 105; and Korean identity, 32–33, 42–44, 46–49, 52–53, 195–96; and language, 31–34, 37–38, 41–42, 211*n*52; *Mihatenu yume* [The Unfinished Dream], 52, 55–56; and *Minto*, 126; name of, 220*n*36; politics of, 56; prizes won by, 18, 23, 33; Sōren and, 7; Yū Miri and, 160
Ri Takanori, 12
Ritual to Invoke Native Land Consciousness, 40
Royal family, 163, 170, 226*n*22

Said, Edward, 12, 13
Saitō Satoru, 162, 168–69, 171
Sakurai Yoshiko, 172, 175
Salp'uri (dance), 129, 131, 146
San Francisco Peace Treaty (1952), 5
SAPIO (magazine), 172
Saran he/aishite imasu [*Sarang hae*/I Love You] (Chong Ch'u-wŏl), 103
Sartre, Jean-Paul, 46
Saussure, Ferdinand de, 110–11
Science: economics and, 79; Kin Kakuei and, 58, 64–66, 71; literature versus, 65–66; surveillance and, 69–70
Scott, Joan, 125
Sekai [The World] (magazine), 195
Sexism, 186–89
Sexual abuse, 157–58, 163–64. *See also* Incest
Sex/Sexuality: in *GO*, 200; ideologies of, comfort women and, 186–89; in Kin Kakuei, 61; metaphoric uses of, 17, 155–56; in "The Red Fruit," 121; role in literature of, 16–17; in Yi Yang-ji's work, 128, 131, 135–39, 141–43, 151–53, 224*n*55
Shamanism: Chong Ch'u-wŏl and, 100–101; and folk culture movement, 40–41; and mourning, 39–40; psychiatric symptoms and, 138; Yi Yang-ji and, 129, 131, 133–34, 137, 139–40, 144

Shigo jiten [My Personal Dictionary] (Yū Miri), 170
Shilla period, 36
Shimon ōnatsu seido ni hantai suru naze naze shimon? onnatachi no kai [Why Fingerprints, Why? Women Against the Fingerprinting System] (organization), 113
Shinchō [New Tide] (journal), 195
Shinchō 45 (magazine), 173
Shin Nihon bungaku [New Japanese Literature] (magazine), 55
Shinse t'aryŏng (ritualistic mourning), 38–41, 43–45, 47, 51, 105
Shishōsetsu (personal narrative), 33, 38, 43–44, 62, 105
Socialism, 56
Song Mi-ja, 86–87, 88
Song Shin-do, 1, 228*n*48
Sōren, *see* Zainihon Chōsenjin Sōrengōkai (General Association of Korean Residents in Japan)
South Korea: Japan and, 5–6, 22, 78–79; Suh brothers incident, 56; voting rights in, 192; Zainichi Koreans and, 4–7, 22, 119, 194–96
"The Stone Path" [Ishi no michi] (Kin Kakuei), 65, 66–73, 82–88
Structuralism, 111
Stuttering, 59–61
Suh (Sŏ) brothers, 56, 214*n*4
Suh Kyung-sik, 11
Suzuki Michihiko, 27–28
Swift, Jonathan, 149

Takeda Seiji, 52, 54, 59, 62–64, 71, 72, 80–81, 127–28, 160, 175
Takeuchi Yasuhiro, 110–11
Technology, *see* Science
Tendo Arata, 157
Textbooks, Japanese history in, 127, 132, 159, 172–75, 185
"Third-World Literature in the Era of Multinational Capitalism" (Jameson), 48
Time, 147, 153–54
Trauma, 81–82, 158–61, 166–67, 171, 182–84
Trauma and Recovery (Herman), 158
Tsuchi no kanashimi [The Sadness of Soil] (Kin Kakuei), 81

Uchida Shungiku, 157
Ueno Chizuko, 174
United States, 12–13, 27
Uri Yoson Nettowaaku (Uri yŏsŏng